BEYOND DUTY

For AJ
and those who have fought and those who have fallen
in the First Battalion, Twelfth Regiment of the First
Cavalry Division

BEYOND DUTY

LIFE ON THE FRONTLINE IN IRAQ

SHANNON P. MEEHAN

WITH ROGER THOMPSON

polity

First published in 2009 by Polity Press

Polity Press
65 Bridge Street
Cambridge CB2 1UR, UK

Polity Press
350 Main Street
Malden, MA 02148, USA

ISBN-13: 978-0-7456-4672-5

A catalogue record for this book is available from the British Library.

Typeset in 10.75 on 14 pt Adobe Janson
by Servis Filmsetting Ltd, Stockport, Cheshire
Printed and bound in United States by Odyssey Press, Inc.,
Gonic, New Hampshire

For further information on Polity, visit our website: www.politybooks.com

ACKNOWLEDGEMENTS

We gratefully acknowledge the support of the Polity staff and editors, in particular John B. Thompson, who provided strong guidance and a clear sense of vision for the project, and Sarah Lambert, who worked so hard to make the book possible. We are grateful to Justin Dyer and Marianne Rutter for helping move this book forward, and we thank Jeremy Clement, who made the connection that ultimately led to this project and enthusiastically supported it from the beginning. We also thank the peer reviewers of the book, whose thoughtful commentary helped us shape its final version.

Deepest gratitude to Roger Thompson: with me from the start, we saw our vision through. I am blessed to have undergone such a project with you, and I am thankful for your wife Laura Thompson's considerate manner as well as her insight with the text.

Many thanks to John Thompson and the members of

Polity, for their guidance and support of our project. We are extremely grateful.

This book would not have been possible without the hard work and dedication of Steven Roberts, Charles Armstead (Sgt. 1st Class); Brandon Duvall, Hugo Garnica, Marion Deboe (Sgt.); Robert Smith, James Szabota, Robert Steffen, Serge Kavenaught, Jerry Tkel, Joshua Rudicil (Spc.); Isaac Warner, Chad Vos (Pfc.); and my entire platoon, *Wolf Pack*, of Delta Company. This includes Cpt. Paul Carlock, whose guidance and mentoring friendship will forever be appreciated. To Lt. Col. Morris T. Goins, leader of *The Chargers*, whose steadfast courage in the gravest of times enabled us to accomplish the unimaginable. Also, to my great friends and fellow leaders Luke Miller, Josh Southworth (Cpt.); Nicholas Poppen, David Nguyen (1st Lt.); Hollie Clevenger (Sgt.); and all those in 1-12 Cavalry who worked with me in support of the mission. Your tremendous effort and commitment to the mission made such a story possible.

I would like to thank all my former coaches, teachers, and professors at Drexel Hill Raiders, Upper Darby High School, and Virginia Military Institute, for helping to shape the direction of my life, and for all of their insightful stories and advice that I will always remember. Thank you.

I wish to express my tremendous gratitude to AJ, the wife I left behind while serving our nation. I am forever indebted to you for enduring a treacherous fifteen months alone, left to bear the burden of daily life never knowing what my future would be, and for caring for our families with complete understanding and compassion. I love you with all of my heart.

Thank you to all of the doctors and nurses who treated me at Fort Hood. From the neurology department to orthopedics and physical rehabilitation; I will always remember the care and concern with which I was treated.

For all in my family before me who willingly served our country proud, including Ed Williams (Air Force); William Henry, Larry Lynn, my father Louis Meehan (Army); Ed LeSage, Eddie LeSage, Tommy Lynn, Tom Reynolds (Marines); Buzzy Lynn, Louis Joseph Meehan, Steve Phipps, and Paul Weinberger (Navy). For all their stories untold.

Roger Thompson – I would like to thank the many people who saw versions of the manuscript and provided suggestions and encouragement, among them the HIU Crew, David Rachels, Bonnie Watkins, Brian and Phil Watkins, Mary Russell, Tim Riemann, Thane Keller, Peter Cook, and J.J. Cromer. I would also like to thank both the Virginia Military Institute Ski Team (for their patience and enthusiasm as I worked throughout many of our weekends together) and the staff of the Palms (for providing me with a quiet afternoon space for working through the final revisions of the book). I thank my Department and the VMI for their ongoing support of my work, and Rika Welsh for providing such a great space for writing during my time in Cambridge. To my family and the Ter Poortens, I offer my sincere thanks for your interest in and support for the book and for the many suggestions for how to think through some of it. It means a lot to me.

I want to express my deepest thanks to Laura, who sacrificed much. I so deeply appreciate not only your thoughtful readings of the manuscript, but your understanding and patience during some of the intense periods of writing that took me away from home. I know it was a lot to ask during difficult times. Finally, I want to thank AJ and Shannon for their willingness to talk so openly about their lives and to share their story. I hope we have honored your experience, and I hope we have made a difference.

AUTHOR'S NOTE

Beyond Duty is a work of nonfiction. All events included in the text took place and have been retold to the best of my memory and with the help of several others involved in the events. Names of Iraqi citizens and U.S. fallen soldiers, as well as many routes and roads, have been changed within the text. Conversations presented in dialogue form have been re-created from my memory with the intention of appealing to the core of what was said, not to represent a verbatim account.

Diyala Province

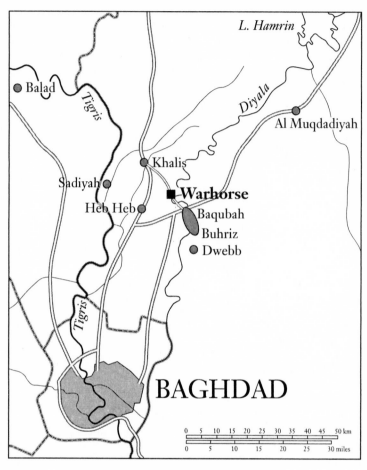

Area of Operations

PROLOGUE

The day that I served as Company Commander, I painted my helmet gold. The sun blazed with a temperature of 124 degrees, and my men teased me, laughing at the gleaming helmet. Even so, when I crawled into my tank with my fellow soldiers, my friends, we all took a moment to recognize the fact that today was different. Today, I was commanding them in battle.

I was a platoon leader, but when my Company Commander had returned to base to refuel his vehicle, he appointed me to lead the company while he was gone. Our orders were to shut down Baqubah, a shattered city now more dead than alive, and clear insurgents and Improvised Explosive Devices (IEDs) from a section west of Route Highlands, a major north–south artery running through the city. We arrived in tanks, Bradleys, and Strykers. The tanks were both heavily armored and heavily armed, and they were able to protect the men in ways that Bradleys and Strykers could not. The last Bradley to see action before our mission was burned to a skeletal frame by a large IED, and al-Qaida had given Strykers a particularly bloody reception to the city. Within hours of their first patrol through Baqubah, two Strykers were catastrophically destroyed. One was cut in half, and the other was flipped in an explosion. Our soldiers died in both. Tanks, then, were the best option for battle, but we needed the Strykers and Bradleys to transport the men.

As our company rumbled into position, I maneuvered my tank southeast to the intersection of Route Highlands and Route LeBarge, an east–west road. The company fanned out northward, each platoon assigned to a different street. I directed the company's movements from my tank, and my job was to support my men when they faced resistance. Within minutes of our mission beginning, it was clear it was going to be a difficult day.

The men were encountering a new IED every few yards, making their movement painstakingly slow. More distressingly, however, one of the platoons had, shortly after our arrival, been engaged by an al-Qaida Rocket-Propelled Grenade (RPG) team. The enemy had waited on a rooftop, and they fired on my soldiers. All I heard was an explosion echoing through my earpiece and one soldier shouting, "Contact RPG team! Southwest!" I heard Blue Platoon open fire from their Bradley armored vehicle with a 7.62 machine gun, streaming bullets through the air. Then I heard them unleash their more powerful 25-mm cannon. The force of their response demonstrated to me they were under heavy threat. I could hear the enemy continue to fire RPGs and their AK-47 rifles, and I got the report that two of my men had been slightly wounded in the initial attack, one with a broken nose and one with a separated shoulder. When it was clear that the cannon would not be enough to suppress the RPG team, they called me for support.

I asked them for as much information as they could provide. I needed to know the exact makeup of the enemy, the exact location of the building with clear and accurate coordinates on our grid, and the full nature of the injuries of my soldiers. The radio vibrated with updates, but gunfire drowned out their reports. The platoon leader's commands mingled with the sound of the cannon, and, in pieces, details filtered back. Finally, above the confusion, I heard the information I most needed. I heard the grid coordinates. I called for our best option, our best weapon. I called in a missile strike.

The insurgents have no defense against our missiles, but ordering them requires certainty. I had to be sure that the enemy was substantive and contained enough to warrant the strike, and I had to be absolutely certain that the coordinates were accurate. I confirmed the location with the platoon, and, with gunfire still sounding in my earpiece, I called the battalion Tactical Operations Center for the strike. Then, I waited.

Two minutes later, the missiles came streaking from the northeast. They arrived with virtually no warning, the sounds of their rockets filling the air only moments before a deafening impact. In the seconds after the strike, the radio was silent, and less than a mile from my location a small cloud of smoke and dust rose from the neighborhood of the engagement. I called to the platoon asking for a report. For a moment, the radio remained quiet, and I worried that the worst had happened. I imagined that the coordinates were wrong, and that my men had taken the hit. I worried that I had failed my men and that I had violated the great trust a commander establishes with his soldiers. I called again for a report, and this time, the platoon called back. The target was destroyed. The building was leveled, and the RPG team was obliterated. My men were safe.

That moment built my confidence. I had been successful as a platoon leader. It was known that I would shortly be awarded the Army Commendation Medal with Valor, and I had developed a reputation as an officer capable of executing demanding missions. My soldiers had begun to call me Capone because of the mafia-like control I had over the area of my command. So, when the Company Commander was called to return to our Forward Operating Base to refuel, re-supply, and debrief battalion, I was put in charge.

For the first time, I now had responsibility over eighty men, four tanks, three Bradleys, and four Strykers. My soldiers were divided into several platoons, and each platoon was supported by different vehicles. Red Platoon had Strykers. Blue Platoon had Bradleys. My platoon, White Platoon, was a tank platoon. One of my tanks led the way for each group, and a single soldier served as point man, moving a few paces in front of and to the left of the tank. His job was to identify potential IEDs. He scanned the ground for copper wires, a sure sign of an explosive device buried in the ground, and when he found them, he would call in to me to request Explosive Ordinance Disposal. After the IED was destroyed, the soldiers behind the tank would enter each building along the street and clear it of any threats. I was directing a large-scale, coordinated mission in a notoriously dangerous area of Iraq, and my command was an integral part of a broader attack involving our entire brigade. I knew it was an opportunity to demonstrate to all the men my ability to lead, and it was my best opportunity to show them that I could be trusted to do what was best for them.

The first moments of my command were overwhelming. My company, Delta Company, dubbed the Death Dealers, was working in conjunction with other companies to clear this section of Baqubah. To my north was Bravo Company, and to the south was Charlie Company. As Delta commander, I choreographed an elaborate dance, ensuring that each of my platoons moved at roughly the same pace in order to prevent one from accidentally moving ahead and coming into the line of fire of another. At first, I had to rein them in. The natural instinct is for each platoon to move at its own pace down the street, but that endangers the mission and other men. From my tank, I directed each group to ensure that they worked together. I had to fashion a team from platoons of men who wanted nothing more than to finish the mission as quickly as possible without regard for the other platoons. Each group moved down a street, calling their coordinates back to me, requesting the destruction of the numerous IEDs and demanding support when the enemy engaged them. My headphones buzzed with their voices, and I tried to negotiate the new terrain as acting Company Commander. I tried to make sense of their voices, and I tried to execute a mission that was already encountering significant resistance.

If all my teams moved together, we could ensure that an area remained clear and that platoons could quickly support each other in the event of a particularly difficult engagement with the enemy. So, I coordinated my platoons and reported the progress of my company as a whole to the companies to the north and south and to my battalion leadership. The plan was for a systematic clearing of Baqubah, and after about an hour of my command, as I began to understand and resign myself to the rhythms of a mission, our company gained confidence in the process. More importantly, my soldiers gained confidence in my ability to lead.

The success of the missile strike on the RPG team offered a clear sign to the men on the ground that I could be trusted to protect them. My men believed that I would provide the support they needed, and they now moved as a disciplined team down the streets. They began to trust my guidance, and they responded by tracking in textbook fashion westward across the city. Our company was working well, and I knew I had a type of control and confidence that comes only from succeeding in a difficult mission. I had a sense that I was living a vocation that was meant for me. I felt like I was embodying the ideal of the American Soldier. I believed that I was doing the right thing.

Three and a half hours into my command, a new IED call came over the radio. My White Platoon sergeant had found another wire. This one, though, was different. I had to ask him several times to describe what he saw. A mound of newly disturbed earth was in the middle of the road. A copper wire, not even vaguely hidden, ran from the mound to a building to the northeast, and then up the side of the building to the second story and into a window. That window had a clear view of the area of disturbed earth.

What my sergeant described was not at all normal, and, given the number of more cleverly disguised IEDs along the route, I was having difficulty making sense of what he was describing to me. The mound and the wire running from it were both in some ways typical. That the wire led up to a window was not entirely typical, but it made some sense given the view it had of the mound. I asked again for him to explain it to me, and I tried to picture what he was describing. It just seemed so obvious. It was as though whoever had devised the IED had made no attempt to hide it. The mound of dirt was obvious, the wire was not hidden from view, and the whole contraption seemed too easy to identify.

I called the situation to the battalion Tactical Operations Center (TOC). The entire mission came to a halt as I discussed the situation with my battalion leadership. It only took a few minutes before another report came back. Locals indicated that the house was an IED factory. The battalion command reported that they believed it to be a terrorist cell. The adjacent companies were pulling ahead. Any more delay and we would corrupt the mission for the entire battalion. The time to decide was running out.

I knew now what I had to do. I had to destroy the house. I could not risk sending men into a house that was an IED factory. I simply had to eliminate the threat altogether. Still, that wire running into the house bothered me. It was all so obvious. Why was it not hidden any better? What was the catch?

I began to sweat. This decision seemed heavier. The earlier missile strike was a no-brainer. My men were under direct fire, and the location of the enemy was clear and the danger was certain. This house, though, was a mystery. I was having a hard time picturing exactly what my sergeant was describing to me, but I knew one thing. I wasn't going to let fear of making a bad decision control me. I had to protect my men. I couldn't understand why the IED would be so obvious, but I knew I wouldn't risk a life trying to find out.

I worked through it all in my head one last time. The house had a wire running from it to a mound in the road. The area was saturated with IEDs, and my men had already been attacked by an RPG team. Locals and my battalion command suspected the house was either an al-Qaida stronghold or an IED factory. My men were concerned about it, and thus far, they had conducted the mission with a systematic certainty and professionalism. Perhaps most importantly, I felt my men's lives were at risk. I couldn't send them into that house. I couldn't risk that.

I made a final call into the battalion TOC. The response was simple and clear: "We support your decision." I called for the missiles, and we all waited.

Somewhere to the north, about twenty miles from our location, two GPS-guided rounds turned toward our location and fired from a 155-mm cannon on an artillery vehicle. They lifted from the vehicle and rushed over the city. Behind them, small contrails etched their paths in the sky.

For two minutes, I waited in silence with the men in my tank. The platoon had pulled back and cleared the area around the target. My men had gathered inside their armored vehicles and locked all hatches to protect themselves from the blast. One of my tanks positioned itself on a rise so it could watch the strike. They waited and watched, and my radio was silent as the entire company anticipated the strike. No chatter. No sound. Just the certainty of imminent impact and utter destruction. I looked at my friend Garnica, the gunner in my tank, and I wiped my brow. The heat in the tank was oppressive. I dropped my head, and I wondered if I had made the right decision. I wondered if I had, in fact, done the right thing.

The ferocity of missile impacts turned my attention back to the radio. The explosions rattled our vehicles, and I waited to hear confirmation that the correct target had been hit. Dust and debris rose above the city and mingled with the haze of the afternoon sky, and my radio fell silent.

The silence lingered for a few seconds before my platoon sergeant radioed in. A successful strike. Target destroyed. For a moment, I felt relieved that the missiles flew true. All the doubts I had vanished, and I felt renewed confidence in my decision. Then, within a minute, another voice, broken, sounded over the radio.

"Did – you see – that?"

I leaned in, trying to hear the broadcast more clearly. It wasn't coming from my company. It was coming from a tank in Bravo Company, just to the north of my men. Even though they had nothing to do with the event, they had a clear view down the street, and they saw the missiles strike.

"Did you see that kid?"

I grabbed my headset, pressing it hard against my ears, trying to hear what they were saying.

I heard them say it again, "Did you see that kid?" and this time, with awful certainty, came a response.

"There were a lot more in there."

The words hung in the air, and I looked at the men in my tank. A new silence settled in. A deeper, more devastating silence. One that joins men together. One that conspires. One shared by all of us soldiers, from any war, who have witnessed the unspeakable and who, in our attempts to cope, pledge to each other, with simply a glance, not to say a word, not to resurrect what we have destroyed.

This is my voice rising out of that terrible silence.

This is my story trying to order the ruins of that day.

1

They call us "butter bars," newly minted second lieutenants in the Army. The name refers to the two gold bars on our uniform that indicate our rank, and it reflects a general skepticism about our ability to lead. It suggests that we're soft. It suggests that we're inexperienced. It suggests that we'll make bad decisions.

Even so, we've all been through officer training, so, when we are called to leave the States and lead our first missions, we are, if nothing else, eager to put into practice all that we have learned. I know I was anyway. I had been looking forward to my chance to prove myself. I had been wanting to demonstrate my ability to take charge and show the men who were now under my command that I was worthy of following. So, when my company left Ft. Hood, Texas, in October 2006, to begin our deployment to Iraq, I was excited to see action.

We flew first to Maine, where we were scheduled to catch a plane to Kuwait, and we traveled in silent expectation of the war. The only sounds on the flight were the buzzing engines and the vibrations of the plastic walls of the plane. I sat next to my Company Commander and my platoon sergeant, and we hardly said a word. I was thinking forward to Iraq, trying to imagine what we were heading into and reflecting on Baqubah. Our mission had been changed just two weeks before our deployment, and we had been told very little about the city. What had been made clear, however, was that our time was going to be difficult, and I tried to imagine myself leading my platoon into its first engagement with the enemy.

When the plane finally landed in Maine, it was almost dark. We disembarked, walking down a set of stairs and out onto the tarmac. A dark line of trees hemmed in the airport, and the sweet smell of spruce trees hung in the cool air, fragrant in their expectation of the night. We walked across the tarmac and up a set of stairs into the airport. At the top of the stairs, a large group of primarily older men had gathered. They were part of a veterans' group, and they had organized a final farewell party for us. One end of the airport had been roped off for the event. They had music playing, and food and drinks were arrayed on tables. Donuts, white with powdered sugar, were laid out on silver trays at the end of one table. Large, soft chocolate cookies were on white, lacey doilies at the other end. Coffee simmered in silver pots. Bottles of juice were stacked in bowls of ice. Around it all, generations of fighting men and their families mingled.

Most of the veterans were in uniforms representing their particular wars and an age of conflict that bore little resemblance to today. They wore their medals on their chests, and, moving about shaking our hands, their voices trembled with proclamations and advice. For me, with my shining new gold bars, they seemed to have only one thing to say.

"Be a leader," they said.

Each one of them, to a man, told me something like "Be a leader."

"You're in charge now. Do what has to be done," said one.

"Make the tough calls. Lead," said another.

I hadn't left the States yet, and here, in an airport in Maine, the weight of the war was being impressed upon me. The men, most of them graying, greeted me with serious expressions and meaningful eyes that were intended to be heavy and profound, and they tried to impart, with a kind of knowing certainty, their final version of what mattered. They wanted me to believe that they knew the place I was going, that they knew the experiences I was about to have, and that they could, with simply a penetrating look and an assertive voice, teach me how to act, how to do my job, and how to be a soldier.

I ate the cookies, and I shook the men's hands. I felt the calluses on their palms and nodded when they pointed to their chests to show me their decorations, and I tried to be appreciative. I tried to remember that these were the men of the greatest generation and the toughest wars. These were the men whose histories shaped policies that, in no small part, were the roots of the current conflict. They had stories to tell. They had lessons to share. But, here, in Maine, they were reduced to shadows and declarations. They had only final words, and the stories that danced behind them were trapped by the lilting airport music and the necessity of making us understand that they, too, had been in war, that they, too, had been soldiers. They were not sending us off to war. They were resurrecting their pasts, and their words were the thin remnants of the stories that once animated their lives. They were phantoms. They were lamentations.

I wanted to respect it all. I wanted to feel the sincerity and conviction with which they spoke, and the depth with which they meant it, but I didn't. I felt sad. I felt removed. The old medals on their chests seemed like so many old tales, and I found myself wanting to be back on the plane and wanting to begin my work as a soldier.

I had been preparing for that work for most of my life. I had not always planned to be a soldier, but my family had shaped me with a clear sense that I would one day lead. I don't know that they imagined that they were doing that, but it was in the messages that I heard every day, and it was in the ongoing expectation that I was the great promise of the family. I was the golden child.

In high school, I was a wrestling star. My meets were covered in the local press, and I was held up as an example of what our community was capable of producing. I was the great potential of Upper Darby, Pennsylvania. The city, just outside of Philadelphia, had been a mill town that had long since lost its glory. Neighborhood bars dotted the streets next to empty storefronts and dollar stores. Cobbs Creek ran brown through a slim line of trees cutting across the city. The story of the town's founding, apocryphal I'm sure, was that a man named Darby took the land that would one day grow into a city for a debt from William Penn, and, in some ways, the town had remained like its namesake. It was always on the margins. This was not the town that William Penn, the great American, founded. It was the town that Darby, a name lost to history, established, and it was a tough town.

At meets, I would wrestle against opponents from the posh suburbs of Philly. I would be on the mat, and I'd know that I was wrestling a kid with more means than me, and, most likely, more opportunities. He certainly trained with better equipment and worked with higher paid coaches. I came to represent, to my family and the people who followed my career in the local papers, the ability to succeed despite limited means. I broke my school's record. I broke county records. I was enshrined in the high school Hall of Fame. A banner with my name on it was lifted to the school ceiling.

I emerged from a down-and-out neighborhood, and I triumphed against the odds. I was the pride of Upper Darby. I was the American dream.

I embraced the role. It was attractive to me. It made me feel special, and it provided me with a clear narrative by which to live my life. Everything I did I could fit into that story, and I began to see my life as enacting a kind of family prophecy. I saw myself rising from the rubble of a depressed city and a family scraping by. Alongside that image of myself, however, I carried a strong sense of responsibility, especially to my father.

My father was the director in my life when I was young. He pushed me to succeed, and he instilled in me a sense of duty and a sense of honor. He, ultimately, guided me to wrestling. He saw some talent in me, evidently, and I think he believed that wrestling would teach me discipline and focus. So, he encouraged me to pursue the sport, and he had sacrificed his own work in order to help me. He was a photographer, and in order to attend my competitions, he turned down jobs and commissions. He cheered me, he consoled me, and he kept me focused on the honor of my work.

He had been a soldier. Out of high school, he had enrolled in college at Temple University, but after only a year, he dropped out and enlisted. Two of his close friends had been killed in Vietnam. One had been the child of Italian immigrants who sent their son to war. They were proud of their adopted American identity, and they flew an enormous American flag from their house. When their son was killed, my father attended the funeral, and he stared at the flag. The war was real to him. College was some strange shadow of reality. His obligation was to his friends. He wanted to honor their lives. So, he left school and enlisted, and he went to fight a war.

He was sent to Korea. Throughout the Vietnam War, the Korean peninsula remained unstable, and U.S. troops were rotated through the country. There were skirmishes. There were battles. When the North Korean soldiers feared defeat in an engagement, they committed suicide. They held grenades to their heads, and they pulled the pins. My father had pictures of their bodies, grotesque forms bound so deeply to a concept of honor that violent death was preferable to defeat. My father, however, did not talk about the pictures. My mother showed them to me. My father didn't discuss what he saw or what he felt, but I had a sense growing up that the war was just below the surface of his life. It was in the pauses in his speech. It was behind the lessons he tried to teach me. It was sometimes in his eyes, like the rough surface of a lake in a fall wind. Memories seemed always to be rippling across the blue and gray. I wanted to hear his stories. I wanted to know why he cried when he watched war movies. He never said, though, and he changed the subject when I asked him about his life as a soldier. He did not give it voice. He did not talk about it. He did, however, talk about honor.

For my father, any sport, especially wrestling, was about honor, and by the time I was a senior in high school, my wrestling career and my dreams of an honorable life were the center of everything I did. I suspect they may have been at the center of my father's life as well. I was successful, and my father was proud. I wanted to stand out. I wanted to be what my family had asked me to be, and the newspapers seemed to love it. In the weeks leading up to my senior season, I spent hours each day preparing. I disciplined my body with brutal workouts. I skipped class to run stairwells and lift weights. I shed weight by pushing myself through long, evening sweat sessions. I told myself that I would be the best and that I would make my family and my father proud. I sat awake at night with my younger brother Patrick, describing the pain of my body, the brutality of controlling my weight and ripping muscles to build them up, but I reveled in the possibilities of my future. I told Patrick how I would succeed, and he and I planned my triumphs and celebrated the fact that I was going to make a name for myself.

Now I had my chance to do that in Iraq. I had a chance to make a difference, and I wanted my family to know that I was finally going to lead the life they had imagined for me. So, in the month before my deployment, I flew home again. I had been married barely a year, and my wife, AJ, wanted to be sure I reconnected with my entire family before I was deployed, so she helped me arrange a small farewell party at my parents' house. My brother and the rest of my family gathered in my parents' kitchen. My closest friends from high school, Matt and Dave, were there. AJ, standing against the faded kitchen cabinets, tapped her fingers on the baby-blue countertops. Eight of us were squeezed into the tiny space, all laughing and trying to avoid the obvious fact that I was about to go to Iraq. When news about the war flashed on the television, and images of the desert and tanks and soldiers rushed across the old set's screen, the room hushed. AJ quipped at the irony, and she strode across the room and turned off the television.

My mother, at that moment, handed me her crucifix. She had been given it for her confirmation when she was a girl, and it was pink. I held it in my hand, and I looked at her. She told me she'd pray for me, and she told me that she knew that God would be with me. I could feel the edges of the crucifix in my hand. I said then that I appreciated everyone's support, and I tried to let them know that I was thankful for their influences on my life. Standing in my family's kitchen, my mother's Christ in my hand and the smell of her cats in the air, I felt guilt. I felt selfish for wanting to fulfill the family dream. I felt selfish for choosing a life that would demonstrate that I was a success. I felt ashamed that I had written a script for myself that would now take me to war and leave my family behind. I worried that my story would leave my wife lonely and my family despondent. So, later that night, I tried to change the story.

I stood in the kitchen with my brother. It was near three in the morning, and my friends had left after having spent the night with me and AJ drinking at our favorite bar, R.P. McMurphy's. A band that had played at our wedding went through a couple of sets at R.P.'s, and we stayed until they finished playing before we went home. My parents were asleep, and AJ had gone upstairs. I reached into the refrigerator for a beer. When I turned around, Patrick was crying. He was weeping, and he kept saying the same thing over and over again. He kept saying, "You can't die. You can't die." His body shook. It was a violent, primal cry. It was fear and grief rushing to the surface, and I didn't know what to do. He needed my comfort. He needed to know that I was going to be okay and that I, the brother he loved and looked up to, was going to return safe. But I didn't know what to say to him. This moment was the culmination of all of those expectations. If I came back from Iraq decorated, I would be fulfilling the family dream. I would be proving my family right. If I was killed, I would still fulfill the family prophecy, but I'd be a martyr. I'd be the promise of my family lost to a greater glory. Patrick saw the family story in front of him. He saw me rising at that moment, but all he could imagine was the loss, and I knew I couldn't tell him that that wasn't going to happen. I was going to Iraq. I was commanding a tank platoon, and I was going to be fighting a war. I didn't feel like I could just tell him everything was going to be okay. I couldn't tell him I wasn't going to die.

So, I changed the family story. I asked him to ascend. I told him I needed him. I told him he had to take care of AJ for me. I told him I needed him to take control. He looked at me. His weeping stopped, deep sobs suddenly silent. He nodded at me. He put his arms around me, and he told me he'd be in charge.

Less than an hour later, we wandered into the living room. My father and mother were now awake. The house was cool. I had a 5 a.m. flight, so they had awoken early to say good-bye. When my father started to cry, I immediately wanted him to stop, and I found myself trying to change our family story. I told him the same thing that I told my brother, that I needed him to be strong, and my father, with that war look at the edges of his eyes, stopped his tears. His lips thinned. He was another generation of soldier. He knew what I was asking, but, unlike my brother, he knew I couldn't change the story. He knew I couldn't, with just a wish of words, make my guilt go away and my history vanish. He said he'd honor what I asked of him, and he told me that he would see me soon. He knew that I needed him to be proud of me. He also knew I'd lived my story too well. I couldn't change it now.

In Maine, surrounded by aging soldiers, I remembered my father's eyes. I imagined the stories behind them, and when one more old man took me by the shoulders and warned me with a stern voice, "Don't crack. They'll rely on you," I tried to see the stories in his eyes. I told him I appreciated his advice, but, in fact, I didn't. I couldn't connect his life to mine, and I couldn't see in his face the face of the soldier who one day left college to honor his friends who had died in war. The music in the airport stopped, and someone announced the departure of our flight to Kuwait. My men lined up, and I turned away from the old man. Someone started the music again, and I headed toward the plane, leading my men into the Maine night and off to war.

2

The golden arches of McDonald's glow even in Kuwait. We were in a desert, we were far from home, and we were on some base whose location I didn't even know, yet we were being bombarded with reminders of home. The Army had made every attempt to make the base seem safe and removed from the war, but it resembled a kind of staged show of American reality. The coffee shop was in a trailer, Harley-Davidson motorcycles were sold and shipped directly in the States, and the McDonald's sign was inscribed with Arabic, except, of course, for the giant glowing letter "M." That was in English. Very large and very bright English.

I had spent most of my flight to Kuwait with my earphones on, listening to Green Day and the Boss, preparing myself for the weeks ahead, and sleeping, sometimes glancing up at the in-flight movie. X-Men: The Last Stand was playing, the first movie, I think, to show soldiers in the new Army uniforms, called ACUs. I didn't much care to hear what Wolverine had to say, so I watched the show with my music playing in my ears. Occasionally during the flight, I would turn off my music and talk to my Company Commander and my platoon sergeant about our mission. I wanted to know what was going to come next. Both of these men had been to Iraq before, so I thought that by talking to them I could make some sense of the mission. One thing became clear, though, and that was that the only constant truth you could count on was that you had no idea how the operations in theater were going to go. Daily expectations of a plan ensured frustration. Uncertainty and waiting were all you could count on.

I already had some sense of that when our mission had changed abruptly two weeks before our deployment. Originally, we had been assigned as the Quick Reaction Force for the theater. We were to be stationed in Kuwait, and as QRF our mission would have been to provide rapid support for any group in the region that would need it. We would essentially be on constant standby, stationed in Kuwait and living in the artificial America. In the weeks leading up to our deployment, however, the situation in Iraq worsened, and our mission changed. We were told we were needed in Baqubah, and Kuwait transformed from our permanent home to a brief training stop. In all, we only spent twelve days there. The 5th Battalion, 20th Regiment replaced us, taking over the role of theater Quick Reaction Force before we were flown into Iraq.

The daily ritual in Kuwait was marked by long stretches of time doing nothing. We gathered for meals, and we attended a brief class or two each day that oriented us to the issues and threats in Iraq, but, otherwise, we were left to find ways to fill time. Sometimes, we met in a movie theater, where we watched videos on the latest enemy weapons developments and insurgent tactics. The videos showed how insurgents created IEDs to test our defenses, then they showed the technology or tactics we had developed to counter those new developments.

They demonstrated that the war remained a constant cat-and-mouse game with no clear winner. Each time that we became aware of how the insurgents were fighting the war and changed our activities to account for their actions, they developed new methods of inflicting damage. We saw in clear detail that we were dealing with an enemy who were, perhaps, more organized than was portrayed in the press back home. The films certainly showed that they had mastered inflicting significant damage with minimal manpower.

Other than short classes and videos, however, our days were unstructured, so in an attempt to combat homesickness and in order to provide some guidance to my men, I asked my platoon sergeant to help me gather my platoon to review Army protocol. My platoon sergeant, Stephen Roberts, had been in the Army for thirteen years by the time he was deployed to Iraq with me. Tall and strong, competitive and hard-working, he was the son of a Marine, and his grandfather had served in the Army. He understood the Army, and he understood why I wanted to have meetings with our men. We conducted the meetings in order to discuss how to apply classroom learning to scenarios we might face in Iraq. Rather than bombard our platoon with information they already knew, we wanted them to have time to talk. We also wanted to provide some structure in otherwise unstructured days in order to keep them focused.

My soldiers, of course, knew they were being forced into review sessions, so Roberts and I ensured the meetings were informal and relaxed. Soldiers see right through bullshit, so we avoided making the topics we were discussing seem more important than they were, and we tried to create an atmosphere where the men could talk openly and provide guidance for each other. Some of the men had been to Iraq before, so I knew we needed to learn from them. We needed to hear their suggestions. We reviewed how to conduct mounted and dismounted patrols. We discussed how to be a combat life-saver and how to react to contact with the enemy. We discussed the videos we had viewed that day, and we tried to make sure the men remained focused. During it all, I found that I was creating a bond with my men. They began to see me both as a leader and as a soldier, and the review sessions were the first real foundations of trust between them and me.

In truth, my men had some reason to doubt me. I had only been assigned to the unit four weeks prior to our deployment, so while everyone else in the company had gone through training together and had bonded in the exercises meant to prepare them for war, I had been trained in a separate unit and was, in their eyes, an unknown factor in their deployment. I was charged with leading them, but they knew basically nothing about me. The time leading up to deployment had offered little opportunity to interact with them in any way that would demonstrate my ability to lead them in combat, so when we were finally sent to Kuwait, I knew I needed to work hard to establish trust. Listening to them was central to that. I realized that in order for them to believe in me, I needed to show them that I believed in them, that I could learn from them.

I was surrounded by many men who had been in theater before. More than half of those who came over with me had already been to Iraq, and they carried with them a kind of resignation to the whims of the Army that I admired and envied, even while I sometimes found it frustrating. They were easy to recognize by their attitude and their uniforms. The Army ensured that they wore a clear hallmark of their previous service. Soldiers who had been to Iraq before wore the 1st Cavalry patch on both shoulders. The rest of us had it only on our left arm. The patch is in the shape of a shield, and it has a black horse's head on it. A black bar cuts across the field of the shield from the upper left to the lower right side. The horse's head is in the upper right-hand side of the shield. It is likely the most recognizable military patch, and all of us were aware of its history and significance. The horse's head represented the long tradition of the American cavalry, and the bar represented the strength of the armor.

Soldiers who had been to Iraq before had a saying that derived from their patches. When they encountered stiff resistance or when they simply felt like things were getting tough, they would say, "Hug your horses." It was a way of getting through the hard times. It suggested they had, in fact, already made it through tremendous difficulty and so had earned the right to have a horse on each shoulder to, in effect, protect them. It suggested their ability to survive and their ability to push through adversity. I wanted to embrace that experience, and I knew I had to be able to relate to and listen to them. I had to respect the fact that many of them had two horses protecting them.

Sgt. Brandon Duvall was one of those men. A California native, he had seen action in a previous deployment in Fallujah and Najaf, two of the most violent cities in Iraq. He had been in the company that had spearheaded the retaking of those cities and had seen more than his fair share of combat. He did not grumble. He did not complain. Instead, he used that experience to mentor younger men, younger soldiers. Including me. He became the emotional center of our platoon as our deployment lengthened, and early on, I realized that his experiences could be pivotal to keeping our platoon working well together. If he were willing to mentor, I was willing to listen.

Duvall worked alongside Sgt. Roberts in the Bravo section of my platoon. I relied on Roberts, both for his knowledge of tanks and warfare derived from his previous action in Iraq and for his candor in communicating to me the pulse of the platoon. Roberts had been running the platoon until

I arrived. For some time, the platoon had not had an officer
assigned to it, so he had been in charge until a fresh new
lieutenant could be found. He was nearly thirty-two. I was
twenty-four. He had the experience of a previous tour in
Iraq during the initial invasion. I had my officer training. He
could have been bitter, or angry, or even simply skeptical,
but he wasn't. He accepted my intrusion into the platoon
fully, and he understood that the best thing for the platoon
was to help me integrate and not undermine my tenuous
authority as a young, new officer. So, in front of the platoon, he was deferential and careful to ensure that everyone
followed orders and the chain of command. Behind closed
doors, often at night, when we would discuss the progress
of the war or the spirit of our group, he would speak to me
frankly, sharing his perception of how everyone seemed to be
doing. He provided me with the real information I needed to
make decisions, and he helped me understand what might
be at stake in those decisions, especially early on. As my platoon sergeant, Roberts' job was to ensure the smooth daily
routine of the platoon, but as my right-hand man, he became
much more than that. He became a trusted advisor.

In Kuwait, I tried to create a foundation for the platoon
by genuinely listening to men like Duvall and Roberts to
establish real faith in each other. I visited them in their quarters, and we talked about football, the women we loved, and
the war. We compared notes on our housing, and we teased
each other about the differences between my privileges as an
officer and their lives as enlisted men. I, for example, lived
in a room with only two other officers. They, by contrast,
lived in rooms with five or six bunks. The disparity made for
easy jokes, and I was quick to engage my men in the ribbing.
It became a daily ritual, and we began to build camaraderie,
the kind of stereotypical fraternal bond that Hollywood so
likes to overemphasize but that is, in truth, something real

and something important. I was conscious that this time in Kuwait, with its long hours of waiting and its repetitious reviews, was an important time to develop trust. It was a time to prepare for war.

It was also time to reflect. Even with the training, the reviews, and the daily interactions with my enlisted men, I spent many hours each day doing virtually nothing. We all did. That nothingness was difficult in Kuwait. The illusion of America that the base created, with its many conveniences and recognizable comforts, made many of us miss home even more. I talked about this with the two other platoon leaders I lived with. In the evenings, we went to the Green Beans Coffee Company, gathered in a group of lounge chairs, and talked about the future and how we were coping with this transition period in Kuwait. We discussed the fact that many of our men were restless and many were beginning to feel homesick. The long periods of nothing to do gave all of us too much time to think about what we were missing back home. The separation from our loved ones was only days old, and the atmosphere of the Kuwait base was enough to keep that separation fresh. We were able to call home and use the internet to communicate with friends and family, and while it was good to hear their voices, it also drove home the fact that we were now just beginning a mission and that we would soon be unable to contact them with any regularity.

I spent many of those long hours thinking about my wife, AJ. I met AJ when I was a junior in college at the Virginia Military Institute and had returned home to Philly for a short school break in October 2003. She lived about an hour from my home town, and we dated for almost two years before I proposed. In July 2005, I had just commissioned in the Army, and I went to the daycare where she worked and lined the hallways with baskets containing hints about where we might be based if she married me and followed my stationing in the

Army. One basket had pineapples in it for Hawaii, another peaches for Georgia, and another apples for Washington. When AJ arrived at work, I asked her if she would follow me wherever I might be asked to go. When she agreed, I asked her to marry me. She said yes.

On the day that we were married, only six months later, dreams of a Hawaii station were long gone. Everyone knew that I would soon be going to Iraq. I had not been given my official orders yet, but I was certain I was going to 1st Cavalry, and I knew they were scheduled for deployment to Iraq in October 2006. So, we began our marriage knowing I'd be going to the war, and as I started my military training in the States, I used to worry about how she would do while I was gone. I knew she was a strong woman, deeply independent, but I feared what my deployment would put her through. By the time we were in Kuwait, I began to worry what would happen to her if I did not come back.

She had already been confronted by the reality of the war a few days into my time in Kuwait, and it shook her. One afternoon, a young mother came to pick up her child from AJ's daycare. When the woman entered the room where her child was playing, AJ could tell that something was wrong. AJ asked a co-worker about the young mother, and she learned that just days before, the young woman's husband and the father of child had been killed in Iraq. AJ broke down. The story finally made real to her the dangers of my deployment, and I worried about what I was putting her through in choosing a military life.

My life in Iraq was just beginning even as she was finally come to terms with what my deployment could mean. On October 19, just a little past midnight, sat in one of the large lounge chairs of the Green Beans Coffee Company, I wrote a final journal entry from Kuwait. The next day, we were flying into Iraq, and all I could think about was AJ. I tried to reassure myself that she would be fine, and I reminded myself why I was here and why I chose this life. I reflected on how thankful I was for her and how much I loved her and our marriage, and I wrote a brief note to her in the middle of my journal. "I'll return home soon," I wrote, "promise." More thoughts about missing home overwhelmed my thinking about the war, and I wrote about autumn in Pennsylvania, trying to resurrect that landscape in the midst of the desert of Kuwait: "I will miss the fall season. I loved it. Upper Darby football games and friends, parties outside, tailgating and visiting other colleges, and AJ coming to visit." All of the memories seemed to reach out to me.

In an effort to get my head back to the mission and in an effort to push home back to where it needed to be, I wrote a final line in my journal. It was abrupt, it was purposeful, and it was an attempt to leave home behind. I wrote, "I am going to war."

I closed my journal, leaned back in the coffee shop's lounge chair for a moment, and finished my coffee. Then, I stood up and left the building. Outside across the street was the McDonald's sign. It was still lit, and I walked under its yellow glow back to my room, AJ still on my mind.

3

We arrived in Baqubah in Chinook helicopters, lifting off from our base in Kuwait and flying into Iraq at night. We flew in the dark in order to minimize the possibility of attacks on us from the ground, and the Chinooks heaved their large bodies toward a moon that made the pure sand of Kuwait glow. As we approached our new home, Forward Operating Base (FOB) Warhorse, the landscape below changed from the desert of Kuwait to the arid, sparsely vegetated land of Iraq, and when we stepped out of the Chinooks, we knew we had landed in a war zone. The perimeter of the base was surrounded by a fourteen-foot-high barrier that was, in some places, five feet thick. Razor wire lined the top of it. Humvees and tanks darted around a motor pool, and brown trailers rose up on blocks in a perfect grid, the only buildings inside the base's perimeter walls. The guard post at the entrance to the base crawled with soldiers, all dressed in the maximum protection they could wear, their faces barely visible below the low-sitting helmets on their heads. FOB Warhorse, set up to provide security for Baqubah and surrounding areas, was always braced for attack.

Baqubah is roughly thirty miles north of Baghdad and is the capital of Diyala Province, a large area of near desert through which runs the Diyala River, a tributary of the Tigris. By the time we arrived in October 2006, Diyala had become one of the most violent and destabilized regions in Iraq and home to some of the most severe sectarian violence. Nearly a thousand civilians had been killed since the beginning of the year, and nearly five hundred Iraqi government officials, including Iraqi police officers, had been murdered. Many of the small villages and a large portion of Diyala itself formed a battleground between two major terrorist groups, al-Qaida in Iraq (AQI) and Jaysh al-Mahdi (JAM). Numerous other smaller but no less violent insurgent groups also operated in the region, but AQI and JAM worked hardest to prevent the establishment of order.

Diyala's geography was the source of many of its problems. It shares its eastern border with Iran and its northern border with Kurdistan. The Tigris marks its western boundary and flows south to Baghdad and the sea beyond. These boundaries represent significant cultural boundaries as well as physical ones, and early in the war the province became a flashpoint for the clashing of various factions in Iraq.

The primary internal conflict was between the Sunnis and the Shias, and the smuggling of Iranian arms through the province exasperated the problem. The Sunni Muslims are the largest denomination of the Islam faith worldwide, but in Iran and Iraq they are the minority. Even so, they exercised considerable control over the country, and, despite being outnumbered by the Shias, have ruled over them and at times brutally oppressed them. The Shias make up around sixty percent of Iraq's population, and years of oppression created the considerable tension that escalated to violence in the months after the U.S. invasion. Shias saw the invasion as an opportunity to seize control and finally gain power in the Iraq government. Many also saw it as an opportunity for retribution.

Jaysh al-Mahdi, a Shia Muslim organization with close ties to Iran, formed after the Coalition invasion and is a loosely controlled group of militants affiliated with the radical cleric Moqtada al-Sadr. Al-Sadr gained control over an area in Baghdad that became known as Sadr City, and while most of the press around al-Sadr and JAM centers on Baghdad, JAM activity in Diyala was pronounced and oftentimes more violent than in Baghdad because JAM insurgents were attempting to seize control from Sunni Muslims. Al-Qaida in Iraq is Sunni, so as al-Qaida continued to build its network of terrorist cells in Diyala from which it could launch attacks into Baghdad, it came into increasing contact with JAM operatives.

Each group sought power in a decidedly different manner. JAM members often worked within the system. They joined local government and rose to positions of power. From those positions, they oftentimes exacted revenge on the Sunnis by denying them access to U.S. aid or by arresting, beating, and torturing them. Al-Qaida, on the other hand, worked from outside the system and launched attacks intended to disrupt the functioning of the state. Al-Qaida has received more press in the States probably because of 9/11 and other dramatic attacks, while JAM activities are often virtually invisible. For coalition forces, al-Qaida was often the direct threat, but JAM was an insidious force whose workings boiled beneath the surface of the social structure until military intervention was the only option.

Conflict between the Sunnis and the Shias escalated throughout the years leading up to our time there, and Baqubah in particular became a strategic point for the launching of terrorist operations throughout Diyala and in Baghdad. Al-Qaida established a strong foothold in the area, taking control of many small towns, to the degree that some, like Hadid, were viewed as essentially unpatrollable by the Iraqi Army. In April 2006, just six months before our arrival, the notorious leader of al-Qaida in Iraq, Abu Musab al-Zar-qawi, declared Heb Heb, a small village that would eventually fall under my area of responsibility, as his headquarters. Al-Zarqawi had planned bombings and attacks that had killed thousands of soldiers and civilians, and he was purportedly the man speaking to the camera as he beheaded Nicholas Berg in a horrific video shown around the world. He hoped to estab-lish an essentially independent region that would function as the headquarters and training grounds for al-Qaida.

While al-Qaida took control and secured several small villages in Diyala in 2005 and 2006, they used Baqubah as a base for many of their attacks in Baghdad. When those attacks continued to increase in scale and frequency, the U.S. Army finally made a decision to aggressively root out the enemy in Diyala. Our reassignment from Kuwait to the Diyala Province was part of an attempt to bring the virtu-ally lawless Diyala under control. Everyone knew it was not going to be easy.

By the time we arrived, however, the Army had had some success. Soldiers from FOB Warhorse were slowly and sys-tematically uncovering terrorist safe-houses in Baqubah, and al-Zarqawi had been killed just two months after he made Heb Heb his headquarters. On June 8, 2006, U.S. jets dropped two bombs and two missiles on an al-Qaida safe-house just north of Baqubah. Soldiers swooped in on the scene and found several bodies, including those of al-Zarqawi's wife and child. They found al-Zarqawi himself still alive, though mortally wounded. He survived an hour longer, and in that time, al-Zarqawi made a final declaration. Fight the enemy, he insisted, and destroy the Americans. He died encouraging the war, and my company and my men would cope with that dying command for the duration of our time in Iraq.

In the months after al-Zarqawi's death, the violence in Diyala did not abate. Indeed, the violence between the Shia JAM, with reported support from militants in Iran, and the Sunni al-Qaida escalated. Several hundred coalition soldiers were killed, and uncounted civilians were slain in sectarian and terrorist violence. We arrived at a time when the Army recognized the need to seize control of the region, and our company was one of many tasked with making the area safe again.

Our company, Delta Company, had an expansive area of operation. It covered a portion of Baqubah, a city of 315,000 people, and stretched westward nearly twelve miles all the way to the Tigris. From the center of Baqubah, our area stretched north nearly thirty-seven miles. Within that area was Heb Heb, al-Zarqawi's self-declared center of operation for al-Qaida in Iraq, Sadiyah, a town controlled by Jaysh al-Mahdi militants and known to have a concentration of what the U.S. government called High-Value Individuals, and Khalis, a city that was a perfect microcosm of Baghdad in its demographics and one that was often saddled with out-of-control sectarian violence. Forward Operating Base Warhorse was just to the north and west of Baqubah, and from it, we ran our missions into both the city itself and the countryside and villages in our area.

Our company was a tank company, and we were the 12th Regiment of the 1st Battalion, part of what the Army calls a combined arms battalion. A battalion is typically the smallest military unit capable of functioning independently and is composed of several companies. Each company is in turn composed of platoons. Our company consisted of two tank platoons and one infantry platoon. Each tank platoon consisted of sixteen soldiers, four tanks, and four humvees. The infantry platoon consisted of forty-five soldiers, six humvees, and four Bradleys, small armored vehicles used to transport soldiers. In all, then, our company was around eighty men, and it was responsible for an area roughly the size of Long Island. We were, obviously, stretched thin.

In order to manage the area, each platoon was assigned its own area of operation, effectively breaking the company's larger area of operation into manageable parts. My platoon, White Platoon, was designated the "Company Main Effort" platoon, meaning we would patrol the largest and most problem-ridden section of our area. Being designated the Company Main Effort platoon is an honor. It meant that my Commanding Officer believed that we were capable of handling the brunt of enemy action. It meant that he trusted us, but it also meant that we would be under significant stress.

I would rely on the men in my tank to get me through the stress that we would encounter. Cpl. Hugo Garnica was my gunner, in charge of operating our main cannon. Like Sgt. Brandon Duvall, he had seen action in a previous deployment in Najaf during some of that area's biggest fighting, and he was a seasoned, thoughtful soldier with a sense of humor that mirrored mine. Marion Deboe, a calm and assured soldier who, along with Garnica, became one of my reliable friends, handled the dirty work of prepping and loading the main weapon. A native of St. Louis, he was working his second deployment and was a steady, trustworthy soldier. Specialist Robert Smith we called Smitty, and he was our tank's driver. Southern by birth and by pride, he spoke in drawls and worked incessantly, a virtual perfectionist. The four of us formed a team that, unlike some other tanks, created a strong sense of brotherhood between us. We relied on each other. We trusted each other.

The faith that we put in each other was apparent to our Company Commander, and it probably led to us being designated the Company's Main Effort. We led a platoon that would be assigned the widest area of operation and, at the time, part of the most dangerous. My platoon's area included the village of Heb Heb and stretched to Sadiyah, which hugs the Tigris, but our center of gravity was the town of Khalis, a hot spot patrolled by other platoons as well that was about ten miles northwest of Baqubah and seven miles northwest of FOB Warhorse. It was viewed by both the Sunni and the Shia as vital for control of the region, perhaps even more so than Baqubah proper. The town was effectively controlled by a Shia majority backed by the Shia-dominated Iraqi Army and Iraqi Police in the area, and Jaysh al-Mahdi ran portions of the town. The town was strategic because it provided access to key roads from Baqubah to the more desolate northern Diyala and to the southwest, past a Sunni-dominated area called the Iron Triangle. Revenge and retaliation in the hopes of controlling the town dominated local politics, government, and military and police activities.

The Iraqi Army stationed at a Khalis base reflected its sectarian-fueled conflicts. The ranks of the Khalis Iraqi Army were dominated by Shias, though some soldiers were Sunnis. Shias were suspicious of the Sunnis and consistently accused them of being al-Qaida in Iraq members or sympathizers. No evidence, other than rumors perpetuated by the Shia command, existed to substantiate these claims. Sunni officers and soldiers lived in constant fear of kidnapping or loss of their jobs simply because they were Sunni. Reports of Sunnis kidnapped at Iraqi Army or Iraqi Police checkpoints around the Khalis area were all too familiar.

Pockets of Sunnis lived throughout Khalis, but the majority of them lived just outside the town in small Sunni-dominated neighborhoods. Going to and leaving from these areas often meant passing checkpoints, and the Sunnis were quick to suggest that the Shias running the checkpoints were affiliated with or were active members of Jaysh al-Mahdi. Fighters from JAM would venture into Sunni areas of Khalis and Sunni villages like Heb Heb and Hadid to incite conflict with their Sunni enemy. The Khalis Iraqi Army did little, if anything, to counter Shia-led attacks in the area, arguing they did not have the manpower or weaponry to protect themselves. They were, however, eager to patrol Sunni strongholds like Heb Heb and were quick to use force there. Iraqi Army patrols in Shia-dominated regions were never done independently of U.S. forces, and they regularly conducted the patrols simply to give the impression they cared or were concerned about JAM activities in the area. In actuality, they were happy to have JAM aggressively seek out Sunnis.

This is not to say that the Shia-dominated Khalis Iraqi Army did nothing of value. It was vital in the eventual push to retake a section of Diyala Province along the northern side of the Diyala River. Even though towns in this area varied in their sect-affiliation, there was a strong al-Qaida presence. AQI was persistent in its desire to eradicate Shias from the area, and some suggested they were attempting to strengthen their position in order to eventually take over Khalis. AQI dominated the towns along the southern edge of the Diyala River and ran rampant in Baqubah, so the move to the northern side of the river appeared to be an attempt to gain ground along the route to Khalis. In response, the Iraqi Army in conjunction with the 5th Battalion of the 82nd Airborne conducted Operation Church in the area in August 2007. The one-day engagement saw some of the heaviest fighting by the 82nd during its entire deployment. The operation resulted in the capture of three ranking AQI terrorists, the killing of thirty-three other AQI members, and the seizure of numerous weapons caches. The Iraqi Army was central in the execution of that operation.

While the tension between Shias and Sunnis in Khalis had a long history, the volatile situation was made worse after the U.S. invasion because of the city's proximity to Camp Ashraf, a primary site of the People's Mujahedin of Iran (Mujahedin-e Khalq, or MEK). The MEK consisted of Iranian ex-pats who fought alongside Saddam's regime in the Iran–Iraq War in an attempt to topple the Ayatollah of Iran. The motives of this group are complex. Although Shia, its primary objective is to control Iran, so its enemy throughout the region is JAM, with its connections to the Iranian military. The MEK began to see that perhaps the best way to defeat JAM and limit Iran's influence in Iraq was by aligning itself with al-Qaida. The MEK is notoriously skillful at intelligence operations, and, by working with al-Qaida, who had a strong system in place for executing deadly attacks, it saw an opportunity to destabilize both Iraq and Iran.

Our company, therefore, was working in a region with deep layers of distrust and hatred. We were combating the more notorious Sunni al-Qaida and their Shia MEK allies, and we were trying to root out the subtle destructive force of the Shia JAM as they waged their war both on Coalition forces and on al-Qaida and the MEK. Even within these groups, other splinter organizations operated, and trying to draw connections between them was often not only fruitless but undesirable. Some groups worked so independently that attempting to associate them with larger terrorist operations could lead to real misunderstandings of how the region was coping with war. So, we focused our efforts on seizing control of each town or village by uncovering the terrorist operations within them and restoring the rule of law. We helped local officials locate and arrest any militants who had surreptitiously ascended to positions of power within the government, and we directly confronted al-Qaida and its associated groups.

Of course, on the night we arrived in Iraq, I could not fully appreciate the complexity of the problems of Diyala Province. I certainly could not anticipate the degree to which terrorist organizations had infiltrated the local governments. What I knew, stepping off the Chinook and making my way to my bunk that night, was that the next few months were going to be intense. I knew, as well, that I would have to ensure that my men worked within our protocol in order to effect real change. I knew, finally, that we needed, whenever we could, to avoid some of the mistakes of the battalion we were replacing. That battalion, in the closing days of its deployment, created significant animosity in the community, and some of the terrorist organizations decided that we needed to be taught a lesson about who was really in charge of Diyala.

That lesson became very clear within our first two weeks in Iraq, when an extraordinarily powerful IED called an Explosively Formed Projectile (EFP) destroyed a humvee from the previous battalion and killed three soldiers in it. An EFP is an extremely sophisticated and dangerous weapon that blasts molten copper into the area around it. The molten copper can pierce most of the armor on our vehicles, and the detonation of an EFP signifies that violence in the area is escalating. Because of its sophistication and its cost, it also signifies Iranian involvement in the attack. EFPs were trademarks of JAM, and they were usually constructed by JAM terrorists who had trained in Iran and brought EFP technology back to Iraq. When EFPs were detonated, our highest-ranking officials were notified, and our soldiers knew that we were being sent a message. In this case, the Jaysh al-Mahdi message was clear: leave the area.

Only a couple of days later, we received the same message from al-Qaida. Our platoon had just finished a joint operation in Baqubah, and we were returning to FOB Warhorse. The air was dry, and the temperature had already risen past

100 degrees. We rolled back toward the base along the main road connecting Baqubah to the rest of Diyala Province, and just outside the city limits, al-Qaida had left a gruesome sign.

Decapitated heads lined the highway. They were the heads of Iraqi Police, national policemen whom al-Qaida killed for working alongside Coalition forces. Flies filled the air around them. Al-Qaida insurgents wanted us to know, and they wanted the people of Baqubah to know, that they had no intention of ceding power. They wanted us to know who really ran the town, and they wanted us to see that we could not protect the men who had volunteered to fight with us. They, like JAM, wanted us to know that they had no intention of leaving without a fight.

4

Forward Operating Base Warhorse is barren. The ground is dirt, and nothing grows within its walls. Military vehicles line the roadways, ready for excursions into Diyala and Baqubah, and the buildings, the soldiers, and the vehicles are all the color of the countryside – desert brown. The base had been scraped out of the Iraqi landscape shortly after the U.S. invasion, and from its founding to the time of my arrival, it remained a place where soldiers spent more time on patrol outside its walls than living inside them. The result was that Warhorse had few amenities. No food courts, no theaters, no particular access to the comforts of a place like the Kuwait base or even a base like FOB Anaconda, a sprawling FOB that seemed like Disneyland when compared to Warhorse. Located in Balad, Anaconda had movie theaters, fast-food restaurants, a hotel with a swimming pool, and a well-equipped and -staffed hospital. Warhorse had none of these.

Warhorse was surrounded by two layers of defensive walls made of HESCO baskets. HESCO baskets are large wire containers with a liner, and though they vary in size, they are typically six feet high by four feet deep by four feet wide. When filled with earth, the baskets are extraordinarily effective defenses. They can be stacked, and the base's outer walls were sometimes four baskets high and two deep. The inner walls, which surrounded the residential area of Warhorse, were two high and one deep. Within this second wall were rows upon rows of trailers, and against each one of them, sandbags were stacked shoulder high, providing the only real protection from enemy rounds or ordnance that might land within the walls. Each trailer looked identical to the next, and each was covered in sandbags, dirt, and dust.

I lived in a small trailer with another lieutenant, Scott Siggins, who worked as our company intelligence officer. Later, he would become Blue Platoon's leader. Siggins, a Texas Tech grad, was about the same age as me, and he was a field artillery officer. His primary job as our intel officer was to compile and analyze intelligence reports from the field, but it was far from what he wanted to do. He wanted to be with the maneuver forces, either infantry or armor, and he would eventually get the chance to head up Blue when the previous platoon leader simply didn't perform well. Siggins was serious about his work, but he was also not always particularly precise in all the things that he did. He was a bit of a mess around the trailer, and though that trait was sometimes a bit irritating, it actually worked out well for us, because I, in my stress, often found it comforting to clean and arrange things, even his stuff. He never did get himself a blanket for his bed, so AJ eventually sent him bedding, including a blanket that her grandmother had made especially for him.

All in all, Siggins and I made good roommates, and our trailer, like all of the others, became a kind of home, even though tiny and made only of thin, painted steel. They were called "CHU's," an acronym for Containerized Housing

Unit, a name that bespoke its lack of homeliness. Our CHU was number 129, and it was identical to 128, 127, and every other trailer in the FOB. We all lived in them, and we all came to know every detail of every corner of our new homes.

When I first entered my CHU, it was dark. I turned on the fluorescent light, and to my left I saw a mangled metal bed frame and a brown, soiled mattress. A broom leaned in a corner, and a bucket full of dark water stood in front of me. A small drip of water fell from a leak in the ceiling and splashed in the bucket. The interior of the room was vacant, and the air was stagnant. All I heard was the sound of my boots on the floor and the occasional drop of water. I looked across the twelve by six foot metal room, and I knew we would not be able to live there without somehow making it our own.

First, Siggins and I secured beds. We threw out the old bed frame and mattress, and I found a cot, a board, and a new, clean mattress, thin and blue stripes, not unlike the mattress I had slept on for four years in college in the Virginia Military Institute (VMI) barracks. Next to my bed, I placed a desk, and above the desk I hung a poster of the Philadelphia Eagles and the brown wrapper of a Hershey's chocolate bar. Hershey, Pennsylvania, was the location of the wrestling state championships, and I hung the wrapper as a reminder of my commitment to work through adversity and to learn leadership. I also hung, before any of the others, a poster of my wife. She was wearing a VMI uniform, unbuttoned so that her body showed beneath the gray jacket. She was bent down and forward, leaning toward the viewer, and smiling. It was a seductive reminder of home, and it was the last thing I saw every night. Before I went to bed, I said goodnight to my wife, then I turned to Siggins, said good night to him, and told him, sometimes wryly, sometimes sincerely, that AJ said goodnight to him as well. Sometimes we would stay awake for hours, talking across the darkness in the room, sharing stories from our past, thinking hard about our futures. For the next year, that was my routine, and CHU 129 and the dry, endless earth of Warhorse was my home.

I wondered, at first, if the land outside Warhorse would look any different. I imagined that the barrenness of the site might have been due to the fact that, in excavating it to make a base, the Army had simply built on exposed dirt without thinking about aesthetics. My first time outside the walls, however, demonstrated that the landscape inside was simply no different than that outside the walls. It was sparse, it was isolated, and it was hot. It was incredibly hot.

Our uniforms provided no comfort in the heat. Our ACUs, the newest military fatigue, covered our entire body so that none of it would be exposed to the sun. Over our ACUs we also wore our Improved Ballistic Armor when we went outside the wire. We usually called it our OTV, or Outer Tactical Vest, and it consisted of a vest lined with Kevlar mesh. Inside the Kevlar mesh we would slip in protective plates capable of stopping 7.62 rounds, which were the typical ammunition of AK-47s, the primary weapons of our enemies. One plate in back, one plate in front, and two under the arms. They weighed seventy-five pounds, and they made the uniforms even more uncomfortable to wear.

None of us seriously complained, of course. We all griped occasionally, but the protection far outweighed the discomfort. Indeed, the plates we wore were newly developed to provide extra protection, so we were thankful that we were using the best equipment. Even so, the first time I prepared to leave the gates of Warhorse, I knew I would be uncomfortable in the heat. I also felt, slipping in the plates for the first time, that my life could end in the war. Holding the plates in my hand was an acknowledgment of how frail my body was, how incapable it was of confronting the weapons of war. So, in preparation for my first time out, I wrote a letter to AJ, a final note in the event that I was killed.

Most soldiers write this type of letter at some point. It's a melodramatic moment, one that we all remember, but one that we also feel is necessary. We want to know that if we die, we did not leave anything unsaid. We want to know that we can offer comfort and express our love one last time. We want to send out our voice one final time. So, we write our letters, hoping they are never opened, and we leave them safe back at the base. I left mine in my desk drawer, and I told my Executive Officer where it was and asked him to ensure it made it to AJ. Then I went out to meet my company.

We all gathered next to our tanks and humvees. The company we were replacing was with us, there to guide us on our first few missions into Diyala Province. We discussed the day's objective, which was simply for the outgoing company to introduce us to the area, then crawled into our vehicles.

I rode with a platoon leader in his tank. We traced out the area called the Iron Triangle, the name for the set of three major roads that constituted the primary conduits between the cities of northern, eastern, and western Diyala Province. We rumbled along these major highways, and the man I was replacing oriented me to the local towns we were passing. Here is a Sunni stronghold, he would say, or here we suspect that JAM has taken control of the police force. He was helpful and informative, but it was also clear that he, like the other men of his company, was ready to leave.

They had seen significant action during their deployment, and some of the men of the company did not hide their hostility toward the people of Diyala Province. When they came across a local businessman selling gasoline, for example, they dumped out the gasoline and set it on fire, declaring that the fuel represented a threat to their safety. On one occasion, during the time that we overlapped with them at Warhorse, my

Company Commander traveled with them to a small village. There, they were greeted by a barking dog. Their Company Commander dropped to one knee, leveled his rifle, and shot the dog twice, killing it. He simply did not tolerate distractions or perceived confrontations, even those from a dog.

Word of U.S. military misdeeds born of frustration spread quickly in the small towns, and anger toward American forces escalated. Al-Qaida's lining the road to Baqubah with the heads of decapitated Iraqi Police was perhaps the most startling response to our presence, but by the time my company began operations in the area, we were confronted daily with suspicion, distrust, and, not infrequently, profound hatred. When we drove into Sadiyah, for instance, children threw rocks at us and drew their fingers across their necks to simulate slicing open our throats. While some of this hatred certainly emerged from a deep skepticism of American motives for invading Iraq, many of these daily reactions to us were fueled by the rash behavior of the previous company in the weeks leading up to their departure. They simply had not respected many of the townspeople. None of us judged that company's actions. We had not experienced their stress or their suffering, and we were just beginning our tour in a place that we knew would be hostile to us. We were keenly aware, however, that those men's actions created another barrier between us and the locals, between progress and peace, and none of us were happy about it.

When I finally began my own patrols in Diyala, then, my primary goal was to establish trust, especially with the local leaders. I knew that I had to repair the damage some previous soldiers had caused before we could effect meaningful change. Trust would create dialogue. Trust would reduce violence. In order for me to try to earn that trust, however, I would first have to demonstrate to my chain of command that I was a good leader and a good soldier. I challenged my men to work with me on this, explaining to them that I thought the best way for us to make a difference was to work with the local leaders who could be trusted instead of against them by simply imposing our will. My platoon stood with me, and we very quickly established ourselves as a strong, reliable platoon within the battalion. We conducted our daily patrols professionally and efficiently, and we focused on the idea that our primary mission was to provide security to the people of Diyala and Baqubah.

Early in our time, we had our first real chance to create meaningful dialogue with the people in our area of operation. In mid-November, a prominent sheik's cousin died, and a memorial service was scheduled. The sheik was a central figure in Sadiyah, the town where even the children threatened us, and I knew we needed to make a connection with him. So, in order to show our respect for him and his family, I asked my entire platoon to attend the service. It was held in the court-yard of the sheik's residence. Two rows of chairs two chairs deep were set up facing each other with a small space between them. We entered the courtyard, and we took seats in one of the rows. Only men were allowed to sit, and the women of the family went from man to man serving chai tea.

The memorial service was less a formal, speech-giving or preaching affair than an opportunity to gather and talk, so I spoke with the people around me through my interpreter. I was careful to follow local customs surrounding this type of service, having learned from my translator how best to act respectfully while there. I wanted to show the sheik, his family, and his community that I appreciated their rituals, and I wanted him to know that I would make an effort to learn his customs and his language. When I spoke to the men around me, I gave my condolences, and at the end of the service, the sheik came up to me. He expressed his gratitude, and he invited us to dinner. I accepted.

The meal was my first exposure to the daily life of an Iraqi. The gathering was lively and animated, and the room was filled with smells I did not recognize. We stood with the sheik and his family at a large rectangular table. Bowls of rice, meat, and dates were arranged in groups at various parts of the table, and men gathered in front of them. When the most senior or most respected member of that group began to eat, the others could begin. When he finished eating, the others had to finish as well. I stood at one end of the table, a position of respect, and my men followed my cues as to when and what to eat. When we were served goat meat that was green, apparently from age more than from seasoning, most of us had to prevent ourselves from recoiling. The goat, however, appeared to be a luxury, and it represented the significance of the gathering and the importance of the sheik. We all ate it, some, like me, in smaller portions than others. Deboe ripped pieces of the meat from the goat and, studying it closely first, eventually swallowed pieces of it whole, trying to avoid having it in his mouth for too long. Duvall and Garnica, knowing they were being offered a special meal, smiled at Iraqis gathered around the table, nodding their thanks and approval even while avoiding thinking about what they were eating. Though we all feared food poisoning, we all expressed our gratitude, and throughout it all, we remained standing, eating with our hands, digging into bowls shared by other members of our group.

I talked to the sheik from time to time throughout the meal, and during those brief conversations, he occasionally expressed his concern about how the American soldiers had treated his people. I tried to assure him that I wanted things to be different, and I promised him that my goal was the security of his town. I suggested that in the future we might establish town meetings where we would be able, on the one hand, to hear his concerns and the concerns of the town and, on the other, to explain our methods for establishing order. He agreed, and in the following weeks we initiated a series of town meetings that would ultimately help bring Sadiyah under control.

The meal at the sheik's residence signified that our compassion and hard work could lead to meaningful interactions with the Iraqis. It also signified that even a small platoon tasked with securing a large area could make a change. I knew it was early – we had only been in theater for just over a month – but I was encouraged, and I let my men know that I was hopeful. We were engaged in combat regularly, and we were conducting raids and arresting terrorists who wanted us all dead, but we had within a short period of time demonstrated to a part of the population of Diyala Province that we wanted things to be different and that we wanted their help in making their cities and villages safe.

While on patrol on November 22, six weeks into our time in Iraq and not even two weeks after our meal with the sheik, we happened upon another funeral. This time, nearly forty sheiks had gathered, and as we approached them, they came to us with their concerns. Where was the money for the road projects, they wanted to know, why had the water project not begun yet, and why were we detaining one of their sheiks? I talked with them, and, because of the goodwill our platoon had started to build, they trusted that, even if I could not bring about the change they wanted, I would bring back answers to their questions. Later, when the sheik who had been detained was released, I personally escorted him back to Sadiyah. Even though it was not part of typical protocol, I wanted to show the townspeople that our platoon wanted things to be different.

After talking to the sheiks at the funeral, we drove back to the base. A late afternoon sun hung low over the land. I reflected on the fact that our platoon had started to form genuine relationships with the people of Sadiyah. I felt proud, and when we turned our vehicles into the base, I remembered that tonight we would be able to relax and enjoy ourselves. No one had paid much attention to the time of month, and no one had paid much attention to the fact that it was the end of November. It was Thanksgiving, and we had been too busy to even realize it. It seemed almost like a surprise party when we finally walked into the mess hall that evening and found a celebration.

Streamers of fall colors laced the ceiling, and cornucopia filled with squash, apples, and orange flowers graced the center of each table. Colorful tablecloths stretched beneath them, hiding sterile metal tables, and the entire hall smelled of turkey. The enlisted men sat at the tables gorging themselves, and the officer of each platoon served his men. I ladled gravy onto my men's mashed potatoes, and I filled their glasses with cider. Deboe teased me, asking for refills, demanding more food. Duvall laughed at Deboe's insistence. We all talked about home and our holiday traditions, and we reminisced about football and autumn air.

We also celebrated a promising start to our time in Iraq. We felt like we were making connections and helping the people of Diyala feel safer. We felt that we were making a difference, and I, and many of my men, felt a strong sense of purpose and a strong sense of vocation. I felt like I had been destined to be here to help this country, and I felt like I was fulfilling a higher calling. So, I celebrated with my men, gave thanks for our own safety, and embraced my role as someone who could make a change, believing fully that we were going to transform our small corner of Iraq. I knew I was in the right place, even if it were not home.

5

The success of our platoon, however, made only a small impression on the large area my company was working in. Since the beginning of October when we had arrived, kidnappings and killings in Diyala had escalated. Children and educators had been killed, Iraqi police remained targets and were being murdered, and civilians were subject to kidnappings and bribery as the insurgents continued to expand the war against the Coalition forces. Our own military reports showed that over one hundred Iraqi police had been killed throughout October and November, most of those by al-Qaida in and around Baqubah. By early December, the power of the new Iraqi Army was being directly challenged, and we would be needed to help them regain their superiority in battle. In December, as the air cooled and the deep heat of November faded, my platoon would be sent to a battle in Dojima, a small town on the northern edge of our area of operation, in order to help the Iraqi Army subdue an al-Qaida force that had killed several Iraqi soldiers.

Dojima had been a mystery to me for quite a while. It did not have the reputation of a place like Khalis or Heb Heb, both of which were essentially controlled by al-Qaida, but we knew it contained the remnants of some of Saddam's Army. It was a primarily Sunni town, and its residents had been relatively successful under Saddam's rule. Many had been officers under Hussein and apparently stayed loyal to him. In the years after the invasion of Iraq, the Dojima townspeople maintained and polished a picture of Saddam, refusing to tear it down. As a result of the town's connection to Saddam's military rule, many of its neighborhoods reflected wealth not seen in most of our area of operation, and we, for the most part, spent little time there.

My platoon's mission into the town that day was to offer support for an Iraqi Army unit that had been decimated by al-Qaida fighters. Iraqi Army soldiers had chased the al-Qaida fighters through a part of our area and finally pinned them in a house in Dojima, but from that house, the enemy had mounted a sustained defense that resulted in increasing Iraqi Army casualties.

My platoon was sent to support the Iraqis because we had been assigned as the battalion Quick Reaction Force. For several days, our sole job was to stand ready to support other units. We spent our days together waiting for a call to assist other units, and most of the time, we played cards, we talked, and we read. Duvall shared stories about his previous action throughout Iraq, and Roberts talked about his previous action as a master gunner. I learned about my men during these times, and we hunkered down and waited for a call for support. If a task took longer than five minutes to accomplish, we simply didn't do it for fear that we'd get a call during that time. We didn't shower, we didn't make phone calls home, and if we needed something to eat, we sent a runner to the mess hall to pick up fifteen meals and bring them back to us. If we wanted to feel clean, we washed our faces with wet wipes. Some of us slept in our uniforms so that if a call for aid came at night, we could simply pull on our boots and go. Our job was to be in our vehicles within moments and be on the road to give aid in less than fifteen minutes.

The day we were assigned to be the Quick Reaction Force, we drove four tanks and four humvees from the motor pool and parked them next to the HESCO baskets surrounding the CHUs. The motor pool was thick with mud because our section of Iraq had seen considerable rain as winter set in. The ground of the motor pool, when dry, is covered in a fine dust that is, in some places, knee-high. An endless train of eight-ton vehicles crushed the earth each day, grinding it into a fine silt and reducing it to the consistency of baby powder. When rain mixes with it, it creates a pasty mud that adheres to anything. We slogged through it to our vehicles, and it sucked at our feet and legs. We grabbed at handles on the vehicles with both hands, yanked ourselves out of the deep mud, and pulled ourselves up and into our tanks and humvees. We drove ourselves to the HESCO wall nearest our housing units. We parked our tanks and humvees in a neat line against the exterior of the wall.

We cleaned and prepped the vehicles for several hours. They needed to be in what we called Red Con Two condition. Red Con One condition means that the vehicles are completely ready to roll, including having their engines running. Red Con Two is one step below, basically being ready to roll within just minutes but without the engines fired. We cleaned the windshields and headlights and removed caked mud from the front of the humvees. We placed our body armor in our vehicles, and we ensured each person had night-vision goggles and two-day supplies of food and water. We prepped the mounted weapons, and then we all retreated to our CHUs and waited, leaving behind one soldier to guard the convoy and our equipment.

All of us carried walkie-talkies, and two men at a time were assigned to listen to Charger Net, the radio frequency that carried most of the signals being broadcast in our area of operation. My soldiers took shifts listening, scanning broadcasts for any sign that we might be needed. We would, of course, be informed by the battalion command if we were to be "spun up" to render aid, but we liked to have some sense of what was happening in the area and, with any luck, get some advance warning that we might be called upon. The men listening to the radio would let me know if anything sounded like it was getting out of control or if anything unusual was happening so that we could prepare ourselves.

We had already been on the Quick Reaction Force assignment for several days before anything unusual happened. Each day we had been spun up several times to support to the Explosive Ordnance Disposal unit. We escorted them from their base to the site of the explosives they were sent to disarm, then we escorted them back to their base. It was routine, it was unremarkable, and it was largely safe work. The Ordnance Disposal teams worked within areas that had otherwise been cleared of threats, so our job was to make sure they simply made it to their site safely. Each day passed without notable event.

In the late afternoon sun of December 14, things changed. We were spun up to aid Iraqi Army soldiers who were outmatched, and we became engaged in a pitched engagement. I rode in a humvee to the battle, and Roberts took a tank. Typically, the platoon leader took the tank and the platoon sergeant was in the humvee. The reason is to protect the platoon leader because the tank is safer than the humvee. I thought that particular arrangement, though, did not fit our platoon well. I wanted to be able to interact with soldiers on the ground, and getting in and out of tank is far more difficult than it is from a humvee. Additionally, the maneuverability of the humvee ensured that I could get to the soldiers I wanted to talk to quickly. Equally important, assigning Roberts to a tank utilized his strengths. He was a master gunner who had already seen action in Iraq during a previous deployment. He had significant achievements commanding a tank and controlled the weapons with deadly precision. I thought that not putting him in a position to use his skills was foolish, so we inverted the typical way that platoons spun up, and we played to our strengths. I had special skills in communicating and interacting with Iraqis. He had special skills in the tank weaponry. Our platoon was strongest in this alignment, and we spun up in two humvees and two tanks.

We rolled quickly to the Tactical Operations Center, where we received a briefing and our orders. The TOC officer pointed to a large map that covered an entire wall and described what he understood to be the layout of the battle. Our job, he said, was to provide support for the Iraqi Army and the U.S. soldiers with them, and we were to eliminate the enemy that the Iraqi Army troops had been unable to subdue. I knew the battle was serious because the two televisions in the room both showed images of the battle in progress. Usually, they were tuned into something like football games, so the fact that they showed the battle meant the soldiers there were facing serious resistance. By the time we left the walls of Warhorse, it was still before five p.m., and over the radio, we could hear that a battle was raging in Dojima.

The trip to Dojima took about fifteen minutes. It should have been shorter, but burned-out humvees and other detritus from the battle filled the street and blocked our way. As we rode, we listened to the sounds of war on the radio. We could hear the popping sound of AK-47s, and we could hear the Iraqi Army troops call out their commands in Arabic.

Occasionally, we heard the American soldiers reporting incidents. By the time we arrived, we knew that the Iraqi Army had blundered and had suffered significant losses because of its own lack of training and discipline.

I directed our vehicles up a main street running through the town, and we turned right on a smaller street that was lined with houses. Ahead of us, on the left-hand side, smoke billowed from a house. The Air Force had dropped a 500-lb bomb on it and decimated it. To the left of that house, another house, gray and clearly the home of a wealthy member of the town, rose behind a head-high wall. Iraqi Army soldiers pressed their bodies up against the wall, ducking from the rapid machine-gun fire coming from the house. I could see the flash of the gun in the house, and I could see blood on the street. Several soldiers lay motionless against the wall. Others hugged it, occasionally lifting their weapons to shoot around corners or to return fire at the building above them.

I pulled my humvee alongside one of the Iraqi Army unit's humvees, and a U.S. soldier stepped out to meet me. He was one of the Captains in charge of training this Iraqi Army unit, and he was agitated. He did not smile when he saw me, and when we greeted each other, he took only a second to let me know that his men were under significant duress. He was sweaty, and his brow was furrowed low. We were only forty yards from the wall of the target house, and his eyes moved quickly around the scene while he described to me how the engagement had been going. He spoke quickly, his words dropping like the staccato fire of the AK-47s. I called in the situation to the Tactical Operations Center with my recommendations, and they gave me the green light to attack the target house. I called Roberts, and we engaged the tanks in the battle.

I ordered my tanks to maneuver along the street so that they faced the house at an angle. They rolled to opposite sides of the house, allowing each one to see along one side of the house and the front of it. I sent my humvees to take up positions on the other sides of the house in order to secure the space between the tanks. Along the way, they worked with the Iraqi Army unit to clear our soldiers from being too close to the target, establishing a perimeter and securing it to ensure that no civilians could enter the area around the house.

The house was two stories high and built of cinder block. It resembled a house from a fifties design magazine, modern and rectangular with low-slung, flat roofs. Simple pillars supported a ceiling over part of a patio, and another thin roof-line hung cantilevered out over the rest of it. The wall around the house was substantial, and an ornate metal gate protected the main entrance into a courtyard. The courtyard showed that the house had not been kept in good condition in recent time. Weeds and overgrown grass sprouted from it and between patio stones, but despite the appearance of the courtyard, the house was clearly the home of a wealthy Iraqi.

The owner had been an officer in Saddam's Army and had decided to continue his fight against the Coalition forces by working with al-Qaida. He had become a lower-level leader of AQI, and he used his house to plan attacks. The al-Qaida soldiers now in the house had, during the course of their engagement with the Iraqi Army, retreated here to make a stand. Along the way, they had catastrophically destroyed five Iraqi Army humvees and injured many soldiers. My platoon had been called to end their final stand in the house, and, seeing the devastation they had caused, I intended to do so quickly and efficiently. I called battalion and informed them that my perimeter was established and that I now had a clear and secure target. I received my orders within moments: destroy the house.

I lifted my earphones to my head and spoke into a microphone.

"Bravo section," I said. "Crossfire on target house, simultaneous fire MPAT round on my command."

I waited for a reply.

Each tank loaded a round, then I heard, "Ready."

"Fire on target house," I commanded. "Fire!"

The first of the Multi-Purpose Anti-Tank rounds targeted the rear corners of the house, and each consecutive shot moved forward toward the closest corners and then the front of the building. The tanks were positioned to engage the target in a crossfire, and by moving the rounds from the rear corners of the house forward, they could systematically destroy the building and, we hoped, kill any enemy soldiers inside as each section of the structure was leveled.

The first rounds thudded into the house and exploded. Dust and shards of the building flew into the air and careened off the inner sections of the courtyard wall. The back corners of the building trembled. I watched the walls shudder and surveyed the scene to make sure no one had entered the target area, then I ordered two more rounds, following the same protocol as the first round.

The second volley from the tanks exploded into the sides of the house. Portions of the walls fell to the ground, and two more rounds blasted into the side walls and the front corners of the building. Smoke now rose from the house, and debris fell from the sky and littered the road in front of it. Glass blew out from the windows, and the doors loosened from their hinges and dropped to the ground.

I ordered the tanks to fire at will, and inside the tanks, my men loaded the main guns and leveled the barrels at the front of the house. The shots blew through the structure and left it barely recognizable. Deep holes penetrated its walls, and portions of the roof fell in. The courtyard filled with dust and blasted cinder blocks. A fog of gunpowder floated around the perimeter of the house, and the air smelled heavy and dark.

As the smoke and dust began to settle, we listened for activity inside the house. We heard nothing. Iraqi Army soldiers moved back toward the wall, their boots scuffing against the ground. They advanced with their heads low and weapons up, anticipating machine-gun fire from the house, but the air was still. Plaster and block crumbling from the wall occasionally echoed along the silent street.

I radioed to cease fire, and the U.S. Captain ordered the Iraqi Army soldiers into the house. They moved into the courtyard, weapons high and ready, and, one by one, they entered the building. I waited, listening to the radio for any engagement or any news. I could hear the Iraqis clearing the house, and, within only a few minutes, it was clear that we had been successful. The al-Qaida threat from the house had been eliminated.

More news, however, came from the house. The number of al-Qaida in the house was staggering. They found thirty al-Qaida fighters killed inside, making this engagement the largest Killed In Action mission in our battalion. There were no survivors.

The engagement left me with the concrete sense that despite my desire to form relationships with the local population, many of my men needed to know that I could be counted on to fight effectively, even ruthlessly, in battles. Roberts had been clear about this with me in some of our previous discussions, and I owed to him a clear sense of the ways in which the use of force not only helped secure some situations, but also gave the men around me confidence in the platoon. All the men, Roberts especially, wanted to help the Iraqi civilians. All of us wanted to be the good guys, to be the rescuers. Sometimes, though, that role wouldn't work. Sometimes we had to fight. As a young lieutenant focused on trying to secure peace through negotiation and dialogue, I sometimes wanted to believe that wouldn't always be true. Roberts would remind

me of his previous experiences in Iraq and the hard lessons
of disappointment he had learned. So, I took his words to
heart. The use of force wasn't just about quelling an uprising
or protecting civilians or our men. It was also about assuring
all of our men that we would be safe, that we would, whenever
needed, do what needed to be done. I had to be willing to
issue those commands. I had to be willing to make those decisions. And, sometimes, I would have to make those decisions
when any delay could cost someone his life.

On the ride back to the base, I talked to Roberts about the
worries I had after firing on a house. He and I were growing
increasingly reliant on each other for honest assessments of
our decisions and our plans, so I voiced my concern about
the last engagement. Despite all of my attempts to secure the
area and all the reasons we had to engage the enemy within
the house, we ultimately did not know who would be in it.
We did not know whether we were firing only on al-Qaida or
on others as well. In previous, smaller fights, we could see the
enemy clearly, but this time, they were inside the house and
out of view. We knew we were being fired upon from inside
the house, but we did not know how many people we were
fighting and who exactly those people might be. The fact that
there were thirty enemy soldiers found dead inside the building was, on the one hand, comforting because it demonstrated
that we could be confident in following our protocol. But,
on the other hand, it also demonstrated in a very concrete
way what we do not know in battle. That there were so many
people inside without us knowing it highlighted the limits of
our knowledge. We had seen the enemy. We had been fired
upon by them. But what if civilians had been trapped inside
the house? What if they had had hostages, or what if the
enemy had had their own families there with them?

Roberts and I talked about what would have happened if
there had been civilians inside. We wondered how we would

have handled finding innocent women or, worse, innocent children killed in the house. We could not imagine how we would cope with that, and we simply hoped that following our protocol, which has preventative measures built into it, would ensure that only the bad guys would be killed. We simply had no real answers. We did not think about whether we were always certain who the bad guys were. We did not even know to wonder about that. I didn't anyway.

I had some sense then that maybe this war was different than what previous wars had been. Maybe some of the neat lines that we had been taught between right and wrong, certainty and doubt, clarity and ambiguity simply wouldn't apply here, and as we made our way back to the base, word came back over the radio that the end of our mission hadn't been so certain and so clear. The Iraqi Army had decided to extend the battle. When all the U.S. soldiers left the area, the Iraqi Army unit moved systematically up a street adjacent to the house, and they set fire to buildings along it. Enraged about the fight at the house, the Iraqi soldiers burned homes of civilians not even involved in the fight, innocent bystanders of an engagement that had rooted out al-Qaida operatives. Smoke and fire rose above the city of Dojima, and from our base miles away we could see it all twisting skyward, dark clouds rising on the horizon.

6

While our engagement in Dojima subdued al-Qaida in the far north of Diyala Province, Sadiyah remained a hot spot for insurgent activity, despite our attempts to form relationships there with the local sheiks. My Commanding Officer had had enough. He declared that we were on the verge of a total lockdown of the city. He wanted the IED attacks to stop, and he wanted the JAM militants captured or killed. He simply would not tolerate more attacks or deception by the townspeople. He would not accept their blatant antagonism to our presence.

I knew a lockdown would be disastrous for our relationship with the Iraqi people. Locking down a town meant completely isolating it. Our company would essentially blockade it, prohibiting any traffic to or from it. No communication between it and other towns. No one allowed to leave or enter. No supplies. No mail. No trade. A lockdown aimed for total control, and once the town was secured from any traffic, we would begin door-to-door searches of the entire community. We would enter every house, and we would check every room. We would seek out weapons caches, and we would root out wanted men. We would move methodically and systematically, leaving behind purportedly a more secure, if also a significantly more resentful, population.

My Commanding Officer was right that the town needed to be secured. Sadiyah's JAM repeatedly attacked neighboring towns and Coalition forces, and the city was the source of a large number of the EFPs we were finding in the region. All of us feared traveling the road leading to the city. We called it EFP Alley, and I prayed for my life every time we drove down it. I rode in one of my platoon's four humvees, but I rode in one without the most recent armor. Only three were equipped with the strongest armor because the battalion had yet to update its entire fleet, and I chose the one without the armor because it seemed wrong to me to ask my men to drive a vehicle I was not myself willing to drive. An EFP would devastate any vehicle, but my humvee, with its out-of-date armor, would be incinerated instantly.

So, all of us shared my Commanding Officer's frustration. We were tired of Sadiyah's resistance, and we were exhausted by our heightened fear any time we approached the city. I worried, though, about a lockdown. I feared that we might eradicate the enemy threat in the short term, but I thought we might create more long-term hostility that would eventually catch up with us. I did not know what other solution we could find, but I decided that if we took our concern to the townspeople themselves, we might find a solution together.

I asked my Commanding Officer if I could hold a meeting with the town. I explained that after the recent funeral, I had gained some goodwill with the local sheiks and I thought I might be able to avert a total lockdown of the city. He was skeptical, I think, but he was willing to try. He knew the costs of a lockdown. He knew the time commitment, the manpower, and the equipment a lockdown would take, and, more importantly, he knew the threat it would place the company under, so he agreed to allow me to hold a meeting. He also told me, though, that his patience was at its end. He needed to see results. Quickly.

I put the word out for the meeting immediately. With my translator, I called some of our local contacts in the area to ask them to inform their sheiks that I would like to have a town gathering, and on our next patrol in the town, I made a point to stop and talk to some of the people we had met there before. I wanted to tell as many people as I could, and within a few days the word had spread. Very quickly. The idea of this type of meeting was new to the Iraqis, and local sheiks were very interested in coming to it. More importantly, I heard that the head sheik of Sadiyah embraced the idea of the meeting and planned to attend.

I knew then that we had a chance of making a change. If a head sheik attends, then a real possibility for a change in the city exists. Without his attendance, we simply would have to rely on lesser sheiks to convince their followers that we could be trusted, and we would have to rely on them to communicate our desires to the head sheik. The head sheik, however, has final word on virtually all matters in the town, and his attendance meant there would be no intermediary between him and me. I wouldn't have to rely on lower sheiks to pass on our wishes, and I wouldn't have to worry about miscommunication as word got passed on. I could ask him directly for what we wanted, and I could hear directly from him what he wanted from us.

No less important, the attendance of the head sheik virtually ensured our safety. I knew that a meeting meant exposing my platoon to an attack. We would be out of our vehicles in a particularly dangerous town, and we would be gathered together in a location that the townspeople knew better than we did. It scared me. It scared all of us. When word came that the head sheik was coming, though, that fear largely evaporated. He was held in too high esteem. He was a man of too much power and too much spiritual reverence. We would be safe, and that meant we could concentrate on forging a relationship with him and his people. It meant we could do things to show our trust.

I tried to demonstrate that even before the meeting by the choice of road I took to the meeting itself. We drove to Sadiyah in a convoy of our humvees, all fifteen of my men accompanying me. All of us were eager to see if the meeting was going to help, and, undoubtedly, some of the men were skeptical of my desire to call together the townspeople. We sped from FOB Warhorse and down EFP Alley. Though we had been told to take a different route, we drove EFP Alley to show our trust in the townspeople to ensure our safety on this day. If we expected to be trusted, we need to extend that same kind of trust to them.

When we drove into the city of Sadiyah, it seemed almost empty. We turned down several streets on the way to the gathering place, and we hardly saw anyone. This was a town where even the children mocked, threatened, and threw stones at us, and the silence of the town worried me until we turned down a final street toward the meeting place. Ahead of us was a crowd. Men and women and children pressed in toward the building where the meeting was to be held, and whole families waited for our arrival. When they heard our humvees, the entire crowd turned toward us, some raising their hands and pointing, others grabbing their children and pulling them out of the road.

We made our way through the crowd to the meeting place, and I got out of the humvee and headed toward the entrance of the building. Roberts, Deboe, and my translator came with me. Roberts' job was to ensure that all the men outside the building were kept aware of what was happening inside of it. Deboe's job was security. I chose him to come with us because I wanted experienced men with me. I knew I might ask him or Roberts for advice or their impressions, and I wanted people there who could draw on previous experiences in understanding the Iraqi's positions and requests.

The building for the meeting was a town gathering place. It stood not far from the center of Sadiyah and was a single-story, low, rectangular, cinder block structure. The interior was lined with an assortment of old couches and lawn chairs. All of the furnishings appeared to have been discarded from others' homes and collected and stuffed inside the structure. The walls were cracking in places, and thin lines of light streamed inside, highlighted by small clouds of dust that rose from the furniture and the ground as people moved around. Not far from the head of the room, from where we would conduct the meeting, hung a picture of the head sheik of the town. Standing only twenty paces from it was the head sheik himself, speaking and gesturing to a group of sheiks circled around him. I approached him, moving purposefully.

I immediately took off my helmet and glasses and set them on a table. I wanted to show Sadiyah's head sheik that I didn't need head protection because I believed I was safe here, and I wanted him to see my face. I greeted him, speaking in broken Arabic. In the short time that I had been in Iraq, I had worked hard with my interpreter to learn some basic Arabic, and I now knew enough to carry on short, informal conversations. The sheik appreciated my effort at speaking to him in his own language, and we talked briefly about the plan for the day, at times together in Arabic, at other times through my translator. I told him that we were there to make a difference and that we wanted things to be different than they had been under the previous company who had patrolled the area, and he expressed his hope that today might initiate a change. He also expressed clearly that he expected the respect of our soldiers, and, by doing so, he implied that he, ultimately, had the power to effect the change we all wanted.

The room was loud, so it took a moment to begin the meeting. When I finally started speaking, I surveyed the layout of the room. To my left sat the head sheik. To my right stood Deboe. Next to him stood Roberts, who, throughout the course of the day, moved from inside the building to the exterior, informing my platoon how the meeting was going and ensuring my soldiers were remaining alert and hydrated. In front of me was a room of sheiks. The room was stratified by a kind of unspoken hierarchy so that the most important sheiks were seated directly in front of me, closest to me, and the least important were seated near the back. Sheiks not only from Sadiyah had come, but also those from much smaller neighboring communities, testifying to the significance the area had attached to this gathering. They had come to voice their concerns.

I began the meeting by speaking in Arabic, and when I could I made self-effacing jokes to help demonstrate that my pride would not get in the way of listening to them. They laughed at my attempts at humor, and certainly they also laughed at me, occasionally zinging me with good-natured jokes. While the tone of the meeting was serious, my broken Arabic paired with clumsy attempts to follow local customs and protocols in conducting the meeting lightened the tone while we searched throughout the day for common ground.

I had several major points that I wanted to cover. The primary one was that I needed to impress upon them that the town of Sadiyah was on the verge of a total lock-down. I described what this would mean to the town, and I explained why my Commanding Officer felt it was necessary. I described the threat that Sadiyah posed to U.S. soldiers, and I described the pain the lockdown would cause in the community. No one wanted any of it, and I explained that we, no less than they, did not desire the lockdown. In communicating this fact, I had to avoid making a threat and I had to avoid seeming like I was simply giving the town an ultimatum. Instead, I wanted them to see that I hoped to work with them to find ways to avert the lockdown. So, I provided them with some concrete things they could do that would help me make the case to my Commanding Officer that Sadiyah was on the path to being a safe town.

The first thing I told them we needed to do was to ensure that any interpreter working for the Coalition would no longer face threats or actual retribution. In the previous months, many interpreters and their families had fled local communities to live closer to or within military bases. Their lives were threatened, and, in some cases, they were beaten. I told the sheiks that we needed the interpreters to feel safe, and that ultimately, by hurting local interpreters, they were threatening not just their own townspeople, but their entire towns, because without translators, Coalition forces stood little chance of forming a relationship with the local communities.

When I made this request, the head sheik stood up. He moved closer to me and slightly in front of me, then he spoke to the sheiks. His voice was strong, and it was certain.

"No more threats against Lt. Meehan's interpreters," he said.

The other sheiks were silent, and the head sheik moved back to his chair. It was a simple, direct pronouncement, and the other sheiks would clearly not violate it. I stared out across the room, halfway expecting disagreement or argument. But none came. No one resisted. The force of his pronouncement, the finality of it, and the silence and acceptance that followed impressed upon me the limits of my own understanding of how this town worked, of how any of Iraq worked.

Our forces, in storming the country, had probably imagined a decisive and immediate end to conflict in Iraq. We had all certainly been sold on the idea that the military force of the U.S. was of such greater superiority that any residual fighting would be quickly eliminated and peace would be decisively secured through a process that started with a period of martial law and ended with Iraqi elections. The fact that I was fighting in Iraq so many years after the invasion meant that that initial vision was an illusion. I knew that. But, standing in that room with the sheik, who took complete control of an area simply through one single pronouncement, drove home the point in a way I hadn't experienced before. We didn't understand the culture. We couldn't. It had been shaped over centuries far from us and far from our world. I hadn't seen anything like it before, and no one I had ever known had ever seen anything like it, and I realized, standing in the head sheik's shadow at the front of the room, I probably would not ever fully understand it. I would not even have a real chance to.

I thanked the head sheik for his unequivocal support, and I prepared myself for the next request. I knew it would be much more difficult for any of them to contemplate, let alone accept, so I prepared myself for a confrontation. I told the sheiks that we needed EFP attacks to stop, and for that to happen, I needed them to hand over the man primarily responsible for creating the EFPs and executing the attacks. His name was Abdul Hakeem. He was a Shia who had trained in Iran, and he was a High-Value Individual for the U.S. Army. He had returned to Sadiyah after his time in Iran with the skill and technological knowledge to create EFPs, and he had established the connections in both Iran and Iraq to supply him with the necessary components to build the devastating IEDs. He was to us one of the most dangerous men in Diyala Province, but to the townspeople of Sadiyah he was a great patriot. He represented bravery and pride, and his attacks were legendary in the area. They knew we feared him, and some of the sheiks celebrated his actions because of that. Asking for his people to hand him over was tantamount to an Iraqi officer asking the citizens of Boston to hand over Tom Brady. He was legendary, he was ruthless, and he had become part of the town's identity.

The room immediately erupted with the voices of the sheiks. While some of them likely did not know who Abdul Hakeem was, most of them did, and every one of them, the head sheik included, resisted my request that they hand over one of their own. I was an outsider who barely spoke Arabic and who hardly knew the customs. I had been in the area fewer than four months, and I was just another soldier making demands of them, insisting that my way be the only way. It must have appeared to them a brazen condition to averting a lockdown. Brazen or, more likely, foolish.

I tried to explain that I was not giving them an ultimatum, because in fact I was not. I tried to be clear that EFP attacks were probably the primary reason that my Commanding Officer had lost his patience with the town and that mitigating those attacks would be a way for the town to demonstrate trust. With that trust, I said, I could make the case to my chain of command that the town meetings were a successful way of avoiding conflict. I wanted them to envision the meetings in the same way I did – as a negotiation. But I was too new here. I had only the most rudimentary understanding of the political structures of the town and Diyala Province, and I probably expected too much from all of them. The result was not so much direct resistance as passive resistance. The primary response from the sheiks was to claim no knowledge of Abdul Hakeem. It was as though one of the best-known men of the town and all of Diyala had suddenly become a stranger. Some sat silently, others essentially chastised me for making assumptions about the town and its people, and still others attempted to reason with me, explaining that their hands were tied as they had no direct control over any specific member of their community.

I pressed my point, trying my best to be respectful to the sheiks and their position while remaining clear that anyone making EFPs was a threat to the security and safety of Sadiyah and Diyala Province. By the time the meeting had ended nearly three and a half hours later, my request that they hand over Abdul Hakeem was the only request that the sheiks did not meet. I was thankful for the progress of the meeting, especially the safety we had secured for the interpreters, but I was frustrated by their allegiance to Hakeem. I could not fully understand it, and as we held more meetings in the weeks that followed, I continued to press home the point that we needed the EFP man to be stopped even while I continued to learn that my view of this man was profoundly different than theirs.

In the meantime, the town seemed to shift its attitude toward us. Within a day of our first meeting, the rock-throwing children and threats that used to greet us in Sadiyah ceased. Instead, we were greeted with a kind gesture or we were simply ignored. Some local men greeted us when we came into town and joked with us. Women stopped scurrying away at the first sight of us.

My Commanding Officer recognized the progress the meetings had made, and only three weeks later he stopped discussing any real possibility of a lockdown. I started to feel like we might be able to fight this war in a different way. I began to feel that maybe discussion and sincere understanding could effect change and avert the violence that all of us feared and dreaded. I communicated that hope to my men, and we all began to believe we were making a difference.

Even so, I remained frustrated by the sheiks' refusal to hand over Abdul Hakeem. For me, he was a bad guy. A very bad guy. Part of me wanted to rush into the city and demand his head. It was foolish. That the sheiks refused me every time, no matter the evidence I presented or no matter how clear the threat Hakeem posed to the stability we had created, irritated me. The town seemed not to care, and I refused to accept their positions, whether ignorance or loyalty. In doing so, I was at least in part refusing also to fully appreciate their difficulties.

Just before a new meeting, in early December, I received word that Hakeem had left. He had been forced out of the town by the sheiks, pressed into exile from the area that was his home. The sheiks had found a middle ground for themselves. While they would not hand him over, they would at least remove him from the area. I was thankful to have him out of the town, but I knew he was still in Iraq and still capable of inflicting harm on Coalition forces and civilians. I wanted him apprehended, so while I appreciated the sheiks' attempt to make a change, it still left me frustrated. It highlighted to me that I, in fact, still did not have a full grasp of Iraqi culture. It demonstrated to me that despite the goodwill we had created, allegiance to the local community still had higher priority. It illustrated the layers of commitment created in these small towns and how, no matter how hard I would try, I would never gain full access to them. I could never gain the type of loyalty that a local man, born and raised there, had as a birthright, even if he was disrupting the peace in their city. I was, ultimately, an outsider. I was a U.S. soldier. I was one of the invaders. Hakeem, no matter how many people he killed, was one of their own.

7

On December 22, one of our men, Mark Bosch, was killed during a battalion-sized operation to cut off and secure Tahrir, an enclave of Baqubah. His tank had returned to refuel at a military outpost within the city of Baqubah, and while the other members of his crew remained inside the tank, Bosch, sitting atop the turret, was hit by mortar fire. The outpost had been ambushed, and one of the mortars, falling like a dark bird from the sky, landed directly on Mark, killing him instantly. His body slumped and fell into the tank and onto the lap of one of his crewmembers.

No one knew what to do. No one could know what to do. The real battle of the operation raged in Tahrir, and while the outpost had been subject to ongoing attacks, it was supposed to be safer than the frontline. Bosch and his men were refueling. They were resting. They were waiting to return to battle, but the battle, the war for which there is no real frontline, came to them, and it killed Mark in an instant, in a moment when no one, not one soldier in that tank, expected it.

This is what the war was becoming. Since the days of
the initial invasion, the war had become increasingly dif-
fuse, spread out across multiple regions with no real centers
of gravity. No certain ones anyway. They shifted. They
changed. Take Fallujah, and Baqubah broke down. Take
Najaf, and Baghdad flared up. Draw a firm perimeter around
the Green Zone in Baghdad, and the outskirts of the city
devolved into a Wild West while the soldiers and civilians
inside the Green Zone moved about in a kind a false and
imagined security. A tentative security. One no one actually
thought was real, but one we held to.

All of us learned to live in that imagined security. It animated our daily lives. Whether we were Justice Department
civilians in the Green Zone, or we were soldiers on patrol in
Diyala, all of us in Iraq developed a certain comfort in the
daily uncertainty. It wasn't complacency. We didn't one day
simply forget that we were at war and that we were under
duress. Instead, we became used to the pressure bearing
down on us. It was like a wound that, raised and seeping,
you one day forget you have, even though each day you go
through the routine of washing it, dressing it, and pressing
down on it to make the certain pain of it disappear for one
moment, as though by one final push of pressure, the thing
will finally heal. It doesn't, but that relief mattered, and we
all pressed down on our wounds and looked up and away and
hoped that at any particular moment, we would not see that
flash from the sky. We hoped we would feel only a moment
of relief. Bosch never did.

Mark Bosch was a corporal in third platoon, Bravo
Company. His platoon had actually been part of Delta
Company leading up to our deployment. He trained with us,
and he worked with us. In Iraq, though, the Army had moved
his tank platoon to Bravo Company and moved one of Bravo
Company's infantry platoons to Delta in order to even out

the forces. Bosch had been working with Bravo since we had been in Iraq, but he was one of our men, and he was one of our best.

Bosch smiled a lot, and he was, in soldier's terms, "squared away." He worked hard, followed commands, showed initiative at the right times, and kept his gear in perfect order. He was organized, and he accomplished even the most mundane and monotonous tasks with good humor and a positive attitude. He was tough, and he was brave. He was an ideal soldier, and all of us, from his fellow enlisted men to the officers he worked under, loved him. We all looked forward to spending time with him, and if the opportunity would have ever presented itself, I would have tried to bring him into my platoon.

I learned early on that both Bosch and I were newlyweds and that we had both come to the war having left our wives before our first year of marriage had ended. We connected. He told me about his bride and her family, and he told me that he knew a bright life was ahead. He told me that sometimes he wondered what her life would be like without him and his without her, and he looked focused and certain when he talked about the possibilities ahead. He listened to me tell him about AJ and the life we imagined for ourselves, and he nodded when I told him that I felt selfish for pursuing a life as a soldier.

Bosch had been stationed in South Korea early on, and while he was there, he met and eventually married his bride. She was Korean, and Bosch was deeply devoted to her. She seemed a dedicated, doting, and loving wife, often sending him messages and gifts, and Bosch's love for her shone in his face anytime he talked about her. They had recently moved together stateside just before he was deployed to Iraq. Mark talked about returning to her to begin his life with her. He hadn't wanted to leave her for this war. She was a foreigner in the States, and he worried about the stress she was under. She had little support in America, and he had been deployed so soon after their wedding that he knew she probably was not happy. She was likely lonely, and she undoubtedly did not yet feel like she had a home. How could she? She had just been married, and she now lived in a different culture separated from the husband who had brought her there.

He must have yearned for her touch sometimes. Sitting in his tank on some dark nights or driving across the dry Iraqi land in a humvee, his mind must have drifted back and lifted his heart with it. He had to wonder sometimes what she, a foreigner in America, would do if he were taken from her. Maybe he dreamed about it, maybe he cried with her on the phone, maybe, late at night, while the rest of us slept, he wrote her letters that told her about their futures, about his dreams for them. Maybe in some hard moment, when the heat and the pressure and the weight of the war felt most real to him, he doubted whether he deserved her or, worse, feared that the war would make him less real to her. He wasn't. He wouldn't be. But it's what we all felt on occasion. We all felt sometimes that the war might not simply rip away our lives, but rip away who we were or who we might have become. We held onto our soldierly hope, our ideals that make us believe that our training has made a difference in our lives, that our experiences will make us into men and maybe into leaders. But we fear the nights, and we fear the times alone, waiting and wondering about what might have been and what might still be. We dress our wounds, pressing hard down on them, hoping that the dark bird won't swoop down on us and lift us like shadows from a scorched earth

I didn't actually hear that Bosch had been killed until Christmas Eve, but all of us in my tank had figured it out sooner than that. When the mission in Tahrir began, my platoon set a cordon around the city and simply waited and watched for enemy forces trying to escape the battle. Most of the action was deep within the city, and from our positions on the borders of Tahrir, we saw very little direct enemy engagement. At one point, three insurgents mounted a small attack on one of my platoon's tanks, and Duvall opened fire on them with the .50-caliber weapon that is mounted on our turrets. Duvall, his experience guiding his actions, countered the attack quickly. His weapon immediately overwhelmed the enemy. Later, further north up our cordon, another minor attack occurred, but generally, the eastern side of the city where we were waiting was quiet, and we spent most of the mission simply watching our buildings, scanning them for threats.

Mid-way through the mission, though, we heard an order passed to our Company Commander over the radio. He was to return to FOB Warhorse immediately. I listened to the call from the battalion, and I looked to my men.

"Wonder what's going on?" I asked.

It seemed strange to me that our Company Commander would be called to return to base in the middle of our mission. One of the men in my tank shrugged his soldiers. Deboe turned in my direction and said, "Bet someone in the company was killed."

We were all quiet for a second. I did not know if that were true, but this was Deboe's second deployment to Iraq, so I trusted his instincts in situations like these.

"They always call the Company Commander back when someone's been killed," he said.

"Yeah?"

"Yeah," he said. "They always do."

We continued to listen to the net for details, but we heard nothing more about it. Still, we had all grown still. We had all decided that something had happened to our platoon in Bravo Company. Bosch's platoon. I knew from listening to the net that Delta had not seen any significant engagement, but Bravo was in the thick of things. If our Company Commander, the leader of Delta, had been called back to base because of a death, it could only mean one thing – one of Delta's men who had been assigned to Bravo had been killed. We all hoped that we were mistaken, but it was the only thing that made sense. We watched the perimeter buildings of Tahrir and thought about the man who must have died. A haze drifted up from the fields outside the perimeter and crept across the town. Smoke from the attacks within the city mingled with it, and the day passed under a heavy, thick sky.

When we finally received word that the mission was complete, the sun was low and orange. Our line of tanks cast long shadows across the eastern edge of the city, and we turned them north, ready to head home. The rainy season had left the ground deep with mud, and a humid, hazy air hung over it. All of our tanks slid and plunged toward home through the heavy earth. The treads spun up clods of dirt. The tanks sank then heaved up and out of watery holes in the ground. One of the tanks got stuck. I called the base to say that I would stay back with one of the other tanks in my platoon to help extricate it, but it wouldn't budge, so what began as a quick attempt to free a tank turned into a forty-hour ordeal. My men and I established a perimeter and watched, securing the area to make sure that the stuck tank would not be attacked, then we waited as several huge rescue vehicles, 88s, arrived with their massive cranes and tried to pull the stuck tank free. One of the 88s sunk deep into the mud as well, and more vehicles had to be brought to free it also. We waited, we watched, staying awake for nearly two days, finally leaving on Christmas Eve when the vehicles were finally pulled free, covered in the dark, heavy mud of Iraq.

We were all covered in that mud when we arrived back at Warhorse. Our Company Commander greeted us, and there, in the coming darkness and cold air of late December, he told us that Bosch died in his tank at the outpost. A battle erupted at the outpost, and the tank continued to take fire. The men inside the tank tried to find a way to move his body to safety. They tried to find a way to show him respect in the midst of the battle and honor his life by removing him from the scene. Instead, they had to engage the enemy while Bosch's body lie lifeless in the tank. The crew would never fully recover. They would never fight without the image of their man crumpled dead beside them.

For many of us in the company, Bosch's presence lingered with us. He wasn't the one who was supposed to die. He was one of the good guys. He was the guy you relied on, whom you shared stories and hopes and dreams with. He was our hope.

After our Company Commander had told us the news, I found my way back to my trailer. I opened the door, walked past Siggins, already asleep in his bunk, and toward my desk. I reached down behind it and found a cord and plugged it in. Lights on a small Christmas tree that AJ's sister had sent me lit the room. I stared at the lights. The tree sat on my desk, wrapped gifts surrounding its base. A few ornaments, some made by me and my roommate, hung from the plastic branches. The tree trembled and the ornaments clicked together when I turned on the tree lights.

I wondered when Bosch's family would hear. Would they be gathering for Christmas Eve when a knock came at the door? Would they be waking up on Christmas morning, expecting to feel the warmth of family, the stability and certainty of love, when the word of his death would finally slice into their home, changing that day and their lives forever? Would they ever open the packages piled beneath the tree or would the boxes, with their colored ribbons and bows, remain never opened, never touched? Would that family ever hear a carol without feeling the news fall over them again, without falling into the news again?

I dropped down onto my bed and watched the lights blink for a few moments. They lit the entire room with a silent dance of white, blue, red, and green. Shadows from the tree shifted across the ceiling in chaotic patterns, and I stared at the shapes and colors. It did not seem right for me to be watching their show, and I told myself I did not want to see them anymore. I told myself I shouldn't watch the colors of the holidays, so I turned on my side in order to stand up and unplug the tree.

I could not move. I could not force myself out of my bed. I was pinned there by exhaustion and nearly two days straight of being awake and working, and my body melted. I could not feel my legs, and my arms hung heavily against my chest. I pulled a blanket over my shoulders, tucked my chin close to my heart, and drew a long breath of the cool air. The night pressed in on me. I felt the past two days fall over me, and I closed my eyes against the Christmas light, finding my way to sleep.

8

When I was a child, when the snows of western Pennsylvania blew hard eastward across the state and piled like great heaves of white earth against Philadelphia, I would go outside, at night, and watch the white lights that my father had strung across our roof and windows illuminate the shimmering night air. He always made the lights his job when the holidays arrived. He strung them, always white, always simple, along the roofline. He hung them on the Christmas tree as well, stuffing great masses of them deep inside the branches so that the tree glowed from within, as though a great pure fire glittered inside, ready to engulf it and spread out like a new star being born inside our home.

There was nothing more I looked forward to during the year than Christmas. We had those idyllic ones, where family gathered and talked and shared, and even today when I try, I have a hard time remembering any hard feelings, any hard words. I only remember warmth. I would wake up early with my sister Erin, older but no less excited, and my

brother Patrick, and we would make our way to our parents'
room. There, we'd linger, talking to each other on the bed,
first in hushed tones, then in bawling laughter, as my parents
slowly woke up and twisted and turned in their beds, trying
to find a way to sit up among the tangle of all of our bodies.
We'd finally all make it down the stairs together to the
family room, my father with his video camera up and filming
as though he might catch some sight of Santa in our eyes.
Mom moved immediately to the kitchen and made us all hot
chocolate, and we'd all drink and laugh as we unwrapped the
great spoils of the season.

My parents must have saved for months. We always got
the gifts we wanted, and we knew our parents didn't have the
means to pay for it all without a lot of planning. My mom
spent most of the time smiling and narrating, reminding us
of previous years and building the strength of our memories
and of our family. We all shared. We all remembered. We
all felt the family history, and my brother and sister and I
were all aware that part of that history was sacrifice.

I felt that when I woke up on Christmas in Iraq. The lights
on the Christmas tree were still blinking, and I was still on
my side. My left arm, pinned under my body, was asleep.
My hand tingled. I must not have moved during the night.
I rolled on my back and stared at the ceiling. Light came in
through our window, but I could still see the different colors
of the tree lights illuminate the shadows along the corner of
the room, away from the daylight. I had to decide what to
do. Underneath the little tree was a horde of gifts sent by my
family. I didn't know what to do with them. I tried to imagine my family's sacrifice in sending them, my parents saving
their money, AJ planning carefully each gift and spending
money that would have made her life back home more comfortable, but I couldn't really think about that. I could only
think about the day before. I could only think about Bosch.

The violence in our region had been escalating, and we had seen increasing contact with the enemy, but Bosch's death drove home the point that we were in an area that was largely out of control. His death exemplified that. He died away from the main battle. He died in an ambush. He died simply refueling.

We didn't really know who was attacking us each day. The enemy didn't wear uniforms or carry all the same weapons or confront us with military vehicles. We didn't face typical military tactics from a formally trained army. We were being attacked by combatants who were using whatever means they could to inflict damage. We simply couldn't know always who they were. We knew whether we were in a Sunni or a Shia area, and we knew, sometimes even by their choice of weapons, what groups were recruiting and supplying the fighters. When we had solid intelligence, we knew precisely who our enemy was, but on a daily basis, the people who might step up to fight us were anonymous, though no less dangerous for that. Al-Qaida was strengthening, slowly seizing more and more control of southern Diyala in particular, to the degree that all of our missions were potential battles. IEDs were expected. They were the mundane daily experience. Direct confrontation was not daily, but it was increasing and it was escalating. More and more of the locals were being lured in by al-Qaida with promises of work and of pay. We were under no illusion that they were all true believers in the cause. Some were. Maybe most were in any given engagement, but there were always young men among them who were desperate men, children really just trying to find a way to live in a land that we had come to free. Those were the men we were fighting, both the true believers and the desperate poor. Those were the men and boys who killed Bosch.

The thought of news of his death hitting his family settled on me again. Christmas seemed far way, but I began to get uncomfortable in bed and shifted around. I looked around the room and listened to the vibrations outside of a humvee's engine churning by the CHUs. I heard someone call for a hand to help carrying some gear to the motor pool. I didn't want to be in bed all day, even though I didn't know if I'd do anything about Christmas. My mind drifted away from the last few days, and I started thinking about the one thing that could get my ass out of bed. Coffee. Virtually every soldier drank the stuff by the gallon, and every one of us regarded it as a best friend or, on more desperate days, a revered liquid cocaine. AJ had sent me a special holiday coffee with a sweet peppermint flavor, and despite my ambivalence about Christmas, I began to think about it while lying in bed. I thought about the flavor, the heat, and the morning ritual I had established for myself, and I eventually swung my legs out of bed and went to brew the coffee.

Siggins was already gone for his day's mission. The war went on despite our holidays. Our Commanding Officer had granted my platoon a day off because they had worked so hard, particularly in staying back to help the stranded tank, during our last few long days, otherwise we too would have spent Christmas patrolling our territory. I was thankful for the time to rest, but more importantly, I was thankful to have some time alone to try to make sense of where I was.

I had come to the war eager to prove myself and eager to learn. I had just graduated from the Virginia Military Institute, where the ideals of honor and sacrifice that my family had given me had been intensified and solidified. I carried those ideals with me into the Army, and when I was finally commissioned, after months of wrangling to secure medical exceptions due to wrestling injuries, I wanted to prove myself.

I wanted my men to work for me not just because of my rank. I wanted them to respect me. I wanted them to believe that I would make the right decisions for the platoon and for each of them. I wanted them all to believe that, as much as possible within the context of our missions and our objectives, I would do what was right to keep them all safe. Thinking about that on Christmas Day, reflecting on my history and my dreams of becoming a leader, the fact of Bosch's death made that seem impossible. Those men that day had done nothing unusual. They had not breached any protocol. They had not broken any cardinal rule. They had been doing their job, and they were doing it the right way. But, a man still died. A great man still died.

Of course, I knew that happened. I knew it had to happen. We were fighting a war, and we were fighting a war that blurred the typical boundaries between safe and unsafe areas. Bosch's death, though, confronted me with the unsettling reality that none of us were really safe, no matter what illusion of security we had established for ourselves, and none of us could promise safety to our men or to the people who surrounded us. Our good men would die, and they would do so when they were simply sitting, waiting, and doing what they were supposed to be doing. I worried what that might mean for us, for my men, and I wondered what that meant for the people in Iraq. How many good men and women, how many playing children, would die while they simply did what they were supposed to be doing, while they were doing what they needed to do to live in a country at war?

My family's sacrifice, all those years growing up, seemed ridiculously small in the face of that. I didn't appreciate it any less. In fact, I admired it even in light of what I was learning about this new place and myself. But, the contrast couldn't have been more stark, and, moving about my CHU on Christmas morning and thinking about Bosch and home, I knew the war had already changed me. It had already made me feel smaller, and the miniature Christmas tree lighting my stark room seemed a dim reminder of home and all the hope for the life of honor I had imagined for myself.

I don't know how most of my men spent their day off. I don't know which of them slept and dreamed of home or wept over the death of Bosch. I don't know which, if any of them, celebrated Christmas. I saw some of them at meal time, and we talked about how, despite the dining staff's best effort, Christmas dinner didn't feel much like a special event in FOB Warhorse's mess hall. Like Thanksgiving, the dining room was decorated with colorful streamers and table clothes and centerpieces, but unlike Thanksgiving, none of us were much excited by it. Deboe kept his head down and focused on his food. Duvall looked around for a minute and muttered something about how cold it was. Roberts just went about his business, and I, surveying the room, reflected on how Thanksgiving had snuck up on us. We had been surprised by the decorations and festivities. This time, though, we were all exhausted, and we had all been in touch with our families and now felt the distance between us and them, and no amount of garland or music was going to make us feel great.

AJ spent Christmas with our families, trying to stay connected to our lives as a married couple. The previous year, we had shared in each other's Christmas rituals. AJ had similar holiday traditions to my family's. She and her sisters, Brie, Kate, and Leah, would gather with her parents, and her dad would pull out the video camera while her mom orchestrated the opening of packages. They opened their gifts one by one, and the opener sat in a special chair, the center of all the attention. That year, only days after our marriage and only months away from my deployment, AJ and I savored the closeness of our families and tried to imagine what our future would be like, knowing that the next Christmas I would more than likely be in Iraq. Neither of us really knew what to expect. Neither of us, especially not AJ, expected to feel the sense of loss. AJ is strong. She keeps herself planted in the present, and she has little interest in emotional imaginings of unknown futures. She's too independent for that. She's too pragmatic. And, she's too careful about letting herself fall into the terrible uncertainty of living the life of a soldier's wife.

She celebrated Christmas with our families, then, but she tried hard to send Christmas out to me. She sent mounds of gifts, and when I finally stepped away from my CHU for a while, I thought about her effort and her strength, and I went back inside to open them. I set up a video camera to film it all, wanting to show her and the rest of my family how much their generosity meant to me. For over an hour, I slowly and deliberately opened each gift. Books about filmmaking and movies, CDs, a football autographed by Brady Quinn, the Notre Dame quarterback, that AJ had gotten me, and trinkets meant to make me feel like I was far from the war all began to stack up on the desk and floor and bed amidst the rubbish of wrapping paper and ribbons. I played Christmas music that AJ had sent me, and sometimes I hummed along. Each time I opened a gift, I doted on it, turning it around in my hands and holding it up to the camera, thanking the gift giver with smiling words. I laughed when I opened a Gwen Stefani CD, not precisely the most manly and soldierly of music, and I told AJ that I wished I could be home with my family and hers. When I stood up to turn off the camera, I looked back at the small tree and all of the gifts, and I felt Iraq fall away. Christmas came to me, and I forgot, for just a brief time, that I wasn't home, that I wasn't with my family.

The past year saw me move from my home in Philadelphia, to Kentucky for training at Ft. Knox, to Ft. Hood in Texas, where I joined the company with whom I'd be fighting a war. After a long, virtual nine-month honeymoon with AJ, after we moved across the country and finally settled into a home in Texas, I left for the war. Now, on a cold day in Iraq, I could remember the warmth of home and I could remember one of the reasons I wanted to do well. I wanted not just to make the men in my company proud. I wanted my family to be proud. I wanted my father to see in me something of the honor that he had gone to his war seeking, and I wanted my mother to see in me the strength and independence of a soldier. I wanted AJ to see that strength and the resolve to help change a country, to help people who we had been convinced were long suffering to persevere and triumph. They were probably selfish impulses. They involved my own desire to become a leader, and they involved my own desire to make a mark, no matter how small, but I hoped they were still somehow positive, that they weren't simply self-absorbed. I wanted to embody that sacrifice that my family had taught me and that the narrative of my college experience at VMI had reinforced, but I knew there were limits to that. I knew that no matter how much I valued that idea of sacrifice, I did not want to be that soldier who left his family forever and left behind him only a story of ruin.

Christmas Day moved into Christmas Night, and after dinner at the mess hall, I walked out across Warhorse, taking a circuitous route back to my CHU. I walked beside the HESCO baskets and watched humvees arriving back from patrol dart toward the motor pool. I watched small groups of men wander back from their meals and laugh and joke as they headed back to their trailers. I walked up a small rise and turned out toward Diyala Province spreading out in front of me past the baskets and the wire. The night was cold, and the base was dark, and beyond I could see the scattered lights of the remnants of villages near the base. I wondered what was happening with the families in those homes around us. It was not Christmas here. It was just another night amidst war, and theirs and our lives simply passed under the cold stars of winter. Tomorrow we would be out on patrol again, and each day after that we would move further and further away from Christmas, further and further away from the loss that shaped our first holiday in Iraq. I looked one last time out across the land, and I tried to find some way to smooth it all out and make that loss disappear. A soft moon began to rise, and I imagined a great blanket of snow covering the province, leveling it with a perfect, sparkling white.

9

A cold winter rain fell the first day my platoon operated as the sole force in our company's area of operation. Christmas was behind us, and most of the company began 2007 with orders to participate in a battalion mission in another part of Iraq. My platoon had been tasked with staying back and keeping Delta Company's entire area of operation secure in the absence of all the other platoons. We would be in charge of an area over one hundred square miles by ourselves for somewhere between seventeen days and three weeks. While being tasked with protecting the region intimated that the Company Commander trusted me and my men in particular for a difficult job, the prospect was daunting. I knew that communication with my men would be key. It would keep them focused and, perhaps more importantly, it would keep us all united in our missions. I wanted to be transparent in my plans for the days ahead, so as soon as we had heard that we would have this assignment, Roberts and I met with the men to let them know. I pledged to them that I would communicate with them, and I asked them to push hard while the rest of the company was away. I told them that keeping an area secure would be easier than trying to regain an area that had gone out of control, and I told them that that might mean we would have to extend missions and spend longer days outside the wire. I told them that I knew I was asking a lot of them, but that I felt that working harder to make our presence known in the area would help subdue any threats and ultimately keep us safer.

All of the men, despite obvious concern over the stress and fatigue that our plans would create, agreed that we would be wiser to prevent an outbreak of violence rather than relax now and have to try to subdue an uprising later. No one was happy, but everyone was dedicated and focused, so when the rest of the company finally rumbled off to engage the enemy elsewhere in the days after New Year's, our platoon prepared for lack of sleep and long patrols in Diyala.

The brutal rains of winter did little to help our job. Sheets of it came down, and the motor pool was so deep in mud and water that some of the tanks sank up to their turrets. They looked like ships floating in a brown sea. The 88s extracted those that sunk, their cranes clattering throughout the day as they lifted and heaved vehicles from the quagmire.

Prepping the vehicles in the rain always took a little extra time, and knowing that we had weeks alone ahead of us did little to motivate any of us to move any faster. We all worked silently. Each one of us had a set of specific jobs we had to do to prep for a mission, and each man executed them with mechanical precision and timing without needing to say much to anyone else. One man prepared his section of the tank just in time for the next man to come and prepare his. Each knew his role. None of us needed to ask others for guidance. Smitty checked to ensure his line of sight was clear for driving, and Deboe checked the area around the main gun to ensure he could quickly and efficiently load the weapon. Garnica set up his gunner's station, checking both the daylight sights and the night-vision and cleaning off the vision blocks. He checked the rapid fire co-ax gun to make sure it was properly loaded, and I made rounds to make sure no one needed any additional support. Working with Roberts I also made sure each man had squared himself away. We trusted each man to do his job, and our platoon moved as a unit in a silent, elaborate dance. All the while, the rain fell, and a cold air settled down over the base. Both would last for three weeks, soaking us for the duration of our time alone in the area.

While our Company Commander was away, our company's Executive Officer, Nick Poppen, assumed the role as our leader. Poppen was a few years older than I was and had just finished school at Oregon State. Before the deployment, some of us wondered how well he would handle the stress of being XO in theater, but when we arrived, he quickly put us all at ease. He was efficient and precise, and he was, above all things, dedicated to helping any of us on the ground and on the frontline. He compiled intel reports and provided accurate pictures of areas we would be working in. He was calm and assured, and he truly wanted to help us in any way he could.

During our time as the company's sole force in the area, Poppen drew up daily mission plans, and he did so in consultation with me and Sgt. Roberts. He knew that we had intimate knowledge of the area of operation, so while planning the sorties into the countryside, he asked us for advice on which routes to travel and which cities to visit. The entire goal was simply to make our presence known and, whenever possible, continue to root out the enemy. We wanted to be visible to as many of the Iraqis in our area as possible so that they would not notice the absence of so much of the company. As a result, we planned our routes with extra attention to trouble spots like Sadiyah and Khalis. If we had a mission that headed anywhere near the town, we would add an hour or two to the mission simply to track through the city. We took different roads than we normally took, cruising in convoys through densely populated regions, oftentimes not even stopping. We simply wanted the people to see us.

We also scheduled observation posts. Observation posts typically are missions whose purpose is simply to observe a particular section of the area of operation. Typically, the Posts were along main supply routes, and they usually ran deep into the night. They frequently passed without incident, and the nights in our tanks were long and, during this time, cold.

Early in our time alone at Warhorse, we scheduled an observation post along the route to Sadiyah. We had traveled the road nearly daily during much of our deployment, but the EFP threat that continued to hang over the area meant that observation of the road was necessary. We wanted the people of Sadiyah and surrounding communities to know that we were out, even at night, watching for activity.

My men prepared the tanks, each man following his unique checklist of tasks, and as dusk set in, we rolled out of Warhorse toward Sadiyah. We stopped a few miles south of the town and, moving our tanks to the side of the road, we began our vigil.

Garnica, my gunner, took the first watch. He crawled into his seat and surveyed the land around us through a set of night-vision optics that were standard equipment on our tanks. As he took his position, we all settled in. Deboe pulled out his iPod and started some music. We had wired the tank with our own little sound system, so Deboe attached the iPod, and heavy hip-hop bass thumped out of the speakers. Smitty, our driver, whipped his head around and stared down Deboe. Deboe smiled back.

"Jesus Christ," Smitty said. "You have got to be kidding me."

"Jesus loves you!" Deboe yelled. He pointed at Smitty, nodding his head to the bass vibrating through the tank.

Smitty frowned and turned away. I could hear Garnica laughing from his gunner's seat.

Smitty spoke with a strong Southern drawl, and his disdain for some of Deboe's music had already been well established. Deboe, strong and assertive, typically humored the rest of us by listening to things like Green Day or even my new Gwen Stefani CD, but tonight he had jumped into the tank and announced his right to roll out some new tunes. Deboe made Smitty a musical target, hurling the sounds at him with good-natured taunts, occasionally rapping with the music and staring down and pointing at Smitty. Smitty's thick mustache twitched. He only had one defense. He started talking.

"The last turkey I shot," he said, "spun and danced and clucked like a madman . . . ."

I stared at Deboe, and he stared back at me, eyebrows furrowed, his head still nodding to the music. He looked back toward Smitty.

"What did you say?" Deboe asked.

"I said," Smitty repeated, "the last turkey I shot spun around like a cat in heat."

I could hear Garnica laughing again.

"Smitty," Deboe said, "What the hell are you talking about?"

"I'm trying to tell you what happened."

"What happened when?"

"When I took out that turkey."

Deboe looked at me again, incredulous. I shrugged. He looked away and reached for his iPod. He turned down the volume.

"Are you talking about turkeys?"

"Yessir. Turkeys are good hunting."

Smitty looked up and out, like he was dreaming of home. Deboe looked at me once more, and I shrugged again, and then Smitty just started talking. He talked about turkeys and the woods. He talked about deer and his dogs. He talked about his father and how, once, when he was a child, he pulled a trigger on an animal before he even knew what he was shooting at. All the while, we listened, and we laughed, and occasionally we dropped our heads out of respect for his losses and his memories. We all took shifts scanning the area, staring out across the night, but even then, we listened. We all wanted to know his story.

I wondered that night what it would mean to lose one of my men, and I began to wonder if my bond with them would affect my ability to make decisions in the future. I prided myself on making objective, rational decisions, and thus far in battle I had remained calm and clear-headed. As I grew closer to my men, and as I sat in the tank that night, I wondered, though, if that would always be the case. Would I always make the right decision? Would I even know what that meant?

That question settled especially heavy on me a week after the rest of the company had left. We heard stories of mounting casualties from the action Delta was involved in, and we heard that a platoon leader, Lt. Hadley, had been seriously injured. His tank had been destroyed by a large IED, and he had been medivaced to the hospital at Forward Operating Base Anaconda. All of his crew had been injured, but Hadley's injuries were the most serious. A head injury, and at the hospital, they treated him and observed him for a few days before sending him back to Warhorse. He would not return to action for a few weeks.

We all made a point to see him when he returned. We wanted to show him support, and we wanted him to know we were there to listen to him if he needed it. We were greeted by a different man than we knew. Before the injury, Hadley was a vibrant, aggressive soldier. He was like a line-backer, always chasing the enemy and always willing to take the fight to them. The Hadley who returned was a shell. His eyes stared, vacant of any of the energy that used to define them, and his face was flat. He didn't smile. He didn't frown. His lips were drawn straight across his face, and they hardly moved. He talked about leaving, and he focused on finishing his time and returning home. The desire to execute missions and the desire to try to establish peace had vaporized, and in its place was a utilitarian worldview, one based on self-preservation and the safety of only his group of men.

None of us judged the change. He had endured significant trauma, and his view of the war changed immediately. In his face, we saw a new, single resolve: get home. Get done and get home. That was all. His purpose had nothing to do with the war, and it had nothing to do with our orders, and it had nothing to do with the ideals that many of us held in our hearts when we went into the countryside hoping to make a change. We all understood the shift, to a degree anyway, but I worried. I worried what that might mean to our missions, and I wondered if I would respond the same way if I was injured. I wondered if I might one day have to choose between an imminent threat inherent in a mission and a retreat to safety. I wondered if I might one day have to choose between simply getting my men home safe and finishing a mission. I looked at Hadley's expressionless gaze, and I saw the possibility of my own failures. I didn't know how I would respond. I knew what I wanted to believe, and I knew what I thought I would do, but seeing him and thinking back to our nights on patrol, working beside my men and living their stories, I didn't know. I didn't know if I would ever have to choose a mission over my men.

10

By the time that the rest of the company returned to Warhorse, my platoon was exhausted. We had been working long shifts, trying to keep the area secure, and we were ready for support. Of course, the men from the rest of the company were returning from a major operation, and they returned heavy and tired. They needed more support than we did. As a company, we were all growing increasingly weary from battle, and nothing suggested that Diyala was improving. Indeed, the rest of the company returned with stories of increasing resistance in other parts of Iraq as well.

A major military surge had begun in Baghdad, and the enemy, fleeing Baghdad, was creating chaos throughout Iraq, especially Anbar and Diyala Provinces. Under pressure from politicians and policy makers, and after months of requests and demands from the military, the President announced that Baghdad would be retaken. That city, he declared, would be safe, and from there, the military could launch a more extensive surge into the rest of Iraq. While

Baghdad was being taken, though, we would have to bide our time.

The surge in Baghdad would be a major problem for us, and we knew it. Diyala, and Baqubah in particular, had long been the home base and staging ground for many terrorist and militant operations in Baghdad. Insurgents planned operations and amassed their men and weapons in Baqubah and surrounding towns and villages, then, at the appointed time, launched their attacks into Baghdad. With the surge in the capital, we knew what would happen. Any al-Qaida fighters in Baghdad would retreat to the relative safety of Baqubah, and when they did, they wouldn't stop the attacks. They would simply launch them in their own backyards. Baqubah would become little Baghdad.

In late January and early February of 2007, we began to feel the side-effects of the Baghdad surge. Baqubah became increasingly dangerous, and our battalion, the only one in charge of not just Baqubah but the most populated and dangerous part of Diyala Province, began to see casualties mount. Baqubah became our focus as we tried to stem the tide of the enemy resettling there. We sent daily missions into the city, but for each operation we conducted and for each al-Qaida operative we subdued, twenty more would flood in from the south and take his place. We were, simply put, outmatched, and, despite the resilience of our battalion leader, our battalion started breaking apart. Attacks in Diyala climbed to over twenty a day, and casualties mounted. By the end of the first week of February, our battalion had lost several men, and nearly a hundred civilians and Iraqi officials had been killed. In one particularly brazen attack fourteen civilians in Baqubah had been killed.

As a lieutenant, I did not have access to much of the intelligence that my senior officers shared, but I knew from their expressions and from their increasing agitation that the war, in Diyala anyway, was not going well. As a battalion we became increasingly focused on al-Qaida and the youths it recruited to fight for it, and some of the small successes that our platoon had seen build up over our first months in the area began to evaporate simply because, if for no other reason, we did not have the time to continue to nurture the types of relationships with locals that had proved so successful earlier. Our entire battalion was increasingly stretched thin, and the Army simply did not have enough troops to send for reinforcements.

Delta Company had, in some respects, been fortunate. While virtually every other company was running missions into Baqubah each day, our company was tasked with maintaining the rest of Diyala. The area, of course, was vast and violent, but the center of gravity for enemy activity in the region was Baqubah, so any stress we felt in trying to maintain peace in the area of operation was insignificant in the face of the daily battles raging in the city of Baqubah itself. We heard stories coming out of Baqubah, and they horrified us. In one event, a soldier died while trying to return to base at night. His Bradley flipped on the edge of a canal and careened into the water, upside down. As men tried to rescue the driver, who was pinned underneath the water breathing from a small pocket of air within the Bradley's cabin, other rescuers shifted the vehicle, and the air pocket slipped away from him. He drowned, pinned upside down in the dark, cold water of the canal.

The surge in Baghdad was the priority, so any additional forces were being sent there, and our battalion was left largely to fend for itself. Resentment and desperation began to grow. Most of us felt like the forgotten battalion. We were left alone, responsible for an enormous area and tackling an increasingly violent and numerous enemy. The American surge to the south created a corresponding enemy surge, and we were on the frontline of the enemy migration largely without support. In Baghdad, a battalion or two might be assigned to a single neighborhood of the city. In Baqubah, there was only us, and we had to secure the city and every town and village eighty miles to the north and east of it.

By the first week of February, my Company Commander had seen enough of the casualties mounting in other companies, Bravo Company especially. The battalion by that point had lost seven soldiers in the past couple of weeks, and many more had been wounded. Bravo, in particular, was being ripped apart. Nearly a third of Bravo's men were either killed or wounded, so even while they were being pressed into the same types of missions that other companies were running, they simply didn't have the manpower to be effective. Worse, they were not receiving reinforcements.

So, my Company Commander went to the battalion leadership and told them that Delta wanted into Baqubah. He told them that we wanted to support the other companies and that we wanted to help secure the city. His decision did not make him popular among many of the men of Delta. Many felt that we had been under enough duress and that sending us into Baqubah was simply putting us into the line of fire without sufficient forces. Others felt that the Company Commander was simply racking up points for promotion. When enlisted men win medals or demonstrate exceptional achievement, they receive points toward earning rank, so they assumed he was trying to win himself medals for personal gain. The truth, however, is that officers do not receive the same incentives as enlisted men. All they get are medals. No points for promotion.

A few of us supported his plan, but only a few of us were vocal about our support. Poppen, Roberts, and I all supported the decision. We felt like we needed to be in Baqubah to help our brothers, and we felt that Delta Company needed to pull its weight in that war zone. We wanted to help secure it. We wanted to keep it from getting further out of control. And we knew it would also help stabilize all of Diyala.

Even though we had not had any company-wide operations in Baqubah, all of our platoons had been into the city many times acting as the Battalion Quick Reaction Force. My platoon had probably already run fifty missions into the city, and all of us knew its state. It was rapidly falling into chaos. We always faced resistance, and we always crossed the paths of IEDs, many detonating as our tanks rumbled by. We had learned what the area was like, and we began to see it as not simply the center of battle, but the proverbial line drawn in the sand. We had to take control of Baqubah. We could not lose it. The influx of al-Qaida fighters and the money that supported them and allowed them to hire essentially mercenaries, though, made any small victory in the town temporary and insignificant. We would seem to take a neighborhood, but the next day, our battalion would face resistance there again. We didn't have the troops we needed to succeed there, and, increasingly, we didn't have the will. We were simply treading water, hoping that after Baghdad was taken, if, in fact, it were, we would be next. We knew that the longer the surge took to take control of Baghdad, the longer it meant that we would be on our own in Diyala, and not infrequently, sometimes at night, sometimes under the winter sun, each one of us wondered if the surge would in fact work. If it failed in the capital, we would never receive the reinforcements we needed. We would never have a real chance to succeed.

On February 6, while the winter rains still soaked Diyala, my platoon was spun up to support another company in our battalion as it conducted a mission into the Buhriz section of Baqubah. We had been worked heavily the previous days, and we had been to this section of Baqubah just a couple of nights before helping to guard a Bravo Company outpost. Bravo had been so heavily worked and had taken such casualties that the leadership decided that they needed extra support just to make it through the night. The Buhriz outpost was regularly subject to attacks and ambushes, and the soldiers stationed there had had little relief. Their exhaustion showed just in the appearance of the base itself. It had received little attention from the soldiers inside it simply because there was no time to clean it up or keep things straightened and in complete order. The men there were simply trying to survive.

When my tank rolled into position, it detonated a small IED, and a moment later, White Two, the other tank sent with me, took RPG fire. Our tanks withstood the blasts, and all night we heard and at times felt explosions and gunfire. We had arrived simply to guard through the night, something we had done before without incident, but here, in Buhriz, the escalation of the war became readily apparent. IEDs had been planted, probably within the last day, and we received fire throughout the night. The area was out of control.

The chaos had started to take its toll on the men of our battalion who had been working daily throughout Baqubah. They had little patience, and when they worked, they weren't going to give the benefit of the doubt to anything that even suggested being a threat. When one of our companies was sent to conduct a mission, we could see the soldiers drag themselves to their duty. They needed someone to relieve them, and though Delta was itself tired from patrolling Diyala, we were more rested than the companies that had been spending time in places like the Buhriz outpost.

My platoon was called to support more and more missions into the city, and one mission in early February illustrated the exasperation of some of the other company's men. Our mission force consisted of my tanks and some Bradleys as well as a couple of Apache helicopters that cleared the route in front of us. The helicopter support signified the level of concern the battalion had about the area. Instead of being sent as a response to a threat, they, like us in our tanks, were sent because the battalion knew the company would encounter significant resistance. They flew ahead of us, and their purpose was to eliminate any threat they saw.

Within minutes of entering Baqubah, we heard the helicopters engage a target. The Apaches buzzed above us, zooming ahead to the enemy, and they radioed to us the location of the target. We wound through the streets, following these directions the helicopter radioed to us from above, and we heard the helicopters' 30-mm machine-guns, powerful and devastating, open up on the enemy. They had found a group of three militants setting up an IED along our route, and the insurgents were in the process of wiring the bomb and finding a place from which they could watch us pass and detonate the explosive. By the time we had arrived, the helicopters had eliminated the threat. All three members of the bomb-making team lay still in the middle of the road. The helicopters requested that we dismount and conduct a battle assessment. They wanted to make sure the enemy was dead and that the bomb had not been fully wired yet.

My White Two sergeant stepped out of his tank and approached the bodies. He walked up to each one. Each Iraqi lie in a pool of his own blood, and holes riddled his body. Each wore tattered clothes, and one had no shoes. They were younger than he imagined they would be, and after he walked to the first two bodies, he wondered if he should even bother checking the third. The gunfire from the Apache machine-guns had killed each one of them instantly, he imagined. The helicopter's gun is rapid-fire and high-caliber, and hiding from it in the middle of a road is impossible. Still he went to the body to be certain. When he approached the last body, he thought something might be different. He bent down next to it, put his hand on the guy's chest, and saw that he was breathing. He was alive. Somehow, he had survived the attack.

White Two radioed back to me, "This guy is still alive down here." For a moment, the radio was silent. No one could imagine how anyone would have survived the engagement. I opened the hatch of my tank and stuck my head out, and some of the members of the company leading the mission, who had arrived in their Bradleys, dismounted and walked as a group toward the surviving member of the insurgent team. We all stared at him for a moment. The bullets from the helicopter had pierced his body at odd angles, some evidently coming down on him from above, and others evidently ricocheting up off the ground and through him. He didn't move, but we could see him breathe. We could hear him take shallow, desperate breaths.

One of the members of the lead company muttered something, and the rest of the group standing there turned away and began to walk back to their Bradley. I looked at them, then at my White Two sergeant, and I realized what they were doing. They were leaving him to die.

I looked back at the one surviving Iraqi. Blood still ran from his body, and his right eye was partially open. I looked up at my sergeant, then I turned to the company men and spoke loudly.

"We can't leave him here," I said.

Several of them kept walking, but one of them stopped and turned to face me.

"What?"

"We can't leave him here," I said again. "We have to get him outta here."

"Are you kidding?"

I stared at him, then looked back at the Iraqi dying in the street. I realized what I was asking. I was asking that we save a man who was moments ago trying to kill us. I was asking for us to take time from our mission to evacuate an injured insurgent. I was asking us to stay out with him until we could medivac him, leaving ourselves sitting targets in the middle of the most dangerous part of the city.

"We have to get him outta here. We can't leave him," I said.

"You have got to be shitting me."

By now, the rest of the men of the other company had stopped and were staring back at us.

"We're not doing it," one of them said.

"Yes, we are," I said. Several of them shook their heads. One of them said, "Fuck," and walked away. "Fucking crazy," he said.

I was the ranking officer on the ground, and what I said had to be followed. I knew I was asking a lot. I looked back to my White Platoon sergeant and saw that while he was clearly uncomfortable with what I wanted to do, he would support me. I knew the rest of the men of my platoon would as well. They might not like it, but they knew me well enough to know that I wasn't going to act rashly. The bomb team had been neutralized. Two of them lay dead on the ground, and the other one, barely breathing, was no longer an enemy target. He was a human, and he was dying. Army protocol was very clear. My job was to render aid. I had to do it. Even if I hadn't wanted to, I had to.

I knew that calling for a helicopter medivac would take too long. We would be waiting on the ground in the middle of a combat zone for the chopper to arrive, and equally important, the helicopter would be exposed to enemy fire as it came in to land. The landing could also conceivably act as a magnet to other militants. They could watch it come in and land from any number of quadrants of the city, and they would be able to zero in on our position. I didn't want to risk that. I didn't want to risk any of our men's lives in trying to save this Iraqi's. So, I radioed into Battalion Command and requested that we evacuate the insurgent by loading him into the back of one of the Bradleys. I heard one of soldiers laugh and say, "that's bullshit," when he heard my request.

The response from battalion was not much better. The young soldier on the radio questioned me why I wanted to do that. He couldn't say it directly, but he clearly thought that we should leave the injured insurgent behind. The battalion had sustained such significant losses in the past weeks that no one who had had any direct contact with the enemy in Baqubah felt much like showing any Iraqi much grace. I could hear in his voice an attempt to offer me assurance, as though he were suggesting that I had done my job in calling it in but that it was okay to indicate simply that the enemy had all been killed. He would die anyway if we left him. Why risk saving him?

I simply repeated what I wanted to do. I didn't want to engage in a power struggle, and I didn't want to acknowledge that he had offered me a way out. I wanted to evacuate the guy. I didn't want him to die, bleeding to death on a muddy street as helicopters buzzed above him and our tanks turned and rumbled away. I didn't want his final vision to be of U.S. soldiers standing above him and determining his fate. It wasn't our job to do so. It wasn't our right.

I knew why the other soldiers wanted to leave the Iraqi behind, but as long as I was in charge, I was going to evacuate him. So, I ordered the men to bring out a stretcher, strap the injured man to it, and carry him to one of the Bradleys. I had one of my White Platoon men watch to ensure the injured Iraqi was properly loaded. I wanted to make sure that the rage that many of the men in that company had started to feel didn't find an easy target, and I wanted to make sure that the anger they felt toward me didn't get taken out on the injured man.

When he was loaded and secure inside the Bradley, we turned the convoy back to the base. It had taken us nearly thirty minutes to evacuate him, and on the ride back to the base I reflected on what I had asked the men of that company to do. I had asked them to make a significant sacrifice. I had asked them to remain in a combat zone to save the life of a man who had been trying to kill them. I had asked them to put aside all the memories of their fallen colleagues and friends and act in a humane way toward someone who may not have deserved such treatment. I had asked them to, for a moment, forget all they had experienced in the past few weeks and to try to follow Army protocol and, more importantly, do what was right. They did it. Not happily. Not even particularly respectfully. But they did it, and I wondered if I had been through what they had, would I have done the same thing? If I had spent the last few months in Baqubah under constant fire and under constant threat, would I have stopped and ordered that the fallen Iraqi be evacuated, or would I have walked away from the blood pooling in the street?

I wasn't sure, but I was certain of the look in the eyes of the men on the ground. Behind the rage and behind the anger, there was something much deeper. There was desperation. They were desperate to avenge the deaths of their men, and they were desperate to survive. They were desperate to get home alive, and if one more dead Iraqi was the cost of that chance to get home, so be it. Even if it meant walking away from a living, breathing man, they were willing to do it. I didn't believe that we could all get to that point, but I feared it. I feared what it would mean when my Company Commander would finally get the orders for Delta to move into Baqubah because I feared what that city would do to me. Would I learn to walk away from a dying man? Would I forget everything else except my own desperation to get away, get home, and survive?

11

Our first Delta Company mission into Baqubah was a large operation. Our Company Commander had successfully lobbied to have us move in to help Alpha and Bravo, and while many of our men were not happy about it, some of us knew we had to do it. Baqubah had disintegrated into a Wild West, and other men of our battalion shouldered too much of a burden of the city. It was necessary that we go to Baqubah, and it was the right thing to do.

We might have asked for better timing, but given the state of Diyala as a whole in the early part of 2007, it could hardly have been helped. On February 8, my platoon and Blue Platoon had been involved in a mission in Sadiyah that resulted in the capture of several enemy operatives. We spent an entire day in the town searching houses one-by-one and rooting out the people we had been sent to capture. While we hadn't faced too much resistance, the door-to-door searching is exhausting and stressful work. Each house is a potential trap, and each street is a potential kill zone.

When we finally returned to Warhorse with our detainees, we had to question them and complete reams of paperwork only to be told that we had to be at a briefing that night for the next day's mission. February 9 would be our first official company mission into Baqubah, and it would involve both my platoon and Blue Platoon, both of us exhausted from the day in Sadiyah.

The mission seemed straightforward. The battalion had identified a house known to be an al-Qaida staging place for attacks in the region. Al-Qaida insurgents had, during the past year, started to reclaim operations by moving into houses and buildings that had previously been detected and taken from them. With the dwindling forces in our area of operation and with the surge in Baghdad pushing more al-Qaida fighters back up to us, they were reseeding previous sites of operation. Instead of finding new places, they were reusing old ones.

So, our mission entailed taking a known al-Qaida target house on the edge of Baqubah in an area called Mujima. The briefing was carefully prepared and detailed. The Company Commander presented us with aerial pictures of the target house as well as specific directions on how to get to it. The house had been well scouted, and we had floor plans and descriptions of the exterior of the building. Some of us knew the target house. We had been to it or passed by it before on other missions when we were working as the Quick Reaction Force, so those of us who knew it offered suggestions for how to approach it. Our Company Commander listened to us and solicited more advice for how best to execute the mission.

The house was a dangerous target, especially because taking it would involve sending men into a building that in the past housed IEDs. Some of the other officers and NCOs in the briefing, particularly those from Blue Platoon, resisted the order to take the house, and, instead of providing meaningful suggestions, offered reasons why we shouldn't go. Blue Platoon would be the force on the ground. Its men would be storming the house, and they knew from previous missions and the state of Baqubah in general that any missions involving entrance into a house were dangerous. Very dangerous. Their concerns made some sense, but our platoons were in no position to question the order. We didn't have the information that some of the senior officers in the battalion had. We knew that they had identified the house as a meaningful and dangerous target, and that meant it had to be cleared and taken. Our CO steered the briefing and redirected some of Blue Platoon's concerns to focus on executing the mission, and despite rising tension throughout the meeting as some men virtually refused to cooperate, we developed a plan for the attack. We would arrive swiftly, we would cordon the house, establishing an inner and outer ring around the building, then Blue Platoon would storm the house. We would rely on speed, surprise, and superior force. We would follow established protocol and training.

When the briefing ended, Roberts and I developed a plan for our platoon and returned to the men of White Platoon and briefed them. We told them the plan and how we had arrived at it, and we told them that we wanted to execute the mission carefully and precisely. Some of the men asked questions, wanting more information about the details of the operation, such as the terrain around the house or the orientation of the gates surrounding the structure. Duvall was clearly concerned about the mission. He was focused and professional, and he didn't question it – he simply asked for detailed and precise information. He wanted to make sure he was absolutely clear on everything so that he knew his role and the role of the men in his tank. The men in my tank, especially Smitty and Garnica, listened intently, and they were clear on the significance of the mission and the dangers of it. They knew the men of Blue were nervous, and they wanted to be sure they would support them well. I left the briefing with my men and walked to my CHU, where, a few minutes later, Siggins joined me.

He had just been made the Blue Platoon leader a week before. Blue Platoon was an infantry platoon, and his men were going to have to search the house. He talked about this mission with me, and as he did, he traced carefully through the plan, double- and triple-checking everything. His face was tight. His eyes were intense and focused. He knew the house had been an IED factory in the past, and he, as well as everyone else, was concerned about having to enter the building. He feared tripwires and booby-traps that would detonate a bomb as they entered, and though he didn't say it, he worried whether his men would be willing to follow his lead. He was new as their leader, and this was a dangerous mission. I knew that feeling, and I shared his concern. I couldn't imagine this particular mission being my first major one with a platoon I had just been tasked with heading up, and I couldn't imagine the pressure he was putting on himself to doing everything right. So, we talked and shared our concerns, then we committed to each other to execute the plan and to follow through and support each other during the raid. By the time we turned in, we felt ready, if still aware of some level of fear about the next day. We slept because we were exhausted, and we slept because we needed to rest before the mission.

I woke up a little after 4 a.m. I heard the sound of tanks, and I knew that my men had already been up and prepped them. They were idling at Red Con One just outside the HESCO baskets surrounding our housing units, so I dressed, pulling on my boots and my clothes that were still dirty from the day before, and I walked into the Iraqi morning. The air was still and clear, and the sound of the vehicles driving up from the motor pool carried across the winter morning. I carried my pistol and my ground helmet with me to the tank, where my men were waiting. I loaded my helmet into a small compartment on the exterior of the vehicle, and I put on my protective armor and strapped my weapon to my leg. I climbed into the tank, keeping my head up and out of it for a minute to survey the area. Four of my tanks stood in a neat line next to the HESCO baskets, and my men were climbing into them. No one said a word. I listened to the tanks and watched a set of humvees dart past us toward the gate, then I dropped my head and lowered myself inside. My gold tank helmet rested on a small ledge next to my seat. I picked it up, adjusted it, and pulled it down tight on my head. I radioed my platoon.

"Let's roll," I said, and we turned our tanks down the road and toward the gate.

We were the first element of the mission to arrive, and we waited until nearly 5 a.m. before the rest rolled into view. We lined up our vehicles in the order most efficient for executing a swift attack on the house. My platoon led, four tanks with White Two in front, my tank as White One directly behind him, White Four with Roberts next, followed by White Three. Behind us, the headquarters element followed in two tanks, and behind them, three Bradleys of Blue Platoon, each holding six infantry for dismounted attacks and three soldiers operating the vehicle, including a gunner manning a 25-mm cannon on top of the vehicle. When all of the vehicles were in order, I radioed to the HQ element.

"Red Con One. Ready to roll," I said.

Each element in turn radioed back, and we signaled the guards at the gate, who opened the barrier. Our engines roared, and we left Warhorse, speeding toward Baqubah.

The tanks rattled with a deafening mixture of clattering treads and vibrations from the engine throttled up. As we neared Baqubah, Roberts and I radioed each other and discussed the best entrance into the city. We had as yet received no resistance en route to the house, and we wondered if we might be wise to find a way other than the one we traced out the night before. The planned street of entry was a known IED alley, and while we had hoped it had been swept and cleared, we talked about the possibility of taking a different route that would be much less likely to have IEDs. We had both been in the area of the target house before, and we had both seen it. We both knew that a canal ran near it, and that along the edge of the canal, on a high mound acting as a kind of levy, ran a road. That road would be clear, and it would likely heighten the element of surprise if we took it.

We radioed our suggestion to our Commanding Officer, who in turn gave us the green light, so just as we entered Baqubah, I ordered White Two to veer from the original course and turn toward the canal. The convoy followed, and the tanks and Bradleys climbed the canal mound and found the road. The rains of the winter season reduced the dirt road to deep mud, and the treads threw up thick clots of earth behind us.

We encountered no resistance along the canal. No IEDs. No RPGs. Not even small-arms fire. The rerouting appeared to work. Across the canal, buildings of the main urban settlements of Mujima rose like uneven sentinels, structures edging up to the side of the canal with dark holes for windows. We saw no one in them, and we hoped we had arrived before most of the town had awoken.

As we approached the target, our tanks came down off the canal road and into a field. A few houses dotted the landscape to our right, and ahead of us a few more rose on the horizon. The road disappeared in the mud of the field, and White Two in front of me had difficulty identifying the way to the target house. Because I had been to it before, I radioed

White Two to move aside so that I could take the lead. I sped past him, and instead of trying to find roads submerged under water and mud, I turned across the field. We bounced over small mounds of grass and scrub, and on the far side, across the open pasture, I could see the target house. I radioed that the target was in sight ahead, and we fell upon it quickly, engines still throttled high.

White Two followed me as I maneuvered around one side of the house. White Three broke off to the right, and White Four followed him. We positioned our tanks fifty yards out from the corners of the house, and swung, in one choreographed motion, our main weapons outward, away from the building. Our job was to prevent an ambush from outside the target. The headquarters tanks and the Bradleys then sped past us and set up an inner cordon, positioning themselves inside our perimeter at the corners of the house and facing their weapons in toward the target. The sounds of the clamoring treads faded away, but the engines still shook the vehicles, and inside the tanks and Bradleys, the gunners and loaders readied themselves in case they received orders to engage. The drivers sat ready, surveying the scene and planning routes in the event that they needed to maneuver their vehicles, and the radio began to buzz with orders and commands. The assault was about to begin.

Inside our tank, we actually began to relax a little. For those of us in tanks, the most dangerous part of the mission is going to and from the target. Unlike the infantry who were about to storm the house and would be outside the protection of the vehicles, we know we are in a strong and safe position once the cordon is set. So, we all leaned back into our duties, waiting. Garnica was at the gun, ready to engage if I ordered him, and Smitty sat in the driver seat, down and away from us, hands off the controls. My loader was Armstead. Deboe, my right-hand man and usual loader, had been moved to gun

for White Two for the mission, so Armstead, a man I knew
well and a man with a previous tour's experience, sat next to
me in his stead. He was a Sergeant First Class and had been
waiting for a leadership position to open up so that he could
take command of a platoon. He lived in the CHU next to
me, and we had spent many days sitting on the steps of our
housing units talking about football, the limits of army life,
and our loves. He was trustworthy, reliable, and strong, and
though I missed Deboe being next to me on this mission, I
knew I had a good man with me.

Roberts radioed to the HQ element that White Platoon
had secured the area. We heard HQ confirm with us, then
with Blue Platoon. Blue Platoon leadership had been less
communicative with the HQ element, so we could hear
that HQ was querying them, making sure that they were
ready. The Blue Platoon dismounts were actually infantry
soldiers from Bravo Company. When some of Delta, including Mark Bosch, had been moved to Bravo to even out the
forces, some infantry from Bravo had been moved to Delta
to act as our dismounts. Many had been especially resistant
to this mission because they had been fortunate to escape
much of the horror that Bravo Company had been enduring
in Baqubah. No one could blame them. By being moved to
Delta they had unwittingly been initially spared the intense
fighting their original company had endured, but now they
were being sent into it. Most of them had wanted to go into
the target house firing. They had wanted it to be treated as
hostile and be allowed to fire on sight upon entering. Our
intelligence on the house, however, did not allow that. It
suggested that the house was being used again by al-Qaida,
but it did not indicate that it would hold a large contingent
of enemy fighters. We could not risk entering the house with
guns blazing. We might kill civilians, and my Commanding
Officer, in particular, would not risk that.

The final Bradley pulled into position, and the order came over the radio: drop gates. The rear doors of the Bradleys fell open to the ground, and the men of Blue Platoon rushed out and through the surrounding gate into the courtyard of the house. They swarmed the building, a low and wide townhouse-like structure.

Inside my tank, we simply waited and listened. The radio was largely silent, but within just a couple of minutes, Garnica and I heard a low thud. We looked at each other. It wasn't loud. It didn't even shake the ground beneath us. It simply drummed across our position and then ended. We figured it must have been a small IED, and I imagined that one of the tanks had simply repositioned itself and detonated a small explosive. A minute passed, and we heard the HQ element radio to Blue Platoon.

"What's going on in there?"

We didn't hear anything. The radio buzzed with static. Then, a minute later, I heard Blue Platoon.

"We're going to need some help in here."

There was another pause, then my Commanding Officer spoke, "What's going on in there? What happened?"

I could hear irritation in our CO's voice. I could hear expectation and concern. He wanted more information. He couldn't see from his position any better than we could from ours, so the only way he could assess the situation was by getting information from Blue Platoon. But the radio remained silent except for the thrumming white noise of static. He grew more aggravated.

"Blue Platoon, I need information. I need to know what is happening."

Static.

I could hear the sound of my own breathing and the rumble of our engine. I looked back at Garnica. He was looking through the optics, checking for sign of any activity.

Nothing. We were all listening, and we were all wondering what the hell was going on.

"The roof collapsed," Blue Platoon radioed in.

I looked at Garnica. He looked down from the optics. I pressed my earpieces harder against my ears. I wanted to make sure I heard everything.

Blue Platoon sounded on the net again.

"We're going to need stretchers."

12

None of us moved. We still did not know what had happened, so all we could do was sit, as still as we could, and listen to the radio. We heard our Commanding Officer issuing orders, and we heard other vehicles repositioning themselves. We heard increasingly panicked voices reporting injuries, and I knew more had happened than just a collapsed roof. I advised my men to stay alert, making sure we did not lose focus, and I continued to monitor the radio. Sergeant Roberts came on over the net.

"Should we move in, sir?" he asked.

I listened to him as he briefly made a case for us to leave our positions to go into the target house and provide aid. The sounds on the radio clearly demonstrated that Blue Platoon was in serious trouble, but I still could not discern exactly what had happened, so I did not simply want to leave our positions. I did not want to expose our force to an attack from another part of Mujima.

Before I could respond, our first sergeant broke into the

net. His voice pitched and desperate, he demanded that we move in.

"We have to get in there. They need us in there."

First Sergeant was well liked by the platoon. He was sincere, a strong soldier, and earnest. His emotions, however, quickly overran him. He was the senior Non-Commissioned Officer, and he was looked to by other enlisted men for guidance and support. When things went wrong, however, he had broken down. In the days after Bosch had been killed, he retreated to his CHU and locked himself in his room. He internalized the tragedy, and it broke him. It shaped not just his view of the war, but also how he had acted, so when he came onto the net, I tried to talk him down.

"We need to maintain our positions," I said. "Give me a moment."

"We've got to . . .," he shouted.

"Wait a second," I said. "We're not going to leave anyone stranded. We just have to do this the right way."

I realized as reports from the target house continued to sound over the radio that we might be needed at the building, but I knew we couldn't leave our positions and expose the entire mission to an ambush. So, I ordered the cordon to be tightened and the tanks to move in closer to the house. Then, I said that each gunner and driver should remain with each tank, maintaining the cordon and ensuring that the elements inside it did not get attacked from another position. The other two soldiers in the tanks could go to the house and render aid. Even with two men outside of the tanks, the vehicles would remain active and capable of defending our position, and our soldiers could still provide help on the ground.

I climbed out of my tank with Armstead. I took my tank helmet off and grabbed my other helmet from a compartment next to the 50-mm gun. Armstead hit the ground running, and I jumped down, reached back down into my compartment and grabbed my M-4 rifle, then I began to run to the house.

My tank was positioned on the southwest corner of the house, and as I ran toward the building, I could see smoke and dust rising up and settling around the area like fog. Most of the structure on the south side was still standing, so as we ran toward it, we could not see what was causing the floating debris. We ran up to the wall surrounding the house, then rounded the corner. The north side of the building came into view and what we saw stopped us.

Nothing remained. Only ruins. Only devastation.

More than the roof had collapsed. Virtually the entire north side had been obliterated. So much dust floated in the air that I could hardly see into the area. Bricks and plaster were scattered on the ground in front of me, and I could hear voices screaming. The house had been utterly destroyed.

I knew then what had happened. The house had been booby-trapped. In recent months, al-Qaida had developed a new method of attack called the House-Borne Improvised Explosive Device, or HBIED. The idea of the HBIED was simple: detonate explosives only after the soldiers were inside the house. Before these had been developed, IEDs were frequently along roadsides or outside structures. They were used to attack convoys, or, in the case of raids, to detonate when the front door or gate to a structure was compromised. While obviously dangerous, these earlier forms of IEDs were far less hazardous than HBIEDs because the only threat was the explosive device itself. House Borne IEDs created a secondary danger. They could effectively use not just the explosives as weapons, but the entire house. They were often set up on internal doorways. Soldiers would enter the house and encounter no resistance. They would begin to move systematically through the building, clearing rooms and checking for enemy soldiers, presumably now less concerned about IEDs because they had encountered none upon entering the structure. Once they were deep inside the house, though, they would trip a wire, and an explosive device would detonate, often against a supporting wall. The structure would collapse, inflicting damage along with the explosive, and more soldiers would become casualties.

The raid on February 9 tripped a House-Borne IED. The entire north side of the building was reduced to rubble, and dust and cries for help filled the air. Armstead's eyes widened as we rounded the corner and saw the devastation.

"Jesus," he said.

We stared at the scene. Part of the wall surrounding the house had collapsed and, through the dust, we could see the outlines of soldiers climbing over it. Two limped toward a Bradley just a bit further north, supporting each other, one with his arms under the other's, lifting and carrying him as the injured soldier dragged his useless legs along the ground. My eyes followed them then returned back to one of the Bradleys.

I could see the silhouettes of men inside, and I could see men helping each other climb in. Near them, someone yelled orders.

Someone else shouted, "We need help here!"

A man rushed toward the sound of the voice, driving his body into the dense air and out of sight. I began to move toward the house and to my left I could make out another Bradley. Two more soldiers, Blue Platoon men, rushed past me. I could not see who they were. Their faces and their uniforms were caked in white dust. Sweat drew black lines across the white dust, their skin showing beneath, but their features were obliterated by the white that covered their entire bodies. Their uniforms were white. Their boots were white. Their hands and arms were white. The dust hid who they were and transformed them into ghostly soldiers in the dark haze of the destroyed building.

I now could hear the sounds of men in desperate pain. They weren't screaming. They weren't even yelling or crying. They were making deep, guttural sounds that rose up from their lungs and their souls. The sounds weren't human. They were animalistic, primal, and desperate. They were loud, cutting through other sounds, rising up above the shouted orders and the crumbling house and demanding to be heard. I hadn't heard anything like this. I hadn't seen anything like this. And I was scared.

I knew I had to move to help, so I began to run toward the house and toward the voices. Ahead of me, I saw another soldier approaching me. I slowed down and peered through the haze at him. I couldn't see who it was, but he was carrying something. He was hunched over, running as fast as he could, but whatever he was carrying in his arms was heavy, and he bent forward with its weight.

I stopped, thinking I would help him and thinking he might tell me where I was needed. More voices rose up around me, orders being shouted to no one in particular. Pleas, really. Nothing sounded like military orders anymore. The other soldier drew closer, and I now could see his face. I couldn't tell who it was. Too much dust covered him, making him another ghost in the darkness. I could only see that he grimaced. His lips were pulled tight, back, and down, and his cheeks were stretched tight against a clenched jaw. I could hear him breathing, heavy and labored, and his eyes looked only forward, focused on the Bradley he was now running toward. He did not look at me, and he did not look down at what he carried in his arms.

I could not figure out what he held. I looked hard at it, trying to peer through the dust and haze. It stretched across and hung over both of his forearms. One end of it bounced as he ran. He drew closer, and his shoulder brushed against me as he continued past me and toward the Bradley. I stepped backward, watching him as he went by. I finally saw clearly what he was holding, and I finally understood why he was hunched over. Through the dust and the darkness of the fallen building, I could see that cradled in his arms, hugged close to his chest, he carried another soldier's leg.

13

For a moment, I did not move. I simply watched the soldier run by me, my eyes tracing his outline as he stepped toward the Bradley and into its hull. He set the leg carefully down inside the compartment, then rushed out and back toward the destruction. My eyes settled on something else inside the Bradley. Next to the leg were the mangled remains of a body. There was no head, and I could not distinguish its limbs from its torso. It was a tangled, bloodied mess. My stomach turned and I felt myself about to puke. I turned away for a moment and bent over in case I retched. My eyes watered. I felt a deep heat wash over me, and I knew it was guilt. I shouldn't look away. I shouldn't be feeling disgust. I knew this was one of the men of my company, and I felt ashamed for feeling my body respond to the small, horrible mound of his body in the Bradley. Blood pooled beneath it, covering the floor of the armored vehicle.

I heard more cries for help. I saw more of Blue Platoon's men now carrying other soldiers back to another Bradley, and

I saw Roberts and the Blue Platoon sergeant directing everything on the ground, trying to maintain order during the evacuation of the killed and injured. One of the Bradleys had been designated for the injured, and another was designated for the remains of those killed in action. The two Bradleys were within view of each other, so when I saw one soldier helping an injured man, I moved quickly to stand between them and the bodies in the back of the KIA Bradley. I did not want the injured man to see what had happened to the other men. I did not want him to deal with that reality while he coped with his own injuries. So, I moved parallel to them, a few paces away, shielding them from the sight of their own dead men, then I stood next to the Bradley, making sure that I remained between them and what was inside the vehicle next to me. I kept my own eyes on the injured men in the other Bradley. If they looked in my direction, I wanted to make eye contact and keep their eyes from seeking out what was behind me.

The degree of devastation settled down on me. The Bradley behind me held the unrecognizable remains of soldiers. I wasn't sure how many. Across from me, another Bradley filled with injured infantry. Armstead came back and stood next to me, and we talked about what to do next. There were too many men on the ground running around. The evacuation had become an orderly search of the ruins of the target house, and having too many men on the scene, especially those of us who were supposed to be protecting the perimeter, was doing more to create disorder than to help bring the situation under control. We discussed returning to our tanks and decided that it would be the best course of action. I suggested that we stay to shield the view of the back of the Bradley until the last injured man was cleared from the building, then we would return to our tanks. Armstead and I turned to look out to our tanks just as the company's first sergeant came rushing toward us. He had his helmet in his hand, and he was crying, tears coursing down his face.

"What the hell happened? What the hell happened?" he shouted.

He kept shouting as he ran, and when he finally got close to us, Armstead grabbed him by his shoulders and shook him. The soldier was a seasoned fighter, in his forties, and we were both stunned by how he was responding to the scene. The explosion was horrible, and the anxiety about returning to Baqubah in the previous few days probably heightened the emotions that all of us felt, but we needed everyone to try to keep his bearing. We needed them to be focused. Everyone on the ground in particular needed to stay in control and keep his composure.

Roberts told the first sergeant that we needed him to calm down, and Armstead got him to look directly at him. He talked to him, explaining to him that an evacuation was being coordinated and that, despite the carnage, Blue Platoon was working effectively to find the injured men. He told him to breathe and to remember his training. He told him to put on his helmet. He told him to return to his tank.

I ordered all the men from my platoon back to their tanks as well. I stayed back a bit longer with Roberts to ensure that all my men were back safe to their vehicles and in order to track down my roommate Siggins. I wanted him to know that we were returning to our tanks but that we had not deserted him, and I wanted to brief him on the security status of the scene. I scanned the land around me, but I could not see him anywhere outside the structure, so I decided to head into the explosion site.

Just inside the courtyard walls, I saw soldiers digging through the rubble, stooped low, searching for men and remains. I walked past them, and, rounding the ruined corner of the house, I saw two more men gathering pieces

of another soldier's body. They didn't speak, and they didn't
look too long at what they found. Next to them, in a heap,
was the torso of a soldier. I now knew that at least two of our
men had been killed. By the time I returned to Warhorse, I
would learn that three had died, two of them from company
leadership. One of those leaders I had seen inside the courtyard, completely unrecognizable as a human being. In all,
most of the men who entered the building had been injured,
seven of them seriously, meaning that the House-Borne IED
had inflicted maximum damage on the raiding party. Nearly
half of Blue were casualties of the explosion.

Standing in the ruins of the building, my mind for a
moment drifted home. I imagined AJ's response if I had been
in that building, if I had left her behind. I couldn't think
of that though. There were men here whose families would
never be the same, for whom February 9 would now be a
horrific anniversary. The air was still thick with dust and
debris, and I simply wandered for a few moments, trying to
find Siggins, wanting him to know that I was there but also
fearing that he may have been one of the bodies, one of the
casualties. I couldn't make sense of it. I could not understand
what was happening, and, more importantly, why I was there.
All my leadership training, all of my feelings of accomplishment and my strong sense of vocation didn't matter anymore.
It all lifted off me and mingled with the haze above the bomb
site, and I wondered who had been killed, who would never
return home.

Three quick blasts brought me back from drifting inward.
Boom. Boom. Boom.

I turned toward the perimeter cordon just in time to
see the turret on a Bradley swing to face outward, south
toward the enclave of Mujima, and open up. The cannon
on top of the turret just kept firing, unloading into the city.
Tracers flew out over the land, tracking the fire. I saw my

tanks begin to move, and then, in a powerful blast, one of the main guns fired into the densely built neighborhoods of Mujima. We were under attack.

All of us in the ruins of the house dropped to the ground. I stopped, looking around to make sure none of my other men were still near me, then I stood up and began to sprint toward our cordon. I had to get back to my men.

I ran past one of Blue Platoon's Bradleys and told the driver there to radio ahead to White One to tell them I was coming. I needed them to know so they wouldn't run me over when I got to them. Then, I rushed to where my tank had been, but as I rounded the southwest corner of the target house, I saw that it had already moved to engage the enemy. The body of the tank rolled forward then back while the turret and the main gun remained stable and locked on a target. My men were fishing for the enemy.

Small-arms fire opened up from the town across the field, and I found myself running toward my tank wondering what was going to happen. I was a lone soldier, sprinting full speed across an open expanse of land, trying to get back to my tank, and the enemy shot freely. I had no cover. I had no real protection. All I imagined was taking a round to the face, the place with the least cover on my body, and I imagined my life ending trying desperately to get back to my command position.

My feet fell hard in the mud, splashing earth around me, and my chest heaved under the weight of my armor. I closed in on my tank, watching it maneuver to fire rounds into the city. Fifty yards. Forty. Twenty. I could see the details of the tank now, each corner on its body, the color, the flecks of mud and dirt gathered on its deck. I kept my eyes on them. I did not want to look toward the enemy. I did not want to see where they were firing from, irrationally fearing that my eyes might betray my position, that one glance in their direction would be my last. I just kept running, focused on getting to my tank, and when I finally reached it, I climbed on the turret and dropped through the hatch into my position, scraping my lower back and arms as I dove in. I heard Garnica open up the main gun again just as I shut the hatch above me, and I felt the tank roll beneath me. My men were doing their job. They were protecting Blue Platoon, and they were executing their jobs with precision.

Armstead got me up to speed. He had identified an RPG team that locked on our forces, so he ordered the tank to engage them. Smitty maneuvered the tank while Garnica took careful aim, waiting for an open shot. When he had one, he fired twice, destroying the RPG team. Still, small-arms fire issued from the town, so we remained alert, looking for the location of the enemy and preparing to engage them.

I knew Armstead had been to the blast site, and at one point, I knew Garnica had left the tank and done the same. They had seen the same devastation and grotesque destruction that I had, and I admired their ability to stay focused. They were doing the right thing, avoiding the mistake of the out-of-control first sergeant who had rushed up on me and Armstead. Our Commanding Officer also remained calm and focused. He issued commands, and his orders buzzed over the net, forming order out of the chaos. Our tanks neutralized the threat from the city, and we heard the orders over the radio for the battalion Quick Reaction Force to roll out to help. We also heard the final orders for the Bradleys to move out and carry the casualties back to Warhorse.

I ordered one of my tanks, White Four, to go with them. I did not know if they would face much resistance on the return trip, but I wanted the men of Blue Platoon to know that they had more tank protection. White Four escorted them, and my tank and the other two from my platoon waited at the scene for the men of Red Platoon, the QRF team, to arrive and search for any final remains of our soliders, while the Explosive Ordnance Disposal team accompanying them scoured the area for more explosives.

We sat mostly in silence, our heads down. At one point, Armstead told me he saw another body inside the house. I didn't believe him at first, thinking that only two men had been killed, but he corrected me.

"No, there was another inside the house. It was the worst."

I didn't look at him. I sunk back in my chair, and we all waited. Red Platoon would occasionally light up the net with a progress report, letting us know where they were, but we just waited, silently remembering what we had seen, trying to push it from our minds. I forced myself to think of other things. Home, football games, people I loved and hated, wrestling matches from high school, even fucking Simpsons episodes, but my mind kept returning to the ripped-apart flesh of the men of Blue Platoon. I couldn't leave them behind.

When the men of Red Platoon arrived, they began their search. They sifted through the rubble, moving systematically from one side of the house to the other. They came with a crane, and for hours the crane lifted sections of the house away from the foundation, and Red Platoon men crawled through the area, finally recovering what was left of the body of the third dead soldier of Blue Platoon. We waited, maintaining the cordon and hoping for them to finish quickly. We wanted to get back to the base. We wanted to get away from this place, but the crane was slow, and the men were deliberate, so we sat in silence, listening to the sounds of the recovery, listening to the remnants of the mission.

By the time we rolled out, evening crept across the Iraqi land. My platoon led the way, followed by the Explosive Ordnance Disposal team, then the crane, and finally the HQ element that had stayed with us to protect the site. We drove through a more heavily populated section of the Mujima neighborhood of Baqubah. Iraqis darted from booth to booth in a market, going about their daily lives. Hardly one looked up at us, and none seemed to know what had just happened.

Just as we left the city market, though, we came under attack. An IED exploded under the rear portion of my tank as I passed over it, lifting and pushing my tank forward. White Two, directly behind me, felt the brunt of the explosion, and his treads lifted momentarily from the ground and his tank bounced slightly off course. Behind us, Red Four swung his turret around. He found the target, a small group of men who had detonated the explosive, and opened fire. Shards of a building blasted skyward, and the militants fell to the ground, but our convoy did not stop. It continued to rush out of the city, toward home, toward Warhorse.

I felt rage. For the first time in my deployment to Iraq, indeed for the first time in my life, I felt rage boil inside me. That final IED brought it out of me, a slap in the face as we retreated to safety. The enemy was far better organized than most people imagined, and they waited for us to leave to hit us one more time, to try to kill us with a final blow as we headed back to base to heal and recover. They were doing their jobs, just as the men in the market went about their day chattering with friends and bartering for bread. Nonetheless, I hated them. I hated them more than the men who planted the bomb in the house, and I wanted them dead. I did not want to be here. I simply wanted whoever had killed our men to be killed.

I had never felt that way. I didn't know I was capable of it, and I didn't know if in the coming days I would be able to lose that feeling and maintain the composure that I prided myself on. I wanted to have something to hold onto, and getting information, amassing data that I could then arrange and rearrange in my head, was all I could think of doing. So, I sat in my tank, feeling the Iraqi land pass beneath us, jolting our tank and collapsing under its weight, and tried to re-create what had happened and tried to imagine ways that things could have been different. I wanted to look at some files, a mission plan, a map, anything that I could put my hands on. I wanted to try to give it some meaning, and when I couldn't, and when I thought about that last attack on us as we left the city, I simply pushed all hope for some sense of it away. I should have thought more about it. I should have put it all into context and remembered that we were in a war where men would die, but I couldn't do that. I didn't know how anyone could. All I knew, and all I felt, was the desire to inflict harm on the people around me. All I felt was a desire to protect myself and my men, and, as our tank bounced across the province on its way back to Warhorse, all I could think was that killing seemed like the right way to do it.

14

On the day that our men were killed in Diyala, the New York Times reported on the rise to power of the Mahdi Army in Baghdad. The story covered Moqtada al-Sadr and his insurgent forces in the section of the Iraqi capital that had become known as Sadr City. Al-Sadr had become the focus of much of the news about Iraq, even as most of the violence in and around Baghdad was waning. The death of our men and the increasing violence in Diyala Province received no coverage. Only hometown newspapers of the slain men made note of their deaths.

I don't know what I had expected. I suppose I thought that the press would flock to cover the horror of the explosion because the whole terrible event marked so starkly the lives of all of us there. For us, we had only before-and-after the 9th, but for anyone else, that day became just another set of casualties of the war. Details were unnecessary. If you supported the war, it was another tragic but necessary loss in the quest to maintain the security of United States and root out the evil of terrorism. If you were against the war, it was another tragic example of the failure of Bush and his cronies. The soldiers' stories, however, were invisible, silent in the face of too much loss, too much war. Readers back home had become numb to it all, and probably still are. Newswires had to have a central figure, a major enemy to report on. Al-Sadr fit the profile. A House-Borne IED did not.

I did not expect deep coverage. I wasn't expecting in-depth interviews or a primetime television newsmagazine report. There were too many stories like ours for that to be the case. Each day, our soldiers faced down the enemy and were blown up. Each day, men died by violence and by accident. Each day, soldiers suffered and civilians died. I wasn't expecting that we would be pandered to or treated as unique. None of us would have expected that. I just wanted to see something like humanity in the news coverage. I wanted to sense some connection between our lives and the lives of our families back home.

The bodies of the men who were killed would be flown back home. Their families would receive them with flags draped over their coffins having waited days to receive them. They would hear stories of the event, I'm certain, and they would feel the war in a way that others don't and probably can't. Others except the soldiers who fought with the fallen men.

We sent the soldiers who had been killed home that very night. I stood with a group of men in a small lane within the grounds of our base, far from our CHUs. We waited in silence and near darkness. Only a few lights illuminated Warhorse so that it would not be an easy target for enemy attacks. A short distance below us, helicopters were landing, and lining the road to the landing pad, the battalion stood in tight formation. Behind us, a vehicle idled, carrying the remains of the dead. We were sending the bodies out that night on a Heroes' Flight. Our small group was acting as pall bearers.

When we had returned to the base earlier after the mission, I made my way to the Command Post. Larger than a CHU, it was made of wood and it sat up on cinderblocks. A row of the Command Posts stood behind a line of two-high HESCO baskets, well away from the rest of the base, and in front of each was the guidon of each company. I could see our guidon in the darkness as I approached the building. Fixed to a small porch on the front of the building, the colors of Delta hung limp in the still night. Red and white, it bore the insignia of our company. The white glowed in the darkness. Generations of men had fought under this banner. One man from its ranks wore the Medal of Honor, the highest award for any soldier. All had seen heavy battle. All had earned the nickname "Death Dealers," and I consoled myself with their history. They had persevered, many in far worse circumstance than ours, and I tried to imagine how our company would adjust and what my role would be in recovering from the blast that tore apart a platoon.

I stepped up onto the small deck and into the building. I walked past a wall of maps and the plans for the day's attack. Details of the operation sat on a desk atop a mountain of paperwork, and I ran my hands over the top of them as I walked into the meeting room. I sat next to Roberts, settling down on a pile of boxes. The boxes were gifts sent by anonymous well-wishers and church groups, addressed to no one in particular, bearing labels like "American Heroes – Iraq" or "Our Troops." They sat in the room, free for anyone to take, but tonight, we simply sat on them, waiting for our Commanding Officer to arrive.

He strode into the room still wearing his helmet, and he announced that we would have a Heroes' Flight that night. The seriously injured men had been flown immediately to the hospital at FOB Anaconda, where they were being treated or evacuated to another hospital in theater. The remains of our three dead would be flown to Germany and then home. A communication blackout had been issued for the base, making sure that no word of the dead reached home before official word could make it to the families. When he asked for volunteers to carry the bodies, I raised my hand. I knew two of the slain soldiers particularly well, despite them being in another platoon. They were in leadership positions, so I had worked with them in coordinating many missions in the past.

We all returned quickly to our CHUs to try to clean up. When I entered my room, I glanced at small table near the door. On it was the notebook of one of the fallen soldiers. He had come to speak to my roommate the night before the mission and had accidentally left it behind when he went. I picked it up and opened it to a page near the end. At the bottom of it, he had written a short note in all caps:

"CALL HOME."

I set the notebook back down, and turned back into my room. Siggins was sitting on his bed, quiet.

"You okay?" I asked him.

"Yeah. I'm okay."

His head was down, and his arms were on his legs.

"If . . . ."

"I'm okay," he said.

"Okay," I said, and I went to clean up.

I wiped my face clean, stripped off my shirt, and scrubbed my chest and arms. Then, I put on my ACUs, grabbed a pair of my gloves, black and dirty, and headed to the landing pad.

We heard the helicopters before we could see them. They sped over the countryside, low and without lights, trying to avoid enemy engagements, and we only saw them when they were close to setting down on the landing pad. We waited until the rotors stopped spinning, watching the blades slowly come to a stop, whipping the air around them. Behind us, the doors to a vehicle opened, and two men lifted out the first body bag and handed it down to us.

I carried one of our soldiers with five other men, all from Blue Platoon. His remains were in a black bag, strapped to a black body board, and we carried him in the darkness toward the helicopter. We could not see the road well in front of us, so we walked slowly, finding our way, until we were on the flight line, carrying our dead past our battalion. Soldiers lined the way, each company in formation, each saluting, their right hands coming crisply to the corner of their brows. Delta Company was on our left, and the men's uniforms still showed the wreckage of the day. Some were blood-splattered. Others were still white from the dust of the blast. Some of the men cried as we walked past.

When each of the dead arrived next to the chopper, our chaplain said a prayer, then our Brigade Commander walked up to each body, leaned over, and hugged the remains. No one moved. No one breathed. We all watched the men get lifted into the helicopters, and we stood at attention as the helicopter rotors began to swing around, picking up speed, whooshing in the night. The force of the air pushed me backward and I stumbled. Roberts caught me, holding me upright while the wind and the might pressed against my body and filled my ears with the sounds of those men's final flight. I felt like a child, collapsing under the force of the swirling air, and as the helicopters lifted skyward, disappearing into the night, I listened to them fly toward Anaconda, away from us, and away from the war.

15

Those three soldiers had died following their mission precisely. They had died doing things the right way and for the right reason. We were taking a house that was a known threat. All evidence pointed to it being so, and all evidence demanded that we neutralize it as a threat. We planned the assault carefully. We executed it perfectly. Still, they had died. Still, they had gone home in body bags.

I knew any war had deaths like those, where following correct protocol and doing the right thing resulted in devastation and tragedy. But this war, without the clear demarcations of a battlefield and with its ongoing shifting battle lines, seemed to lead to more of those. Our protocol wasn't entirely suited to these battles. The protocol itself was in flux, certainly improved since the outset of the war, but still changing, still developing. It had to be simply because the enemy continued to devise new ways of hitting us, new ways of finding our underbellies. I wasn't sure. I knew my Commanding Officers were developing more methods for rooting out problems and for trying to stabilize areas, and I knew that some of the enlisted men's desires to simply stay put and wait or avoid new battlefronts was not tenable. We couldn't stay static. We couldn't simply wait. But with our troops stretched thin and our morale at Warhorse steadily slipping, I wasn't sure what we could do. I figured the best thing I could do was to try to keep my platoon in order.

That was difficult in the days after Blue Platoon's tragedy, to the degree that when a soldier, Dave Nguyen, who had been stationed in Anaconda got shipped to us, we all greeted him with some scorn. He arrived on the day the Blue Platoon soldiers were killed, and Poppen, probably not knowing exactly what to say, told us that he came to join us because he was "looking to get into some action." I rolled my eyes, and a couple other men just stared, and one walked away. Dave looked embarrassed. He knew that wasn't a good introduction, and he knew that we were grieving, even though it was true that he was eager to get out of Anaconda and do more significant work than he had been doing there.

Dave was the son of a man who had been a POW with John McCain for seven years. His father and McCain formed a close relationship, and both Dave and his older sister pursued military careers, Dave at West Point and his sister at the Air Force Academy. Dave came to our company and immediately began work as an intel officer, and in the weeks that followed, he and I would become especially close, sharing the most private details of our lives as we increasingly tried to cope with the difficulties of an out of control war.

When I first met him, though, I glared at him, wondering why he would dare come to us seeking "action" on a day that we were all suffering. I wasn't interested in more intel officers. I wasn't interested in more West Point dandies telling us how to fight a war. I wanted, we all wanted, more men to fight the battles, and we all wanted to seize back control. We also all wanted some time to get away and forget about the war, and as my deployment reached its halfway mark, I and several other men in shifts were sent home for a brief R&R.

When I stepped off the plane in Philadelphia, a bright sun cast long morning shadows across the tarmac. It had been nearly a month since everything that had happened on February 9, and I still felt like something had been blown out of me, like I had been overwhelmed by something darker, angrier, and more desperate than I had ever known. When I arrived in Philly, though, and I felt the cold, clear air on my face and smelled the crisp, tight odors of a city not covered in waste and ruin, I hoped I might be able to change back. I hoped I might be able to find a connection to home and forget about Iraq.

AJ met me at the plane, and we went to get an early lunch. All of downtown Philly stood tall, straight, and gleaming. The bridge crossing to New Jersey seemed to glow. Cars darted about and honked, and they rushed along in their lanes sparkling like gems, no dust on their windshields, no mud on their fenders. The whole city looked so new and bright. I had never thought of Philadelphia as clean and new, but the contrast of it with Diyala's towns made me see it in a new way, and I found myself pulling out my camera and taking photos of the cityscape. I took hundreds of pictures, just of the buildings. They all seemed so impossibly perfect, so impossibly bright. AJ stood by me, laughing, teasing me and pointing out one "perfect" building after another in downtown Philadelphia, and we passed the day wandering the streets before finally driving off to meet friends and family at my sister's bar, Locust Street Rendezvous, where, in the smoke and stench of spilled beer, my brother, my sister, and my best friends Dave and Matt would greet me like a hero.

My sister Erin had always considered herself my protector. She was older than me, and since we were kids she had tried to make sure I was safe. Once, when I was in kindergarten, she had smacked a neighborhood kid who had gotten in a fight with me. He was in fifth grade and much bigger than I was, and when Erin saw that he had hurt me, she stormed out the house, tracked him down, and knocked him around. No one on the street ever bothered me again.

When she saw me sitting at the bar with AJ, she immediately started crying, came over to me, and hugged me, refusing to let go. She knew some of the action I had been in, and it hurt her when she heard about all of the casualties the company had seen. When I had left for Iraq, she had cried hysterically, knowing she would not be able fulfill her role as my protector, and I think her seeing me at the bar waiting to talk to her drove home the point that she had been unable to help me. She, more than just about any other member of my family, knew all sides of me, every layer, the good and the bad, the hopeful and the hopeless. So, she and I talked frankly with each other, and we shared the dark corners of our lives, the shadows of our failures. We spent the entire evening and night talking and, when my friends Matt and Dave and my brother Patrick joined us, we celebrated. We drank. We talked about our family and our friends, updating each other about our lives, and we made sure to avoid the reality of the war.

Erin encouraged me to call my grandmother, my father's mother, but I found it hard to do. During college, I had lost touch with her. We had ongoing difficulties understanding each other, and I had grown comfortable with not being on good terms with her. She, evidently, had felt much the same way, and neither she, nor my Uncle John and Aunt Lynnie, who spent a lot of time with her, had ever met AJ. I think Erin knew I needed to be sure I connected with as much as my family as I could. I told her about what had happened to Blue Platoon, and I think it made more real to her the devastation of the war. The men it killed. The families it ripped apart. I think Erin wanted us to reconcile, and hearing her talk, and thinking back to February 9, I knew she was right. I didn't want to leave anything behind when I left home to go back to Iraq. I wanted to know that I had said everything that I needed to say and that I had said it to everyone who needed to hear it.

We arranged a family gathering at my grandmother's house, and AJ and I arrived before my parents, my sister, my brother, and my cousin Megan, all of whom had planned to come along. I introduced AJ to my aunt and uncle and grandmother, and AJ, talkative and warm, helped ease the awkward first moments of the reunion. We fell into a rhythm quickly, and we listened to each other and laughed, and my uncle, a man I had hardly ever known, treated me like a brother. He joked about our family and made AJ and me feel like we had always been part of his close circle of friends.

As the night wore on, my grandmother took me by the arm and asked me to sit down. I had been showing her pictures from my deployment, and she looked at me and told me how proud she was of me, then she lifted her hand and gave me a small medallion on a chain. It had an image of Mary on it, standing with arms and palms open and down. Around her, hugging the edge of the medallion, a Latin phrase, imperfectly written, stretched from one side to the other: Maria Concepta Sina Peccato Ora Pro Nobis Qui Ad Te Confucimus. Mary, conceived without sin, pray for us who have recourse to thee.

My grandmother told me it had been blessed by the Pope, and I lifted the chain and hung it around my neck. I could feel the cool metal against my chest, and I touched it with my hand. It hung over another necklace that I had been wearing during my deployment, a gold shamrock that represented my family's Irish heritage, and I wondered which one I would continue to wear when I returned to Iraq in just a few days. I wondered if Mary would guide me away from sin or if that shamrock would bring me good luck. I wondered if either would remind me of home when I felt darkness crowding in.

I know it's strange for some people to imagine a soldier essentially taking a vacation from war. It must be bizarre to imagine that a man at war can one day ask to go home for a few weeks, then board a plane and fly home to a family, all waiting for him, all wanting to help make him forget about his battles. We don't, of course, forget. We feel the weight of the daily routine of the soldiers fall off of us for a time, and we feel what it is like to be with people who love us and want us to come home, but we don't forget. In fact, the war shapes what we do when we're home. It structures it, and it makes us do things that we have forgotten to do, have failed to do, or have never thought would be important to do. It makes us look past our own family's sins and flings us back into to their arms, hoping for their forgiveness, hoping for their love.

16

When I boarded my plane back to Iraq on March 22, I was wearing the medallion my grandmother had given me. I left my shamrock with AJ. I found my way to my seat and sat next to a woman. She was middle-aged, and she wore heavy bracelets. I was in uniform, and when she saw me, she shifted slightly in her seat in order to turn toward me.

"Are you going or coming back?" she asked.

"I'm going back to Iraq."

She paused, and she made a gesture like she was going to touch or pat my hand. She looked hard at my face.

"I can tell," she said.

I nodded, and for the rest of my flight to Atlanta, then to Kuwait, and then back to Iraq, I kept thinking of her expression. I kept wondering what she saw on my face. I had cried when I left home, holding AJ for as long as I could before I had to board the plane, but I thought that by the time I was on the plane I had gathered myself enough to resemble the soldier I needed to be. I thought that on the plane,

I had become Lt. Meehan again, ready to return to war. Obviously, I hadn't, so on the flight into Iraq, I wondered if I had returned to my soldier self. I hoped that by going home, I had somehow reversed my descent into anger and desperation and found my calling as a soldier again, but I wasn't sure if I would be able to convince myself still that my purpose was to help the Iraqi people.

I thought that getting directly back to work would help me avoid thinking about February 9, so when a helicopter set me down in Warhorse, I immediately reported back to Company Command and told my CO that I was ready to get back to work. He told me that my platoon was on QRF, and I could expect to get to work right away. Within two hours, just as I finished unpacking from my trip home, we were spun up, and I was outside the wire.

I had convinced myself that just getting back into the routine, working hard each day and pressing myself to succeed, would overwhelm my doubts about my purpose in Iraq. I thought that seeing the devastation in the small towns scattered throughout Iraq would remind me of how fortunate I was and leave me newly dedicated to helping Iraqi civilians. I thought that getting myself back into the action would help me focus on my duties as a soldier. It didn't, though. It reminded me of the hardships our company had endured so far. It brought February 9 and the horrible deaths of the men of Blue Platoon back to the surface. The Iraqi landscape crowded out memories of hope and home.

While I was back home, I told AJ about the events of that day in February. I had timed my trip home to coincide with my friend Dave's wedding, and during the reception, AJ and I stood outside in the cold March air, snow still on the ground. I told her about the bodies of the men I saw. I told her how I felt disgust when I saw them and my shame for feeling that way about people I knew. I told her about my fear and my horror, and I told her that I did not know how I made it that last few weeks I was there. I told her that the day after the attack I wept, crying nearly all day, curled on my bed in my CHU, wondering why it had happened and why it had not happened to me. I told her about my rage and how, now, I feared that my anger would never subside. I told her that I wasn't sure how I was going to get back to where I was before that day.

She listened. Standing on a snow-covered patio while laughter from the reception drifted out and fell in the hard air, she listened to my story and reminded me where I came from and what I wanted to be. She held my hand and touched my chest, and she told me that she loved me. And I believed her.

I held that image close to me when I returned to Warhorse. I tried to use that memory to replace the memory of February 9, and I imagined that if I just got back to work, if I just got busy outside the wire right away, I would leave that loss behind. I was wrong. I had only been back in theater for a couple of days before I began to feel the weight of Iraq again. Baqubah continued to spiral out of control, and the Army, focusing its efforts on Baghdad, had sent us little relief. Additionally, the amount of time we were spending in Baqubah finally became obvious to insurgents and terrorists in other parts of the province, and many started to act with greater courage in executing their attacks throughout Diyala. They knew we were spread thin. They knew we were focused on Baqubah. They knew we could not stop them.

They were brazen in some of their attacks, and my platoon increased patrols in other sections of Diyala, away from Baqubah once again, to try to prevent the entire province from falling into anarchy. Sadiyah had, thanks to our meetings, continued to improve, or, at the very least, had failed to escalate like other parts of the region. The meetings had started to involve other small towns and villages, and, eventually, instead of holding just meetings in Sadiyah, I started to conduct meetings in other towns, especially those where I thought we might be able to undermine an insurgency by being proactive. I had, however, fooled myself.

The early successes of the Sadiyah meetings were predicated on close relationships with area sheiks, but as the region increasingly destabilized, many of the sheiks began to shift their focus from advocacy for their entire community to simply self-enrichment and protection. This was especially true in some of the more ruthless towns in the area, such as Heb Heb.

Heb Heb was an al-Qaida stronghold, and the area around it was especially poor. Most of the people there lived in mud huts, and, as in the rest of Diyala, many had no running water. Not consistently anyway. They bathed in the canals that also served as their sewage system, and in the heat of spring afternoons, a stench rose from the waterways and fouled the air. We could smell the shit. We could taste it. Dogs, hundreds of them, roamed the streets and scavenged for the remains of local butchers who slaughtered goats outside their front doors, bleeding them into the dirt and gravel roadways. Flies buzzed around the mouths of the dogs. The area had always been poor, even under Saddam's rule, but after our invasion of the country, and the destruction of the area's minimal infrastructure, it had fallen into a desperate poverty. Here, in Heb Heb especially, al-Qaida gained a foothold, terrorists promising change to the young men who converted to their beliefs or who would work for them and fight against us in order to earn a living. In the midst of the poverty of a war-torn region, al-Qaida fashioned them into insurgents.

I realized very early in a series of meetings there that we stood little chance of effecting change through discussion and diplomacy. The sheiks and town officials saw the meetings as an opportunity to exploit me and the Army, oftentimes virtually demanding more money or more supplies from us. On one occasion, when we were finally able to secure a $20,000 grant to help some of the local leaders improve a road in the area, the man to whom we gave the grant skipped town and disappeared. Tracking him down was futile. No method of searching for a fugitive like him was in place. No central police force and no central database or call center existed where we could make the event widely known. He simply had taken the money and run, and we would never see him again.

That type of personal corruption extended down to much smaller things, though. When I arrived at one meeting with a small load of blankets, the sheiks scrambled for them, pushing each other out of the way and ripping the blankets from each other's hands. It resembled an air drop of food into a disaster area, with each person fighting for his own survival. The difference here, though, was that the sheiks did not need the blankets. They were doing more than just keeping the blankets for their own families. They were hoarding them so that they could put them up for sale, often in their own shops or kiosks in the market. They were profiteering, and, increasingly, I lost patience with their behavior. I also lost hope that change was really possible through negotiation.

The hope I had once had in the meetings evaporated. I had earned a reputation as an earnest and hopeful soldier – one with no qualms about executing a military mission, to be sure, but one always trying to find a way to work with the leadership of Diyala Province to find better alternatives than military action to solve problems. The behavior of some of the opportunistic sheiks, though, began to challenge my hope. Only thoughtful local leaders would mitigate the desperate poverty of the region, and I had little patience with local sheiks or mayors exploiting that poverty for their own ends.

Ideally, we would have been able to simply root out the al-Qaida members who had assumed leadership positions. We knew who many of them were, and we knew how many of them operated. Unfortunately, some of the key members of al-Qaida in Heb Heb had infiltrated the Iraqi Police, and in recent months, we had been given explicit orders not to arrest Iraqi police officers. We understood why. The war was in no small part a public relations campaign, both in Iraq and abroad. Arresting members of the national police, or even local police, highlighted the depth of corruption, and it suggested the impotence of Iraq's provisional government. Arresting Iraqi police also fueled al-Qaida's propaganda. It used such arrests and any raids on governmental officials as evidence that America controlled Iraq and that the Iraqi government functioned as a puppet state under the direction of President Bush.

The Army, then, was in a tough spot, and we, as the ground troops supporting the mission, were in a bind. We couldn't go after the bigger name leaders within the government, the ones who may have been coordinating many of the difficulties we were experiencing, without direct commands from the higher levels of the U.S. hierarchy, and those commands were unlikely to come down the line. So, we had to go after the lower levels of combatants, many of whom were probably seeking simply to earn a living more than they were seeking annihilation of American intruders. They, of course, were no less dangerous. Many of them probably did despise us for being there, but even those who didn't were armed just as any other insurgents and were, to some degree, trained to use those weapons. They launched RPGs, they planted IEDs, and they fired their rifles and their mortars at us, some trying to purge Iraq of the American presence, others just trying to get by.

The Army set in place very clear guidelines about who we were allowed to go after and under what circumstances we were allowed to seek them out. Some of that was good, of course. It prevented vigilante justice and mistaken identities. It removed from the ground-level command the capacity to form judgments based on limited information while not preventing us from engaging an enemy that was directly confronting us. On the other hand, it also meant that we were sometimes unable to respond to intelligence that we, on the ground, were collecting. If we found information that definitively implicated a governmental official in a military action, we were being asked to pass that information up to ensure that the information was vetted to prevent us from giving the newly formed Iraqi government a bad image. We were caught in those instances between knowing full well who was responsible for some of our problems and ensuring the public image of a stable, centralized government for Iraq.

Understanding the reasons for not being allowed to make certain arrests, though, did not mean we, as soldiers on the ground, agreed with them. We knew we were leaving dangerous men not simply on the street, but in the police stations and in the government offices, and we knew that they knew we were powerless. Their attacks escalated and at times even seemed to mock us. Unless we caught someone with a bomb in his hands and we could publicly demonstrate it, we simply had to endure and survive while trying to find some other way to root out the bad guys. I decided that the best way for us to force them out was to collect intelligence on them and try to gather indisputable evidence that we could act on.

Early in my time in Diyala Province, I realized that some of the intelligence that we were receiving from our superiors was either out-dated or failed to account for what was really happening in our area. This was not to say that it was not useful in some broad way of understanding the landscape we were fighting in, only that it sometimes failed to get to us in time. I began to realize that to truly help fashion some sort of security in the area, we would need to rely on intelligence that we could gather ourselves.

I was lucky in that my Company Commander had faith in me, and as the spring approached, he increasingly trusted me to gather and act on street-level information that we secured. My platoon had demonstrated that we followed military protocol precisely and we had ensured that we treated suspects that we had arrested respectfully. My Company Commander had also seen some of the positive work that our platoon had done with town meetings, and he trusted that the relationships we had formed with local communities were genuine and, in terms of intelligence, fruitful. Probably equally important, Diyala's rapid descent into increasing violence and the lack of reinforcements meant that, sometimes, local intelligence might be all we had to work with. My Commanding Officer, and later, in the years that have followed, the Army in general began to see that what was needed to win this type of warfare was officers on the ground who could work with locals, think critically about the information that they provided, then act within the parameters of the rules of engagement.

So my Commanding Office gave me some leeway, and in Heb Heb I nurtured a relationship with the mayor of the town, and he became one of our greatest allies in collecting that intelligence. He was a large man and a Shia in a predominantly Sunni area. He was, however, well known for being fair and equitable, and for the most part he was respected by the community. He was also one of the more educated members of the community whom I communicated with, and he was quick to realize that the only way to work on behalf of the people and the only way to help secure the town was to drive out the al-Qaida fighters who were attempting to run it through intimidation in order to ensure their own power and financial gain or fund al-Qaida activities. So, he worked with us to provide information that would help us dismantle the al-Qaida network that dominated the town.

Two months after my arrival, however, he was assassinated. He had left his office at the Iraqi Police Station, and he was driving home. A car drove up next to his, and, leaning out their windows, a group of men with AK-47s unleashed a hail of gunfire. When his car was searched, the Iraqi police found it littered with bullet holes, and the mayor's body was slumped across the seats. Blood pooled around him.

Al-Qaida intended his murder, done in the middle of the day in the middle of a busy street, as a threat not so much to us but to anyone in the area who considered helping us, and it reinforced its control of the area by installing essentially a collaborator as the new mayor. The man was emaciated and spoke quickly. He was bald, and the only hair on his face was a thick, furry mustache. He was conniving, he was selfish, and he was dangerous.

Within a few weeks of him becoming mayor, I decided that the meetings in the town were fruitless, and I expressed to him my irritation and frustration. I couldn't simply end the meetings, but I went to the gatherings firm in my convictions and not in a mood to peddle more cash allowances and grants for pet projects that I knew would simply line the pockets of a few greedy and corrupt men. I went to the meetings unwilling to negotiate. Al-Qaida responded to my frustration.

Early one morning, while my platoon prepared for a routine mission in another part of the province, a group of small trucks and cars sped through Heb Heb toward the Iraqi Police Station. They surrounded it, and, speaking through a megaphone, a man declared that they had come to destroy the station and all of the city offices inside it. They told everyone inside that they only had a few minutes to evacuate and that they would spare anyone who left. Inside the station, a couple of the policemen rushed to the corners of the building, where small machine-guns had been mounted, and they fired on the attacking force. Al-Qaida responded, firing into the building from several angles, pinning down the resistance and then, once again, ordering them to leave the building before they were killed. The police capitulated, and with barely a shot fired, al-Qaida entered the building, ransacked several rooms, then set the entire structure on fire.

The station stood near the edge of town, a smallish rectangle with an open center, so that offices lined an inner courtyard, connected only by a breezeway. Typically, beggars filled the courtyard, loitering and looking for handouts from anyone who came to do business there. They sat in the dirt and mud, kicking out their legs from the edge of the breezeway, sitting against posts supporting the roof. Weeds grew up between stone pavers and concrete walkways.

All of the beggars and all of the city police left the building before the al-Qaida men entered it. Not surprisingly, many of the town officials had not even come to their offices that day. Most city offices were located within the Iraqi Police Station in order to provide safety for town officials while they did their jobs. That day, though, many officials had not come to work, and the mayor, in particular, had been nowhere near the station when al-Qaida arrived. All knew what was going to happen.

When we received report of the attack on the station, I looked to the west out of Warhorse, and I could see smoke rising on the horizon. I knew the fire would be catastrophic, and I knew nothing would be left. At the time, I wondered how many Iraqi police had been injured in the defense of the station, and I hurried my men. I wanted to get there as quickly as possible in the event that al-Qaida was still engaged in a battle with the police or was attacking civilians. I wanted to get there to ensure that al-Qaida did not expand the fight.

When I arrived, though, I quickly learned that it had been a precision attack and that there had been virtually no defense of the station. There had only been desertion and a token smattering of resistance, more a formality to protect a few policemen's reputations than a sustained defense. I couldn't entirely blame those who offered some resistance for eventually retreating. They, at least, knew they were not supposed to capitulate, and they showed, perhaps, some sense of pride in their assigned job to protect the community from terror and intimidation. They also knew, though, that they had been deserted by other police who were either complicit with al-Qaida or part of the organization's rank and file. They also knew that many of their superiors, including the mayor, would provide them no support. They were outmatched and outmaneuvered.

I wanted them to defend their station. I wanted them to show some pride. But, I knew that they had families and that they probably saw the futility of their resistance, and they simply did not believe my platoon, or any other coalition force, could protect them. So, they surrendered and walked away from the station.

From my humvee, I could see that one side of the building had burned to the ground. Smoke still rose and blackened the sky. I got out of my vehicle and walked past a set of HESCO baskets that had been erected to protect the structure from a bomb. They seemed ridiculous now. No one needed a bomb to destroy the police station. All they needed was a megaphone, gasoline, and a few matches. I walked into the courtyard and turned to the left and walked into what had been the mayor's office. The walls were charred and smoke lingered in the air, but it still stood. The desk where the men had fought over blankets, turned on its side, rested on the other side of the room. Mattress springs, used as a couch, still sat on the left, surrounded by a grouping of lawn chairs. It all seemed so ridiculous and futile. We had been conducting meaningless meetings with the town officials in this office for weeks, sheiks sitting on bed frames fighting over cash allocations and blankets, flashlights and light bulbs, all the while demanding more so that they could fill their own coffers or supply their own homes. Now, that room was burned, and it seemed hardly different at all. It seemed small. Insignificant. Meaningless.

I turned out to the courtyard and made my way to my humvee and my men in their tanks. I told Roberts that we had little to do than just gather reports and then head back to Warhorse. So, we collected stories, acting as scribes for the stories of the police who abandoned their posts and those who, behind the scenes, helped execute the attack, and we drove back to base.

I felt like shit. By burning down the Iraqi Police Station, al-Qaida was sending us a message. The message was that despite all of our efforts, it was still in control of the area, and there was little we could do about it. I was in charge of a fifteen-man platoon, tasked with patrolling an enormous territory. We came out during the day, met with our contacts, responded to certain threats, conducted patrols, and generally tried to corral the enemy. We were, however, limited by our size and the times of our patrols. We never ventured out of the Forward Operating Base at night, and we couldn't patrol an entire town, even a relatively small one like Heb Heb. They knew it. We knew it. We were stuck, and I hated it. I hated the corrupt leaders. I hated feeling like my hands were tied by political posturing and public relations. I hated feeling like meetings that had once been productive had been reduced to hand-out sessions. I hated that the hope I once nurtured seemed to have died, and I hated that my own sense of accomplishment was so deeply tied to this place. It was Iraq. It was a war. I didn't want to care anymore.

I felt a dark heat inside me, and sometimes, in the days that followed, I felt aggression boiling. I would go to a small enclosure near some of our CHUs and I'd lift weights, trying to find some place to direct all my energy. The moment the workout ended, though, I'd feel the anger burn again, ripping away inside me. I'd try to find other things to do – talk to some of my platoon or check emails – but none of it provided much release. I felt the war changing me.

One day, as I ate a meal, the TV blared news from the previous day, and I looked up and saw an image of Anna Nicole flash on the large screen. I stared at it. It was a still shot, taken from some paparazzi at some glamour event during the height of her popularity. Her face, nearly white and perfect, had a wide smile across it, and her eyes were looking straight at the camera. She wore red, and her pose, sexual and irresistible, drew my attention.

She had died a few weeks earlier, and the story of her death and the drama surrounding the custody of her child remained headline news. It led evening entertainment and news programs, and her image, living and larger than life, danced across our screens every single night. Her death, real and palpable to so many viewers, including so many of us, shocked me. Not the fact of it. Not the reality of the tragedy and the ridiculous circus her child had been made the center of. It shocked me because it stayed on the air for so long. Each night, presumably, Americans tuned in to hear her story. Each night, Americans pined to know what had happened that day, what new details they could find out about her last moments. Each night, I imagined, groups of friends talked about and discussed her celebrity and her image and her final moments. All the while, their friends, their neighbors, their family died in Iraq.

I knew there was no comparison. I knew connecting the two was overblown and melodramatic. To me, though, sitting in that mess hall, hands smeared with dirt and grease and the scum of the Iraqi canals, it didn't feel trite or contrived. It burned. It stung. And, it pissed me off. I hated Anna Nicole, and I wondered how many people back home dared to turn off their televisions when she came on in order to make the point that there were other stories in the world worth listening to, that there were other tragedies unfolding. Those stories had been made into footnotes, numbers splashed across the screen during the final few minutes of the news each night.

"Four more soldiers were killed today," Katie Couric might say, "and the death toll in Iraq now stands at . . . ."

Perhaps I should have been grateful even for that. Perhaps I should have simply acknowledged the effort to represent the war to the U.S. public in some neat, tangible, compact way. I wasn't though, and I'm still not, and when I saw Anna Nicole that night, and I thought of the men who were suffering and dying, both U.S. and Iraqi, both soldiers and civilians, and I thought of the corruption and the futility of the last few months, I could not tolerate it. Sitting there in that hall, listening to commentators wrangle over the reasons for Anna Nicole's demise, I felt like anything we did simply did not matter. I felt like we did not have a chance at fixing all the broken parts of Iraq.

I decided I had to make a change. If I were going to feel anger, if I were going to see this province unwind around me, and if I were going to leave the base each day knowing that most Americans were watching images of Anna Nicole on television, I was going to divorce myself from external measures of my success. I couldn't control the television news. I couldn't control Baqubah. I couldn't control the Army's orders or the rules that bound me. I couldn't control much of anything, but I could control my platoon and myself, and I dedicated myself to taking back any section of Iraq I could, no matter how small and no matter how I would have to do it. If that meant using force and refusing to engage in circular discussions with known deceivers, so be it. Something had to change, and I was going to try to make it happen, even if I had to punish someone to do it.

17

Green Eyes provided me with the best opportunity for change. I do not know his real name. He came to us shortly after the Iraqi Police Station had been burned down, and he expressed his desire to help us. He was himself an Iraqi policeman, and the destruction of the station left him disillusioned. He could not believe so many of his peers had abandoned their posts, and he had felt his sense of pride battered by his own decision to preserve his own life instead of fighting virtually alone against the al-Qaida force that lay siege to the station. So, he and another man sought us out. They covered their faces to protect their identities, unsure about how to approach us and still embarrassed and fearful. All we could see were their eyes, and Green Eyes, as we called him from that day forward, became one of our most trusted and reliable sources.

My resolve to make a change where I was meant I had to do things differently, and I decided that the best thing I could do to take control was to nurture my own sources and generate my own intelligence. With that intelligence, I would act. I would no longer wait for orders from battalion. I would no longer wait for the lengthy process that typically governed intel. Instead, I would go door to door in towns, build relationships, and seek information. When I got it, I would act on it myself, not by passing it up to battalion, where it would linger, waiting for administrators to vet it. We simply could not do things the way they had been done for so long. With the surge in Iraq simultaneously occupying most of the forces in the area and forcing many of the deadly fighters into Diyala, typical modes of operating no longer functioned. I still ran all operations by my Company Commander, and despite some concerns on his part, my actions in the past and my reputation as both level-headed and genuinely concerned about the people in my area provided him with enough reason to trust me. So, he made an exception. He allowed me to conduct raids, to work somewhat independently. He embraced the intelligence we had been gathering and realized that much of it was time-sensitive and required swift action. He knew, I think, that we would get results even while we followed all rules of engagement, and he knew I would extensively document anything I did. So, he let me run the missions, and he requested that I work with an intel team from battalion so that the information I gathered could be made into official reports. I assured him we would keep him fully informed of all of our actions and that we would follow established protocol in gathering intelligence and executing raids. He wanted us to be safe. He wanted only the bad guys captured or killed. I promised him we'd be professional, and my platoon began a series of night raids that helped us reassert some authority in the area.

Night raids were unusual. They are more dangerous than other raids, and they involve variables that daytime operations don't include. We felt like we needed to use them, though, to help us regain some control in the area. The patrols and our missions in Diyala had become extraordinarily predictable. For the most part, we only left Warhorse during the day to conduct raids, and, unless we were manning observation posts, few of us were ever outside the wire at night. The enemy knew this. They knew where we would be and often when we would be there. Indeed, in the days before we finally left Warhorse near the end of our deployment, spray-painted messages began to appear on the walls of ruined buildings around the base. "The tanks are leaving," they said. They knew, despite the supposedly classified nature of the information, that 1–12 was leaving, and they spread the word with public messages that they knew we would see. If they knew something as significant as when we were leaving, they certainly knew our basic modes of operating and our daily routines. Night raids would be a way to break that routine. They would be a way to surprise some of the men who were causing us the most difficulty, and they would be a way for us to act without drawing too much attention to ourselves.

Green Eyes was pivotal in the night raids. While he provided us with significant intelligence that led us to important arrests, he was important to me personally because my interactions with him gave me the confidence to pursue more intelligence. He represented a side of Iraq I had lost faith in but still existed. He represented the people who wanted to make changes but were powerless to do so. I wanted to act on his behalf, and I wanted to demonstrate to him that we were there to help him. We were there to make a change.

That change was predicated on a significant shift in how I went about my job. I simply had had enough of the liars, the corrupt officials, and the violent gangs that controlled so much of the area. One day, acting on information from Green Eyes, my platoon and I raided a small house in Heb Heb. Green Eyes had informed us that it was the house of one of the al-Qaida members involved in the burning of the Iraqi Police Station. When we confronted the man in the house about the allegations, he denied it. We had strong evidence besides Green Eyes's information, though, so I pressed the point. When he refused to cooperate, lying and virtually mocking me by saying things like, "You can do nothing to me," I snapped.

The moment must have looked contrived, like a staged scene from a cheap movie where the bad cop flies off the handle and shouts at the accused, yelling at him and threatening him. I became that guy, though. I did not know it was going to happen. I did not know that I had it in me. I did not feel like myself. I did not even recognize my own voice. Rage, a long-simmering rage, came up from my gut, and I grabbed the guy by the collar and lifted him off the ground, pulling him toward me so my face was against his. I yelled at him, words spitting out on his face. He cowered. Genuine and deep terror was on his face, and I dropped him to the ground. He wept, and while I stood over him, he confessed his role in the burning. He had been the cameraman. He had videoed the entire thing, and with that tape, he had incriminated himself.

We arrested him, and from him, we gained more information, and that moment marked a turning point for me. I had let the rage come out of me. I had changed. I hadn't exactly lost control. Despite the yelling and the anger, I had still been completely aware of what I was doing, but it was like I was watching me from outside myself. I could think through things, I could see things happening, but I allowed that part of me to explode outward and seize control of the situation.

Part of me wanted this other side of me to take complete control. Part of me savored it. I could feel my body tighten and my face burn, and inside my gut, an anger boiled that finally found some way to express itself. But, afterward, and after each subsequent time when that rage would explode outward and I would transform into a calculated intimidator, I was exhausted. Sometimes I had to sit down. I would pretend that it hadn't affected me, laughing as I would casually take a seat and chat with my platoon, but I was worn out. It was as though in the moment of that release, everything in my body had been funneled out of me. It was an emotional exhaustion. It was a spiritual one. But I courted it. I looked for it, and I sometimes hoped that I would have the opportunity to give that part of myself voice on a mission. I wanted someone to cross me. I wanted to make someone pay, and my platoon, all of my men, fed off of it.

On April 16, Green Eyes came to me with a group of men. One of them gave us startling news. He knew the location of an important Jaysh al-Mahdi figure. Indeed, the man, Ali Hassan Hadi al-Nasir, was a top religious leader of JAM for all of Diyala Province, and our informant knew where he would be that night. He also knew he would be hoarding a significant arms cache. Finally, our hard work in building an intelligence network of locals who trusted us seemed to have yielded a major result.

I asked our informant to come back to FOB Warhorse with me, where, together with the intelligence team, we went over maps and discussed the layout of the building where the JAM leader was staying. The informant provided detailed and precise information, and his association with Green Eyes meant we trusted him. I went to my Company Commander with the intelligence and a request to conduct a raid that night. He hesitated. He knew it would be a dangerous mission. If the leader of the JAM in Diyala was the target, we would very likely face significant resistance. Additionally, our platoon was not scheduled for night missions, so battalion leadership, who were not entirely aware of our increased intelligence capacity, might see the raid on the target as too risky. They would want their own intelligence. They would want to take time to check their own sources. I knew we didn't have that time. My Company Commander knew it as well. And so, bolstered by our relationship, built on the trust he had put in me and in my results, and his belief in the credibility of the source, he decided to okay the mission. He said he'd run static for me. He told me to go get that man.

I immediately gathered my platoon and told the men to watch for our operations orders, which I would post on my door. I wanted everyone to be amply prepared, and I wanted to make sure that each one of my soldiers was clear on our plans and the significance of our mission. So, I told them about our target, and I told them to follow the orders and schedule on my door to the letter. Everything had to be perfect.

The schedule told my men when the vehicles had to be ready, when to form up for a final inspection so that I could ensure that each man had all the right equipment, and when to sleep. I told them to check their Surefire lights at the end of their M-4 rifles, and I told them to make sure that they had extra batteries. I confirmed with them that we had two days' worth of ammunition, food, and water packed, and I inspected the night-vision goggles, the few that we had been issued. When they were all set, and when Roberts and I had checked and rechecked everything they had done, I sent them to bed to rest for the hours ahead.

I stayed awake. I couldn't sleep. I knew that if our information was accurate, we were embarking on a dangerous mission in the middle of the night, and sleep wouldn't come to me. So, I flipped in a DVD of The Dark Crystal, the cult classic film about the conflict between good and evil, and I went slowly through my own equipment, inspecting every inch of it just to pass the time. Sometime after midnight, I got dressed for the mission, and a little after 2 a.m., I stood up, reached into a small pouch affixed to my vest, and pulled out the crucifix my mother had given me. It had been pink when she had given it to me, but I had painted it gold, like my helmet, and it reflected the dim light of my desk lamp. I slipped it back into my vest, patted it through the fabric, and went out to my men.

We left FOB Warhorse in humvees, speeding into a clear warm spring night toward our target city, Qwaylis. Behind me in my humvee sat my interpreter and the informant, both dressed just like the rest of the platoon, except for the mask that our source wore. Accompanying my platoon was a small contingent of men from headquarters, bringing our force from fifteen to twenty-three men. The lone road into Qwaylis had been stacked with barriers, and locked gates crossed it at random intervals. Dogs barked in the darkness, and we knew that the obstacles had been erected as a warning system. They slowed us down, and the dogs, we feared, warned the insurgents in the town of our arrival. When we came to a stack of bed-frames, or huge rocks, or discarded furniture, groups of us leaped out of the vehicles and heaved the obstacles out of our way, throwing them to the edge of the road. We were all sweating from the work and the anxiety, and as we encountered more and more barriers, we began to realize precisely how powerful our target might be.

As the road curved on the final approach to the target house, we came to a sudden stop. A huge pipe as tall as our humvees stretched the width of the road and blocked our way. Buildings were on either end of it, so we couldn't drive around it. We were eighty yards from the house. I could see it in front of me. I hesitated for just a moment to decide what we should do, then ordered us all to dismount and head for the house on foot, leaving our five hummers back with two men each.

I knew this was an important decision. Eighty yards on foot into a hostile neighborhood is a long distance, and while it seemed like the town was still sleeping, I couldn't be certain. I couldn't be sure that we were going to make it to the house without resistance, and I considered the possibility that we might walk into an ambush. We had to make it to the house, though. The obstacles convinced me of its importance, and I thought that if they had seen us on our way to it, we would have already been under attack. We weren't, so we left the vehicles and the safety of their heavy machineguns, and we rushed toward the house, carrying our M-4s high and ready.

We hit the house hard, running down the street as a unit and kicking in the door, infiltrating swiftly. Light from the doorway spilled into the space, but shadows lingered along the corners of the front room. I could hear my own breathing, and a flurry of dust drifted from the shadows.

In front of us in the middle of the room sat the man we had come to find. He stared at us. We trained our weapons on him and told him to drop to the ground. He shifted, his hand dropping. I told him to stay still, my interpreter translating my command, shouting it at him. He tilted his head slightly, then, in one deliberate motion, he lifted a gun and leveled it at the first soldier who had come through the door – Deboe.

I thought at that moment that one of them, either Deboe or the suspect, was going to die, and I was certain it was going to be our target. Deboe had his weapon up, and he only had to pull the trigger to end that man's life. The JAM leader would not have stood a chance. But Deboe did not shoot. Instead, he rushed the target, running straight at him and his gun. The man hesitated, surprised by Deboe's quick move toward him, and in that moment, Deboe closed on him, kicked the gun from his hand, and, in one motion, tackled him and pushed him hard to the ground.

More of the platoon fell on him and pressed in to subdue and disarm him, ensuring we had him secured. Others executed a

search of the house and the area. We had been told we would
find significant weapons caches, and that information turned
out to be true. We found AK-47s, PKCs, many RPGs, IEDs,
as well as JAM propaganda and torturing equipment. The
stash was so sizeable that I knew we had the right man.

We had captured alive the leader of JAM in Diyala, neu-
tralizing him as a threat. The capture would be significant
not just for us, but for the company, because with him
apprehended, the JAM in Diyala would have to reorganize.
That would likely happen quickly, but seizing him would be
a clear message to the JAM leadership that despite the rising
violence in the area, we intended to do our jobs.

We did not have time to celebrate our capture, though. I
knew other JAM militia would be nearby, and I guessed that
more weapons might be in neighboring houses. So, when the
target house was secure, I ordered more searches. In empty
houses around us, we found more AK-47s and RPGs, and
each structure was littered with JAM propaganda. I realized
now that what we had found was not simply a JAM stash and
safe-house. We had just raided a village entirely controlled
and run by the JAM, so we had, in effect, stormed not just
a house, but a community. We needed to leave and get the
captured JAM leader back to Warhorse quickly. If we were
discovered and if anyone realized we had captured al-Nasir,
we might very quickly be fighting the entire town.

I decided to call Company Command for back-up just
to be safe. I went outside and surveyed the area. Dogs still
barked. Across the street from the target house, a tall mosque
stood quiet in the darkness. Four of my men joined me outside the target house, and I, speaking with them, decided to
reconsolidate the rest of the platoon at either the humvees
or where we were currently standing. The mosque across the
street, though, begged to be searched. Speaking through the
interpreter, our informant had told us the JAM kept weapons

inside, but the military had long ago decided to respect the sacredness of the mosques, and we had all been trained not to enter them. I stared at it, tracing its doorways with my eyes, and I wondered how many weapons were inside.

Next to it rose another house. I decided that, given the nature of the area and the number of weapons we had found so far, there would likely be more weapons there. If we couldn't search the mosque, we would search the house next door to it, and, turning to my men, this is what I instructed them we would do. We would wait for the rest of the men to return, move quickly to the house next to the mosque, search it, then return to the humvees and leave as quickly as possible. I radioed the plan, and I walked toward the mosque and the neighboring house with my four other soldiers. We would all rendezvous there.

We began to see signs of the sunrise in the east, the sky glowing in deep, rich tones of blue. The ground in front of us was still dark, but we could feel the anticipation of morning, and with it, we knew we would be back at Warhorse, debriefing and celebrating our significant capture. I looked up, toward the mosque again, not thirty yards ahead of us. I could see more detail on the building, Islamic designs etched into stone. My eyes wandered further up the building. I could see the roofline. The sky glowed above it.

Without a sign, without a sound, without even the slightest indication that we were being stalked, rapid flashes of machine-gun fire lit up from the edge of the mosque roof, and we were under a hail of bullets. Multiple machine-gun nests on the mosque roof opened up on us. We hadn't seen them. We hadn't heard them. Not a sound. Not a whisper, just the sudden screeching of machine-guns ripping off rounds at us. Bullets glanced off the road in front of us, dirt and gravel popping up from the ground, and we instinctively dove for cover.

I dropped behind a pile of shattered cinder blocks. To my right, some of my men hid behind a mound of dirt. We returned fire, but we were pinned hard to our positions. We could hardly move without exposing ourselves to fire. When I heard the first explosion from a hand-grenade, the ground rumbling beneath me, I knew we were in trouble. They had the high ground, and they could see our location clearly. They were keeping us pinned with machine-guns and were going to use the grenades to force us to move, exposing us to their fire.

Roberts radioed for help. He requested support from the Quick Reaction Force and, more importantly, the Air Weapons Team. We continued to try to return fire on the enemy, but their positions were high on the mosque, and we did not have clear line of sight for engaging them. I turned to Deboe and asked him to fire at the positions while I tried to move to a large dirt mound. I rose to a crouch, then looked back at Deboe. He gave me a nod, and I leaped up and ran. I heard the explosions of grenades around and behind me. The air shook, and my ears filled with the rapid fire sounds of the enemy guns and the concussions of grenades.

I hit the ground again just as I heard a man behind me yell, "Man Down, Man Down!" I turned to face the shouting voice. I couldn't see who it was. It was still too dark, and the thin line of dawn still had not crept toward us from the east. I could see the lights of my humvees to the rear, and, occasionally now, I could see the flashes from their guns light up. They opened up on the mosque, unloading on the high towers where the enemy nests were perched. I had a moment to think about what was happening. Between the rapport of the guns and the blasts of the grenades, I wondered why I had stayed so long. I had captured my man. We had conducted a successful raid and nabbed a High-Value Individual. Why did I stay back? Why did I have to search that one last house? Then, above it all, above the grenades and machine-gun fire and shouting men, above my own doubts, I heard the sound of choppers descending down on us.

For a moment, all I could hear was their blades whipping the dark sky. The machine-guns on the roof fell silent, evidently having noticed the incoming birds. The choppers had orders to fire only on targets that they could clearly identify as hostile, and so when the enemy ceased fire, the choppers could not engage them. Our men in the helicopters reported seeing the fighters on the roof and they could see them moving around and in clear positions to engage us. More distressingly, they identified a force in a palm grove to our east, closing in on us, flanking us. Roberts's experience came into play. He recommended that the choppers move further away so that the enemy would re-engage us. As long as they heard the thumping of the rotors, he reasoned, they would stay low on the mosque or in the grove and wait. The Air Weapons Team followed Roberts's suggestion, and when they had left the scene, the enemy immediately emerged from the grove and prepared to engage us. The choppers let rockets fly and opened up with their 50-mm guns, killing eight of the enemy soldiers immediately and wounding another. The birds whipped around, turning back toward us. They had secured our flank. Now, we had to subdue the mosque fire.

Duvall leveled his M-4 at the top of the mosque. Attached to the front of his rifle he had mounted a grenade launcher, and, carefully directing his fire, he sent six grenades into the nests. Flashes of orange lit the clouds of smoke and dust that rose from the explosions, and the sound of debris dropping from the sky filled the night air. We continued to fire into the upper reaches of the mosque, but the helicopters radioed back to us that the enemy had been eliminated. We paused a moment and listened to the space around us, hearing nothing but the barking of the damned dogs. We peeked from behind our barriers, then we finally rose from our hiding places.

The JAM in the city had surprised us and caught me off-guard when I should have been most alert. I had, in my desire to seek out one more cache and destroy more weapons, put my men and myself in danger. I hadn't been complacent. We had executed our mission carefully and professionally. We ultimately left the town not only with al-Nasir, but with eight other detainees. But, I had been too ambitious and stayed too long in the area. I should have left after we had grabbed our man, but I had gotten greedy. I knew we could not have been alone in the town. I should have listened to that instinct more carefully. The enemy in the town was too thick and too well organized not to mount a counter-attack quickly.

I stared at the mosque. We had been attacked from it, and I knew more weapons were in it. Our protocol, however, did not allow us to enter it. We could not chase down any of the men who attacked us from it, and we could not search it for more weapons, despite the fact that it had functioned as a virtual enemy fortress.

My chest was heaving. I was furious that I could not raid the mosque, but I was also scared. I thought during the attack that I might die. When the bullets jumped off the ground all around me and I could feel the blasts of grenades pulse up from beneath me, I wondered if I was fighting my last battle. I had pictured AJ wanting me back home, and only the fear caused by another grenade exploding close to me had knocked that image aside. When I heard that a man had gone down, I feared that I had gotten one of my men killed. I worried that I had failed as a leader and that I had destroyed some other soldier's family. I did not take too many risks on the mission in terms of how we conducted our raids, but I vowed to remember the importance of timing. I vowed to acknowledge to my men my mistake and praise them for their work in taking control back from the enemy.

Ultimately, the mission was a success. We had captured the biggest leader of the JAM, and our company and my platoon would receive wide recognition for it. The injured man turned out to be our informant, a man who had risked his life in providing us with the information that led us to the most significant capture of our company. We ensured he received treatment and protection, and we ensured that our men understood his sacrifice.

Despite the success, though, I felt uneasy returning back to base. I celebrated our capture, certainly, but I couldn't remove from my head the images of the machine-gun fire lighting up from the edge of the mosque. It scared me. It reduced me. I leaned back in the seat of my humvee and listened to the sound of the tires ripping along the road back to Warhorse. I reached back into my head, and I found the anger simmering from the past months of battle. I found the anger I harbored from the death of our men by the House-Borne IED in February, and I let a rage rise inside of me. I closed my eyes. I felt the world turning around me, crashing against me like waves, and I knew that the anger would anchor me, that the anger would keep me from spinning into dark, empty chaos. I numbed myself to every other feeling. I put anger in their place, and, with night air lashing against my face, I let everything else fall away.

18

My men had begun to call me Capone. The name had been in place for a few months, but as April dragged on, I began to embody the role. I spent my days leading missions into the countryside, going door to door talking to the men and women of Iraq, trying to gather enough information to lead a raid. When credible information materialized, my platoon acted, storming buildings and knocking men to the ground, guns leveled at their heads. I shouted. I screamed. I grabbed men by the back of their necks and shoved them into walls. I lost all tolerance for deceit or equivocation, and I executed missions swiftly, efficiently, and violently. I still wanted to make a change in the area where I worked. I genuinely wanted the poor families of the area to live without the daily fear of attack or explosion or kidnapping, but I had adopted a new strategy. Instead of holding town meetings, instead of discussing the trials of occupation with the sheiks, instead of negotiating, we conducted raids, and all the anxiety and all the sheer terror of the night raids fed me with more energy than I could have imagined. It seemed boundless. It seemed insatiable. I wanted my men to see only that side, and to do so, I worked hard to ignore any other part of me. I courted my anger, and I was praised for it.

For months previous to the night raids, I had negotiated virtual cease-fires with towns like Sadiyah, working with sheiks to avert lockdowns. We had been successful in the early days of our deployment. Some of the towns had grown more peaceful, and some of the townspeople had come to see me as someone they could trust. For all of those efforts and for all of the insurgents we had neutralized simply through forming relationships with locals, however, I had never been recognized for my work. Not by the higher-level brass anyway. I valued what we did, and my men appreciated what we had done. My Company Commander even acknowledged to me the value of the work, but, as I found out, no one gets medals for negotiations. No one gets commendations for meetings.

It makes sense. Drawing a clear causal relationship between town meetings and a reduction in violence would be difficult for any Commanding Officer to do. Direct influence is hard to trace at best, impossible at worst. What's more, most commanders are not in the business of encouraging platoon leaders to form close ties with local townspeople. Our explicit goal is to act as the ground troops in battles. Our job is to be the weapon that enforces U.S. military directives. I did not expect commendations for my work early on in Sadiyah or other towns. I simply did it because it seemed like the best thing to do. When I was publicly acknowledged for my actions as a warrior, though, the contrast seemed stark to me. I had saved lives by capturing the religious leader of Jaysh al-Madhi. I had disrupted the JAM network, and it would be months before it could fully regroup. I had also, though, saved lives by having dinner with sheiks in Sadiyah and meeting with families in the houses of Heb Heb, but I noticed right away that while both would save the lives of our soldiers and Iraqi civilians, only one would be tangibly and publicly recognized and rewarded, and that recognition was seductive. It fit my growing rage. It encouraged it, and it made it more desirable to act on it.

I had channeled my anger into action in the past. As a wrestler, I used it on the mat. When I had begun to search for colleges during high school, I didn't seek out a place that would harness that anger. I wanted to find a place that would challenge me, certainly, but I mainly wanted to find a place that valued service as the cornerstone of leadership. My friends all fled to state schools, choosing the lives we all imagine college should be. Late nights. Fraternity parties and sorority women. Heavy drinking and new drugs. I wanted something more than that. I sought out a place that would mold me into a leader and that would challenge me to do more than what my friends were doing. I desired to stand apart, and ultimately I thought that VMI, a military college, would do that.

VMI sits in a valley, flanked by the Blue Ridge Mountains of the Appalachians to the east and the Allegheny Mountains to the west. It rises along the cliffs of the Maury River, marking a stretch of the western border of Lexington, Virginia, the small town that is home to both VMI and Washington and Lee University. The city has the grave sites of both Robert E. Lee and Stonewall Jackson, and it prides itself on its southern heritage. It is, in many respects, the Old South, and for me, coming from a major northeastern city, it was a significant culture shock.

The greatest shock was the VMI training system. I wanted a challenge, but I was not fully prepared for the first-year crucible that VMI calls the "Ratline." Freshmen at VMI are called "rats," and as rats, all first-year students are subjected to intense physical training and intense emotional stress. In the first days at the school, we were essentially stripped of our identities. We referred to ourselves as "this rat" instead of "I" or "me," and for the first weeks, we were not allowed to contact anyone we knew from home. I did not even learn my roommates' names for the first few days. We were all too scared to say anything but "this rat."

The purpose of the Ratline is, essentially, to eliminate individuality so that each cadet learns that he or she has to rely on others. Each cadet's sense of self must be abandoned so that each one realizes that the only way to persevere through hardship is through bonding in a community. The result is that each cadet becomes extraordinarily close to the other students in his or her incoming class, and that bond forms them each of them into a "brother rat," a phrase once made famous by Ronald Reagan when he starred in a film of that name about VMI.

The Ratline demonstrated to me that I could endure significant physical and emotional hardship. It showed me that I could persevere, both through forming close relationships with others and through channeling the frustration and anger at being put through the brutal rite of passage into action and desire to achieve. I became very close to my roommates, particularly Zach Lewis and Brian Gorski. Zach had an unfailing willingness to help other people, and Brian, a former Marine who had returned to college to get a degree, had a steadying and rational perspective on our lives as cadets, and together, we found ways to overcome our frustrations over the daily struggles of the Ratline. As a senior, I passed those lessons on to the rats whom I mentored, particularly Jeremy Clement, who would ultimately become close not just to me, but to AJ as well.

The result of my friendships with Zach and Brian and, eventually, Jeremy was that when I graduated from VMI and commissioned in the Army, I graduated "with Distinction."

They had supported me through my time at school, and I earned a BA in English after having studied at Oxford as well. I also made it through the ROTC program as a "Distinguished Military Graduate." I had been given my choice of branches within the Army, and I had chosen Armor. I saw the military as a way to continue the success that I had had at VMI, and I saw it as a way to try to forge an ethic of service and leadership that my family valued and that VMI reinforced. It was the only real model I had, and my time at VMI convinced me that the Army could put me on a path to become the type of man I wanted to be.

VMI had also, however, taught me something else, or, at the very least, it reinforced something I had learned to do in wrestling. It taught me to ignore pain. It taught me that enduring hardship sometimes required silencing parts of myself that wanted to yell out or to scream. It taught me not to give up, even when everything suggested that I should, and in doing so, it unwittingly taught me that winning sometimes meant numbing myself to the world around me so that I couldn't feel it, so that it wouldn't sink in and wouldn't overwhelm me.

I never thought that lesson would matter. I never thought I'd see it again after my time at the school and in the Ratline. But I did, and as the time of my deployment lengthened, and as my missions into the night and into Baqubah intensified, I found I could do that again. I could shut out all the pain. I could turn off that part of me that felt it and instead convert it into anger, into energy. When I did, I could make it through each day smoother, quieter, and more certain that I would not feel anything like hurt ever again.

I tried to push out the last of my own pain when a man who had worked so hard to help us in Iraq was killed. The head sheik of Heb Heb, Haji Geylan, paid with his life for cooperating with us. His information led to the capture of many al-Qaida terrorists in the area, and he had explained to me very clearly the internal networks that governed the town and the area around it.

Haji Geylan was a strong man. He believed that the situation in Iraq could change, and he believed that al-Qaida preyed upon the poor and hopeless and provided them with easy solutions to complex problems. We worked closely with him, and he, as a sheik, dared to be seen in public with me. He did not think himself above being killed – he knew well he was putting himself at risk – but he wanted his people to know that he would not bow to al-Qaida. He wanted his people to know that he would stand up to the terrorist groups, and he wanted to show the townspeople of Heb Heb an alternative to joining them.

I respected Haji Geylan more than any Iraqi I had met. He and I became close. We shared stories about our families. He explained Iraqi customs to me, and I told him about daily life in the States. He laughed at my attempts to speak Arabic, and he shared with me his frustrations about trying to make a change in his town. We drank tea together, and once, during a dry Iraqi afternoon, we stood in the shadow of a tree and talked about what his life would be like after we had left, what his life would be like after the war. Then, one day, as the sun shone down on him in the mid-afternoon, he was gunned down by the people he had hoped to save, murdered by men who had lost all hope.

When he died, I knew I could no longer form close ties with local men. I felt responsible for his death. I wanted to believe in his confidence and certainty. I wanted to embrace his belief that his town could change if the townspeople could see a different kind of leadership, one based on discussion and trust and respect. I shouldn't have believed it. They murdered him simply because he cooperated with us, and I, in the weeks that followed, decided that I would not only not allow myself to be seen publicly working with a local. I decided that I wouldn't form a relationship with anyone. I couldn't stand the idea that I had caused his death. I couldn't stand the idea that another person with whom I had shared a common vision, a common goal, had been killed.

19

I had learned to numb myself to grief and pain, but I had never learned how to cope with anger, and it began to pour out not just in the work I was doing, but in my journals as well. I had been reading news reports about the war, and I had grown increasingly angry about them. One afternoon while working out, I overheard a television report about Rosie O'Donnell's perception of the conflict. I watched a clip of her rant about the war, and I had to leave the gym. I couldn't stand it. By the time I got back to my CHU, though, I felt like I had to know exactly what she had said, so I logged on and watched clips on the web, all of them streaming in fits and starts because of the poor internet service. She declared that the war was a mistake and that the troops, all of us, in Iraq were responsible for the slaughter of innocent civilians, that we had shed too much innocent blood. I felt my face burn. I felt that I had been doing my job well and that I had worked hard to do the right thing, so when I heard her proclaim her disgust with us, I, feeling as though someone had kicked me in the gut, picked up my journal and lashed out:

> She has no clue what is going on here at all, just as I had no clue before I got here.
>
> But apparently – according to her – we only kill innocent civilians, as she so remarks that all the dead Iraqis are innocent civilians. So was it innocent civilian Iraqis that killed the 3 bravo soldiers four days ago, or was it al-Qaida? Was it an innocent civilian that gathered 20 oxygen tanks together to explode on the 3 Soldiers, leaving them to burn alive until there was nothing left of them except charred, skeletal remains, or was it the terrorist organization of al-Qaida? I would like to take her out on one of the missions where we lost Soldiers and let her live thru that experience and see how she feels then. I would like to rub her face in the mangled remains of my friend and see if HE was killed by innocent, undeserving people. Take a look, up close, at his disgusting mess of a body and tell me that then . . . a body rendered so disgusting and in pieces that I couldn't look anymore b/c it made me so sick to look at what used to be my friend. He made me sick to look at him. I would like to see her there with me then, and then ever again say one fucking word against this war and what we Soldiers do and who we kill, and who kills us. . . .
>
> Do you know how many women screaming crying, life's a wreck b/c son/husband just got kidnapped by terrorists and she is begging for my help that Ive had to deal with. Do you know how many times – on the way back from a patrol me & my platoon while in our HMMVs – have been flagged down by men, women and/or children who are absolutely such a mess they can barely get the words out to tell me the rest of the family was just killed/kidnapped and the terrorists (or innocent civilians) fled this way or that way. . . .

My men – our company have only killed "bad guys" – for a fact.

I was tired of shit like O'Donnell's proclamations. We had all been careful to a fault in executing our missions. We followed protocol, we followed the rules of engagement. We never blindly rushed into a building hoping to round up civilians and torture them. We did not take pot shots at random people walking down the street. We didn't enter cities shooting, any more than we entered individual houses shooting. If the enemy attacked us from a mosque, we did not enter it, despite our own personal doubts as to whether that place remained holy if it functioned as a weapons cache or place from which to attack us. We did what we were supposed to do, and I was confident that we had avoided civilian casualties.

Certainly our intensity had increased. I was angry. I aggressively confronted people who were kidnapping others or hiding weapons or harboring al-Qaida or JAM. I scared the shit out of them sometimes. I yelled. I screamed, but I never struck a detainee. I never shot someone I should not have shot.

Maybe others did. Maybe in other places in Iraq our troops had gone beyond their call of duty and purposefully engaged and killed civilians. Maybe they tortured Iraqis. We had all seen the videos. We had all read the reports. But we also had seen the men around us fighting to do the right thing in the face of uncertainty and the terrible truths of war. I did not know the men who found ways to do the wrong thing. I knew the men who were trying to do the right thing, and, in our company anyway, they were doing it.

Part of the reason was that, especially in Baqubah, there were few people who could in any reasonable way be considered uninterested civilians. The town had been reduced to a virtual ghost town. Sunnis and al-Qaida in particular had driven out nearly a third of the city, and entire sections of the town were by mid-April not simply controlled by al-Qaida, but entirely populated by members of the organization. Many other smaller towns were the same way. Heb Heb. Khalis. Swaths of Diyala Province were inhabited by entrenched al-Qaida fighters. They had fled Baghdad. They had fled Anbar Province and the now infamous city of Fallujah. They had all settled in Diyala, and they intended to make a stand there. They intended for the area to be their capital and their base of operations. If we received intelligence from a credible source that someone was a member of al-Qaida, they were. We found no exceptions, and searches of their houses always yielded either weapon caches, propaganda, or, in many cases, direct resistance and engagement.

All of our missions, however, were not simply combat missions. We were there to secure an area and try to allow those Iraqis who were not disrupting the establishment of law to settle and prosper. While it was clear that the U.S. mission had in many respects gone drastically wrong, most of us still believed we could help the people locally. We were, however, outmatched, so instead of increasing law and order in the area, increased violence settled in.

Early in May, after an exhausting April, the Army had finally sent some reinforcements into Diyala. The Army recognized the trouble in Diyala and probably had for a long time. Under pressure to secure Baghdad, though, it had been unable or unwilling to commit more troops to our region. By May, Baghdad was becoming more stable, and finally a small force of additional troops came our way. The 5th Battalion, 20th Regiment arrived, the same force that had taken over our original mission as theater QRF in Kuwait. It had now arrived to help us try to stem the rising tide of enemy forces. Its arrival, however, was marked by the immediate destruction of one of its Strykers and the death of all of

the men inside of it. The reinforcements, on their first day
in theater, suffered tremendous loss and learned too quickly
what we had already learned – that we were outmatched. As
soon as we would secure a part of a town or a city, we would
have to watch it be lost within a couple of days, indeed sometimes in only a couple of hours, because we did not have
the manpower to keep it secure. The reinforcements, which
were supposed to make us feel better, in fact did the opposite. While we valued the additional firepower, the fact that
even with them we were unable to control the area forced
us almost daily to confront the fact that we simply could not
do what was being asked of us. As more and more enemy
foot soldiers found their way into our area of operation,
fleeing other parts of Iraq, we found ourselves increasingly
frustrated and increasingly demoralized.

Roberts and I worked hard to ensure that, even if the
overall mood of the company was down, our small group
remained cohesive and focused. We could not control how
each of us felt about the state of the area. We could not control what each of my men thought or what they told their
families about our work here. We could, however, control
how we ran our missions, and I, for one, could control how I
behaved in front of them. So, I made sure that I kept focused
on executing well-crafted military missions, and I focused on
communicating those missions to my men. Even if they had
doubts about the state of Diyala, I wanted to make sure they
had no doubts about our platoon.

It worked for a time, and I could tell because our men were
willing to work even when others weren't. On one day in
June, my men went to rescue Blue Platoon from an engagement that had gotten out of control. Blue Platoon had left to
execute a mission in Khalis, a town that had continued a downward spiral that paralleled Baqubah's, and within minutes of
the men's arrival, they had been engaged by the enemy. They

fought off and on throughout the day until it became clear that they would need help. They radioed the base.

I was walking with my Company Commander when the call came in. I had just come from working out and was wearing my physical training uniform. I was covered in sweat and exhausted. My entire platoon had finished two missions earlier in the day, and the workout had been a way for me to relieve some stress and find some relaxation. When the call came in, my Company Commander knew more than the Quick Reaction Force would be needed. He looked at me and told me that I should head up with White Platoon, and he would request Red Platoon be spun up as well.

Even though my men had just come from a long day of missions and even though we were not the Quick Reaction Force, my platoon moved quickly to action. I went quickly to my housing unit and threw on my ACUs over the top of my workout clothes. Other men in my platoon did the same thing, and within just a few minutes, we were in our humvees and ready to roll out. In the meantime, Red Platoon looked for some direction. Many of them seemed uncertain whether this mission actually required them, so they lingered, waiting to see, and my Company Commander, originally slated to ride with them to Khalis, joined us instead, leaving Red Platoon behind.

We arrived in the middle of a major gun fight. Blue Platoon had attempted to clear the area, but too many insurgents had barricaded themselves along their route, and they were firing freely at them. We engaged the enemy immediately, just as air support also arrived. Apaches launched hellfire missiles on one particular house, and we opened up on another set of buildings. By the end of the day, sixty enemy soldiers were killed, many surrounded by heaps of weapons.

My men had reacted to the call for help without hesitation. Blue Platoon had seen significant action, and we knew, especially after the devastating house explosion in February, that many men in the platoon had low morale. My men wanted to help them. They wanted to be part of the group that came to their aid, and they wanted to act professionally. Certainly they were tired. Certainly the prospect of rolling out after a long day in the middle of a long week weighed on them, but they did not complain, they did not hesitate. They acted.

The engagement helped remind us why we were fighting and why we were needed. It reminded us to think beyond ourselves a bit. Often in the Army, a kind of competitive tension exists between infantry platoons, like Blue, and armor platoons, like ours. It centers on the question of who is really fighting a battle. Is it the men on the ground, running across open expanses or through potentially booby-trapped doors, or is it the men in the tanks, rolling through and over roads littered with IEDs and taking on the most difficult places of resistance? The tension, especially after long days of combat, becomes palpable. It becomes something you can feel in a room. For my platoon and Blue Platoon, however, that tension did not exist. We had worked together too much. We had tried to support each other, and missions like the long afternoon engagement on June 5 demonstrated that. My men were not going to let Blue Platoon down. They had been there for us, and we were going to be there for them.

That kind of professional ethic was encouraging, but it would hardly help the overall state of the company and the battalion. We were all exhausted, worn out from daily fights and rising anger. The arrival of reinforcements in early May had helped buoy us for a short period of time, but their tragic first engagement muted that and reminded us that we simply had very little chance of overcoming this area unless major change happened.

In June, rumors started to circulate that that change might be coming. All Army bases, but FOBs in particular, are rumor mills. Soldiers leak information, some of it real but most of it either misunderstood or imagined. It works itself around base within hours, and in June, the rumors of a large-scale change in operations circulated, new versions of the rumor mutating daily. The heart of it, though, was that because Baghdad was finally coming under control, the Army could redeploy forces and continue to push al-Qaida and other insurgent groups further and further from the city centers of Iraq. We all hoped it was true, and most of us imagined something had to eventually happen, but none of us fully believed it. None of us dared hope for it.

Still, we knew something was changing. My Company Commander confirmed that plans were in the works for a major shake-up, and as June continued on, chaos seemed to overtake Warhorse. When men were not out fighting bloody battles, they were trying to negotiate the terrain of the rumors, trying to sort through their futures and praying that if change came, it would be something more substantial than simply shifting a few platoons or the arrival of just a few hundred more men. We all wanted one thing. We wanted to go on the offensive. We wanted to change the battlefield by taking the engagement to the enemy. Instead of heading into a small village or into Baqubah in order to conduct small missions, we wanted to move en masse and retake an area. We no longer wanted to respond to being attacked. We wanted to attack, and we wanted to drive the enemy out of Baqubah and the rest of Diyala. We all knew it was the only way things were going to change.

On June 16, the Army began a major new campaign, Operation Phantom Thunder. We fell under its umbrella. Phantom Thunder sought to expand the successes that the surge, Operation Law and Order, had been having in Baghdad. Between January and June, four brigades arrived in Iraq to help gain control of Baghdad, and in June, a fifth and final brigade, constituting 30,000 troops, flew into theater and provided the Army with the means to expand the battle it had initiated in Baghdad and Anbar province.

As word spread of the initiation of Phantom Thunder, we wondered where the new troops would be going. We knew that Baqubah was the most violent city in Iraq, and we knew that it was serving as the capital of a newly formed insurgent state. We guessed and we hoped that our leadership would not stand for that for long.

Within thirty-six hours, we found out we were right. Some of us heard it from our Commanding Officers. Others read about it on Yahoo News. Still others heard it from friends in other battalions. Word spread quickly. More men were coming. Lots more. Battalions more, and throughout June 17 and June 18, they arrived. Armored vehicle after armored vehicle rolled into the base. Strykers. Humvees. MRAPs, large armored vehicles that were designed to protect soldiers from mines and ambushes. They came throughout the day, rumbling past the gate, men emerging from them and scrambling to get their equipment in order.

An infantry regiment.

Two Stryker battalions.

Much of the remainder of the 82nd Airborne.

Wave after wave of them rolled into Warhorse, plumes of dust and exhaust rising from the base, the smell of diesel floating above the land, and we all understood very clearly and very quickly that something big was about to happen.

Something powerful.

Something decisive.

We all knew the war was about to change for us.

We all knew the Battle of Baqubah was about to begin.

20

On June 18, my men and I pulled on our dark-green Nomex suits, one-piece zippered uniforms made of thick fire-resistant material. They were made especially for tank combat. Created in the event that we needed protection from an explosion that somehow penetrated our tanks' armor, the Nomex suits would supposedly provide us with enough protection from flame that we could either put out any fire within the tank or evacuate the vehicle. We hardly ever wore them. I wore mine so infrequently that the rank insignia on it was out of date, and I used a Sharpie to blacken the gold bar to indicate my promotion earlier in the spring. Typically, we just wore our ACUs and our body armor, expecting that we would at some point have to dismount from the tank or, as was usually the case with me, leave the humvee. The Nomex marked us as tankers. It was our official uniform as the tank section of the 1st Cavalry, and the fact that we were wearing them for this mission meant both that we would be in our tanks for an extended period of time and that, more importantly, we were finally doing the one job we had been specifically trained to do. No more negotiations with locals. No more rushing into buildings on foot. No more short missions that required me to be on the ground coordinating efforts. This time, we would stay in our tanks, and this time, our platoon would lead the charge.

Our current mission, a total lockdown and attack on Baqubah, was called Operation Arrowhead Ripper. One of many subordinate campaigns that constituted the larger, umbrella campaign called Operation Phantom Thunder, Arrowhead Ripper represented a significant symbolic front. Baqubah and the area around it, sometimes called the Baqubah Belts, had received increasing press as an region in which the surge had not worked. In actuality, the often-commented-on surge had not yet reached us. Phantom Thunder officially began on June 16 with a smaller operation to the southeast of Baghdad. On the same day, an Operations Center was established in Diyala, and my Company Commander briefed us on the operation.

The day began with a brigade-wide briefing. Platoon leadership from across the FOB gathered in the Faulkenburg Theater, a small movie venue that had been built on the base. There, the Brigade Commander presented a slide show of the plans for the large operation. He described the mission, and he made it clear our final objective would be the final removal and annihilation of the al-Qaida influence in Baqubah. He wanted nothing less, and he expected us to be focused on our mission. He also called on my Company Commander to address the entire brigade. He wanted him to remind everyone what had happened to Delta on February 9. He wanted each of us to remember the tragedy as an example of the enemy's resourcefulness and the danger of House-Borne IEDs. My Company Commander spoke to us all, and those of us in Delta could feel the earnestness in his voice.

He could still feel that loss, and he wanted everyone else to feel it as well. He wanted the different leaders throughout the brigade to take extra precaution, and he wanted each of us to hear the story of that day so that we would remember that each house could be a trap.

In the afternoon, my Company Commander addressed those of us in Delta separately. The brigade briefing had provided the overall snapshot of Operation Arrowhead Ripper. The company briefing would provide our platoons with their particular operation orders. We met in the Operations Center, sitting in the hodge-podge of collected lawn chairs and gift boxes from home. Our Company Commander was serious. Sober. His face was tight and straight, and he spoke clearly and authoritatively, his voice firm and direct. He wanted no mistakes.

He had prepared a PowerPoint presentation with detailed maps. Some were overhead visual maps, satellite images zoomed in on the area along Route Highlands in Baqubah where our company would be moving. Others were grid maps, showing clearly the scale of our area and the types of terrain we might expect. As he showed them to us, he explained precisely where each platoon would operate, and he explained to us that our company would have some changes to it. We were having a Stryker platoon attached to us in order to provide us with more ground troops. As a result, one of our tank platoons would be rotated in order to work with another company to provide armor support. He looked across the room to all of us, then his eyes settled on me.

"White Platoon will be staying with Delta," he said. Then he looked across the room to another set of platoon leaders. "Red, you'll be going with Bravo Company."

Red Platoon was not happy. No one would have been. They were part of our company. They were used to how we did things, and they were used to knowing how each different platoon operated. Our Company Commander, however, had grown to trust me pretty deeply, and he wanted me not only to stay with Delta but to lead the mission. Our company would lead the battalion into Baqubah. My platoon would lead our company. We would be at the point of the attack on the city. By sending Red Platoon to another company, my Commander was demonstrating his faith in me, not his lack of faith in Red.

When the meeting was dismissed, the leadership of Red Platoon grumbled, but I went with Roberts to brief our soldiers. The significance of the mission was clear, and I knew the men would see it the same way that I did – an opportunity. Here was our chance to take back control, to get off the ropes and lunge forward. I predicted the men would revel in the chance, and I was right. Deboe muttered, "About time," and Sgt. Duvall leaned forward and, with his face stern and focused, said, "Hope they're ready for us. We've been waiting for them."

By the time the 18th arrived, and with it, the long train of forces for the offensive, my men were eager, focused, and even excited. They were not blood-thirsty. They weren't seeking to simply destroy the town. They were, however, ready to be moving forward, and they were enthusiastic about the plan. They saw in it a release from our current position, and they loved the idea that we would be leading the mission into the city that had been the largest problem of our deployment. We met the Stryker platoon attached to us, and we prepared our vehicles.

The heat of summer had long since set in, and temperatures soared past 120 degrees. Inside the tanks, we baked. The tanks were equipped with tubes that carried air directly to us, and in our tanker uniforms, we could maneuver the tubes so that they blasted cool air against our skin. We could partially unzip the uniform, and because they were one piece instead of the two pieces that make up the ACUs, air traveled up and down our bodies, mediating the heat. Still, the air inside the tank was difficult to breathe. Stale. Hot. And stifling.

We organized our small corners of the tank to ensure everything was in its place. I taped maps along the side walls of my little space. On one side, I hung the overhead visual maps that my Company Commander had shown us, and on another wall, the grid maps. Next to the grids, I taped up a blank sheet of paper on which I could write down coordinates quickly while referencing the map in one glance. Above them, I taped my mom's crucifix, a reminder of home and a hope for protection.

It took me less than ten minutes to prepare the area, but by the end I was drenched in sweat and breathing hard, wishing for fresh air. Emerging from the tank, however, brought little relief. While I was glad to be out of the staleness of the air inside the tank, and the odor of four men running nearly a year's worth of missions inside the cramped space, outside the tank a bright sun beat down on me, and the air hung heavy over the land. There was no wind. There was no sound of movement except the clanging of vehicles preparing for battle.

Blue Platoon had been ordered to guard a section of Route Highlands during the night. The men were supposed to set up in a few of their Bradleys along the road to ensure that the enemy did not plant IEDs on the route we were using for the first assault on the city. As I finished prepping my tank, though, it became clear that they would not be ready. They only had three Bradleys to prepare, and fifty men to account for, but the casualties they had suffered in Baqubah undoubtedly pressed in on them like the summer heat, and their men moved slowly, cautiously. So, my platoon was ordered to guard the road, and I readied my tank and another to come with me, leaving Roberts behind to ensure that the last two tanks would be ready to roll when the attack began.

My section, Alpha section of White Platoon, rolled out in our two tanks as the sun was beginning to set. It was nearly six o'clock, and though the sun was low on the horizon, and though the sky had begun to shift from the blazing white of the afternoon to the brooding orange and blue shades of the early evening, the heat lingered. The tanks fired up, and we sped past the gates of Warhorse and down Route Highlands.

We traveled the highway without incident, occasionally passing other companies' armored vehicles along the way. Each company had a section of the road to guard, and we were all maneuvering into position to pass the night as watchmen for the coming siege. My platoon's two tanks, however, traveled the farthest, and we positioned ourselves closest to our battalion's entry point into Baqubah. Because we would be leading the way into the city, we needed to be closest to it, so we passed all the other vehicles, came within a few hundred yards of where our forces would launch the attack, and turned off the road, stopping along it and setting up for a long night of waiting and watching.

We all felt the energy of the coming operation. I could see Garnica tapping his foot, and Private Vos kept shifting in his seat, turning one way, then another. Vos joined us on this mission as our loader. He was young and came from an artillery outfit, and though I was concerned about his lack of experience inside a tank, I knew he would be helpful with grid coordinates and orienting ourselves to our orders. As an artillery man, he had a lot of experience with maps and orienteering. I continued to review the plans, trying to memorize as much of the map as possible, trying to learn every part of it, looking up sometimes to talk to my men or to look out across the road and into the night air. All was still. All was quiet except for the sound of dogs barking, a sound that we had all learned to tune out. None of us slept. We were too wired. We were all expecting our biggest fight.

I thought about the movie I had watched the night before. I had dropped The Thin Red Line into my DVD player and spent the evening watching it while I prepared for the mission. I thought about the different narrative voices of the movie, the varied inner landscapes explored, and I wondered how I would ultimately see this war and how I would finally talk about it when I was done. I knew the heat of the tank wouldn't be what I most reflected on. The physical drain on me was powerful, and I felt it each day, but sitting in the tank on the brink of the invasion of Baqubah, I knew I wouldn't dwell on that pain and that hardship in the years that would come. I knew I'd feel the inner struggle about what it meant to serve in a war where the local men and women sometimes hated me, and those who didn't I could do little to protect. I thought of Haji Geylan and his sacrifice for his people, and I thought of our three soldiers killed on February 9, and I felt the power of retribution rush over me. I felt the loss all over again, and I turned my grief to aggression, knowing that in this battle, I would finally have a chance to strike back. I would finally have a chance to punish an enemy that had, I felt, nicked away at my strength, my certainty, and my hope. I thought that Baqubah might be a bloody fight, and I knew that whatever happened, this battle would probably shape my life in ways that I might never be able to understand. I did not care, though. I simply wanted a chance to hit back at the forces that had pounded us for the past few months.

Sometime between two and three in the morning, the net buzzed briefly with activity. The forces were mobilizing at Warhorse, and within minutes, Roberts was radioing to me over our platoon net. He was approaching our position, so I looked out of our tank to the north and west, and as far as I could see, our Army, vehicle upon vehicle of it, snaked its way in the predawn light toward Baqubah. We could hear it. We could feel it beneath us. We could sense it inside ourselves.

At that moment, I knew things were not going to be the same. I was comforted by the sheer numbers of the operation, and I felt proud, even, to see the convoy of tanks, Bradleys, and Strykers. I think we all did. It reminded me of how I felt about the Army when I first joined. It reminded me of the excitement, and, more deeply, it reminded me of the power of the military. It was frightening. It was daunting. But it was exhilarating.

The Stryker team attached to my company immediately came up to us, and, within seconds, a rush of soldiers emerged from the vehicles and moved toward a corner house near my position. Our tanks moved into position to support them, and I heard a few short blasts, the troops on the ground blowing their way into the building. When they were inside, they cleared it. They used small explosives to blow open doors, and inside they encountered no enemy resistance. They moved, then, to the neighboring house, clearing it as well. I watched more soldiers file into the houses. The corner house would be our staging house. We would launch the full attack when the sun peered over the horizon, so instead of the ground troops waiting inside the cramped and uncomfortable armored vehicles, they massed in the house, sitting still against its walls and barely muttering a word while they waited for the dawn.

We waited secure in our tanks and scanned the area, watching it closely for the final hours before the full offensive. We saw a single bird, black and shimmering, fly past us and into a tangle of brush. Dust billowed across the road and into our section of the city when other vehicles drove past us. The stars slowly disappeared as the early sunlight filled the void and extinguished their smaller, tighter glow. We didn't speak. We didn't joke. We waited, and when the landscape finally turned from black to gray, and the sky showed the first hints of blue, I turned to my driver.

"Let's roll," I said, and our tank moved into position.

The strategy to clear Baqubah was straightforward. Our forces would establish a perimeter around the city to ensure the enemy could neither escape nor flank us. Then, within the city, our platoons would move street by street, house by house, literally sweeping from one end of the town to the other in order to round up or kill any al-Qaida fighters or other militants. Every section of town would be searched. Every street. Every structure.

Each company had been assigned a specific set of neighborhoods, and within each neighborhood, each platoon had been assigned specific streets to clear. Tanks led the way, and behind us, infantrymen cleared houses, one by one, block by block. We encountered very little direct resistance. Instead, we found IED after IED, most wired in the road. To destroy them, we typically called in the Explosive Ordnance Disposal team, who, with small robots would approach the buried IED and detonate it with the use of C4 explosives. With each detonated IED, more and more dust filled the air, so that within only a couple of hours a brown haze hung over the streets of Baqubah.

Most of the buildings of the city were pockmarked with bullet holes, and chunks of them had been blown out by grenades. Many structures had roofs that had already collapsed from explosions during previous attacks, and the entire city seemed like a graveyard. Few people, at this point, wandered the streets, and each low, brown building seemed like the ruin of an old, now extinct civilization. Debris filled all of the roads. Burned-out cars. Plastic lawn chairs. Old neighborhood water tanks. Reams of wire and mounds of steel and iron, twisted beyond recognition. They all littered the roads and the alleys, creating obstacles and hiding spaces for IEDs.

For deep-buried IEDs, we called in GPS-guided mortar strikes. Deep-buried IEDs were the most dangerous, often consisting of ten or twelve large containers of gasoline or oxygen. Their power was great enough to obliterate our 74-ton tanks. When a mortar struck the site, an enormous explosion would fill the air, sending particles of the roadway skyward, littering the ground with brick and pavement and gravel and leaving behind a gaping hole in the ground, sometimes ten feet deep. The deep-buried IED became the most obvious threat to us, though we still worried about direct enemy engagement and, especially those of us in Delta Company, House-Borne IEDs.

Near one o'clock on the first day of Arrowhead Ripper, June 19, my Company Commander returned to base to refuel. He put me in charge while he was gone. It was my first official command of the company. It demonstrated the trust my Commanding Officer had in me, and it meant that I was responsible not just for the activities of my platoon, but for the entire company. I turned my tank from the street I was clearing as a platoon leader and rolled toward the command position along Route Highlands. There, I assumed the role of Company Commander. I was officially in charge, and I wanted to do things precisely and efficiently. I wanted our company to do the best job and to stand out as the most efficient, so I encouraged the platoons to work hard, and I offered them all the support I could.

When an RPG team attacked Blue Platoon, I called in fire, requesting a missile strike that neutralized the enemy. The missile strike on the enemy forces built my confidence, so when, shortly after that, I received the call about the possibility of the House-Borne IED, I felt that I knew the best course of action. My men on the scene described the suspicious wire running half-buried in the street up to the window of a house. The wire looked precisely like an IED wire, and on the far end of it, away from the house but in clear view of one of the house's windows, rose a mound of freshly disturbed earth.

It all sounded so obvious. The wire was not well hidden, and nothing obstructed the line of sight to the road. From that window, an enemy soldier could clearly see us and detonate the bomb. The arrangement, though, just seemed too easy to uncover, especially for an enemy who had become increasingly savvy, and that feeling of it being too obvious felt familiar to me. It reminded me of previous missions. It reminded me of al-Qaida's tactics of luring men to greater devastation by distracting them with a less significant threat. It reminded me of February 9, and it all began to make sense.

They meant for it to be found.

They meant for us to question the wire and then, in our haste, decide to rush into the house. There, deep inside the house, a wire waited to be tripped, waited to detonate a House-Borne IED and destroy all of the men inside.

So, I made the call that would change my life. I ordered the missile strike on the house. I had to. I couldn't risk my men. I couldn't send them into a house with a potential IED inside it. I had seen the horror of that type of bomb. I had seen our soldiers ripped to pieces by that kind of blast, their limbs buried under the ruins of a house. I had seen men crumble under the weight of that attack, and I, like every other platoon leader, had been specifically warned about this danger in our briefing for this mission. So I brought in support from the sky, launching an attack against which there is no defense and through which I knew no one could survive.

And no one did. No one.

Not one person.

Not one child.

I had followed the correct protocol. When the suspicious house was identified, I asked for more information from my men on the scene. I gathered that information, relayed my report to battalion, and requested permission for the strike. They agreed. So I took the final step before calling in the missiles – I sent our Psych Ops forces down the street and in front of the house to warn civilians in the area. Psych Ops consists of a large truck outfitted with oversized loudspeakers hanging all the way around it. The speakers blared a message in Arabic. "Clear the area," it says, effectively announcing our attack.

The truck drove right to the front of the suspicious house, turning so that the largest speakers were broadcasting the message directly into it. Then, the truck turned and continued down the street before swinging around to return. It approached the house a second time, continuing to blast its warning message. Civilians needed to leave the area, it said, because the area had been deemed hostile and an attack was underway that would be catastrophic.

The few people who were further up the street fled. Only a group of boys on bikes lingered. Roberts saw the boys, and, despite the fact that he was going above and beyond typical practice by doing so, maneuvered his tank so that his weapon could be fired down the street. He fired a series of warning shots, high over their heads and away from the group. It worked. They got the point that they were in danger, and they fled.

The street had been secured. I waited to make sure that I received the "all clear" from my men, and when the final person radioed in that his position was safe and locked down, I called in the strike. We waited. We all waited, mostly expecting to hear the enormous explosion of a House-Borne IED, but also concerned, wondering if the decision had been the right one and if all of our men and all the civilians would be safe in the strike. Would the missiles fly true?

They did. The explosion ripped apart the house, and neighboring buildings shook, shedding loose bricks and plaster. A secondary explosion followed immediately, tearing the structure apart, blasting the house to pieces and demonstrating that somewhere in that house more explosives had been stored. The report of secondary explosions validated my decision to call in the missiles, but in the moments that followed the strike a deeper truth of my decision became clear.

Bravo Company's men saw two children round a corner on their bikes just as the missiles flew in and exploded into the target. They rode right next to the house, and when the missiles struck, they were killed instantly, their bodies tossed into the air. When Bravo broke into our net and, in a devastatingly nonchalant tone, announced the hit on the children, our men moved to the target site quickly to assess the damage. There they found more casualties than the kids on the bikes.

They found eight bodies in the ruins.

A family. Children. All dead.

All inside the house.

All killed by the missiles.

All killed by my orders.

21

I once tried to explain to AJ what I imagined had happened inside that house in the moments before the missiles struck. I imagined a family gathered together, eating perhaps, or maybe hunkered down, having heard the loudspeakers but having decided to wait it out, feeling safe inside their own home. They sit, praying, and the father says encouraging words to his children, comforting them. The mother holds a child in her lap and speaks to the others in reassuring tones. Then, in a flash of red searing heat, they're gone. Every one of them.

I know I can't know what happened inside that house, but I also know I can't remove from my head the image of that family gathered together, joined together, in the final moments of their lives. I can't shake it, and no matter how hard I try, I can't project it outward. I can't forget it and I can't make others see it. It simply lingers there, suspended and dark in the shadows of my mind.

At the time, I did not have the luxury to dwell on the strike. I did not have time to feel about it. I had to work. A heavy

silence fell over the men in my tank when we all realized
what had happened. It sunk into me, and I felt it press down
hard on my chest, but outside, on the streets of Baqubah, the
men of Delta Company were still clearing neighborhoods,
and they were still putting their lives on the line. I was still
their Commanding Officer for the time being. I had to act
like one. I had to keep our forces moving. I had to forget
about the house and its family.

Private Vos looked up. He knew we needed to stay at
work, and he heard more requests coming in over the radio.
We were receiving calls from other platoons across the company. Other IEDs had been found. They needed Ordnance
Disposal. I looked at Vos, told him that we were still working and told him to keep the grid coordinates coming. He
did. Though young and only a private, he maintained his
composure and kept the mission squarely in front of him,
leaving the disaster behind. I wrote down coordinates for
the most recent call from a platoon, and he and I checked
and double-checked them. Then, he called them into battalion, requesting support. Above us, Garnica continued his
vigil, watching the roads around us, ensuring that no enemy
approached our tank.

Within a few hours, my Company Commander radioed us.
He was nearly back to Baqubah, having finished refueling at
the base. I began to brief him. I told him about the RPG team,
about the numerous IEDs that various platoons had uncov-
ered, and about the house. I spoke clearly and professionally,
explaining the situation at the house fully. He did not react. He
simply thanked me for the briefing and for leading effectively
while he was gone. He did not seem too concerned about the
house. He did not ask a question about it. He was focused on
the mission. Casualties were secondary and expected.

I returned to my role as platoon leader, turning my tank
away from our command position and toward the streets

where my platoon was working. My street was several blocks away from the home I had destroyed, so I did not see the ruin, driving past its neighborhood en route to my assignment. My tank rumbled past cleared houses and now safe alleyways, sometimes rolling over debris in the road, other times maneuvering around it. Still, we watched for IEDs, knowing that one could have escaped our detection despite the systematic nature of our search. We found none, though, and within just a few minutes I was leading a platoon down a street, creeping along in our tank as the infantry scoured the roads and the houses for threats.

Our platoon was moving more quickly and more efficiently than others. We had to be sure not to move too fast so that we wouldn't create a gap in the long line of teams working east to west across the city, but we moved fast enough that we essentially created a wedge in our forces. Our company came to resemble an arrow as it moved, with my platoon at the tip. Other platoons worked next to us, slightly slower, so that by the time we reached the end of the streets we were working, our forces formed a wedge that separated north Baqubah from south. While not planned, the wedge became an effective tool in minimizing attacks. It prevented the remaining al-Qaida forces from moving between the southern and northern sections of town and isolated enemy forces from each other, preventing them from sharing intelligence. It also essentially squeezed out the enemy as each platoon moved to the west and shut down more and more of the city.

We would be commended for our efficiency, my company in particular being singled out for helping the operation divide the enemy and effectively shut off communication between parts of the city. At the time, however, our quick movement across the city created an almost insufferable circumstance for all of us, especially those of us in our tanks. After we had cleared the area, we simply had to sit in our tanks and hold our positions on the western side of the town. We waited, of course, so that no enemy could retake ground that we had seized. So, we sat, and we baked inside the tanks. The heat had been bad enough while moving through the streets, but without anything to do, and without any action going on with my platoon that I had to supervise, all we could do was sit in the tank and wait and feel the heat wash over us. We sat, and we sat, waiting for other platoons to catch up. We sat for twenty hours at a time, holding our position, wishing that we could simply leave our tanks or drive back to Warhorse. We envied the infantry, something we rarely did, simply because they could be out in the air, not stuck inside the virtual oven of a steel military vehicle.

For those of us inside my tank, the wait was even more awful. It gave us all time to think about the house I had destroyed and the children who had died inside of it. It gave us too much time to remember and reflect on it. Even those inside other tanks were grappling with it. I knew because on one of our few trips to return to Warhorse to refuel, Roberts started to vent about Bravo Company's report of the missile strike when they broke into our net. He didn't like their tone, their complete nonchalance about the fact that they had seen children hit in the blast. He didn't have anywhere else to put his anger about the tragedy, so it landed on the apparent attitude of another company.

I spent hours thinking about the strike on the house, and my emotions spun inside even while I tried to keep a professional composure in front of my men. I knew I still had to be their leader, but inside, sitting in the heat of the tank, I felt anger rising up inside of me. I didn't understand how I could, in a single moment, have the success of being asked to command a company swept away and turned into disaster. I didn't understand why I couldn't just let it all go, like so many of the other people around me seemed to be able to do. Why didn't it faze my Company Commander? How could others seem to consider it just a price of war?

I felt sometimes that I needed to climb out of the tank and get away from the heat and find someplace cool, cold, numbing. I imagined myself in the clear winter air of Philadelphia. I imagined the bright, perfect buildings, the certainty of the city, even when it snowed. I wanted to be there. I wanted to keep my mind there, but I couldn't. The silence was too heavy. No one could speak about what happened. No one could say a word. All that existed was a deep and penetrating silence, the kind where all that is left is you and the fact of what has happened. All that is left is your heart unraveling your actions and tearing open the space around you. The kind of silence in which you wish everything was different, everything was just the way it had been moments before. The type of silence that means your life will be marked forever into before and after and that demands that its certainty be honored. All we could do, all I could do, was say something, anything, to break the silence, but I couldn't. None of us could. We weren't supposed to. We all feared that the minute that we did, that space and all of its facts of what happened would come rushing back into us with such a noise and fury that we'd fall to the ground, broken.

So, instead, we lived in the silence. All of us lived in it. It was our pact. It was our promise. We were soldiers, and we had to fight the war, both with the enemy we had been sent to defeat and with ourselves as we worked alone to subdue the losses that tore at us. So we'd focus on the fight, and we'd fight the war not talking about it.

I wondered if I were really meant to be in charge, if I could lead while feeling anything about what I had done. I had become a minor star in the battalion, a soldier whom the brass turned to when they needed hard work done. I always came through, and my men always worked hard to make us the top-performing platoon. We had been pub-licly recognized as an outstanding group, and my Battalion Commander's evaluations of me spoke to his belief that I was a rising leader with a future ahead of me. The most recent lavished praise on me:

> 1LT Meehan is a superb officer and the best platoon leader of 16 I senior rate in the battalion. Shannon's understand-ing of the complexities of the counterinsurgency fight are well beyond his peers and his ability to leverage kinetic and non-kinetic effect in order to drive a wedge between the insurgents and the Iraqi people is seldom matched. His leadership resulted in multiple IED cells defeated in the bat-talion AO [Area of Operation], and the capture of over 50 insurgents provided key intelligence on enemy forces and contributed greatly to the battalion's mission success. . . . Give him the opportunity to command at the first available opportunity; where he will excel.

I had been proud of the report, but now, reflecting on it while waiting for Arrowhead Ripper to finish, it stung. It didn't capture what the war was about. It didn't give me any greater insight into the complexities of the war, and, despite my ability to numb myself to what was happening inside me, I doubted whether I knew real leadership at all. I did not believe that numbing myself to the horror of killing children would make me a more effective leader. I did not believe that that experience would make me a better soldier, a more experienced officer. I did not believe that the war was shap-ing me into the man I thought I would become. I thought back to the time before the missile strike, before I had issued the order, and I went through it all time and time again.

My men had found a suspicious wire precisely resembling an IED wire.

They found a fresh mound of dirt and noticed the wire running to a house that had clear view of the mound.

We knew al-Qaida had begun to use House-Borne IEDs as a devastating tactic, and that part of that tactic included decoys to lure soldiers to their deaths.

The threat was not the mound. The threat was the house. There was no way to clear it with troops. There was no way to send someone in to scout it. There was nothing to do except follow the prescribed method of dealing with that type of house. The missiles were the only option. I had to call down the fire.

The reasoning sometimes comforted me, and sometimes, someone in my tank would remind me that we did what we were supposed to do. We did what we had to do to protect our men and to clear the area, both of threats and of civilians. They tried to convince us, all of us, even themselves, that we did the best that we could. But no one actually talked about it. No one dared say a word about how we actually felt about it. My Company Commander never said a thing, and I never brought it up to my roommate or to my men. I did not know how to. It had become a void, both in the air between us all and within me, and I did not know how to talk into that void without it collapsing and crushing me. It was empty. It was dark. But it was comfortable because it swallowed everything up. All the feelings. All the pain. All the fear and hurt disappeared in that absolute void and allowed me to continue to march down the streets of Baqubah and not feel a thing.

A couple of days later, I was summoned to go to Baghdad. One of our previous missions had resulted in the capture of a horde of militants, and the JAGs wanted me to come testify against the detainees. I did not want to go. Everyone knew what a trip to Baghdad meant – it meant a vacation. I would be put up in a hotel in the Green Zone, complete with a pool and room service, and there, I would wait for days until it was my time to testify. I could swim. I could lounge in the sun and relax. I could try to live a life away from the war. I could not make myself go, though. I could not imagine leaving my men. I did not want to leave them to fight a battle I was supposed to lead in. More importantly, though, I could not leave behind me the family whom I had killed. I could not picture myself swimming through a lazy summer day, splashing in the water in the free zone of Iraq, knowing that I had destroyed that family. It was more than guilt I felt. It was shame. It seemed like if I went to Baghdad then that that family's death would have been even more meaningless. I could not simply destroy life then go swimming a few days afterward.

So, I told my Executive Officer I did not want to go, and he worked with the JAGS to find other soldiers to take my place. I sent Duvall and Garnica instead. The JAGs were not thrilled – they wanted an officer – but my Company Commander was more than happy to find a way to keep me around. Despite feeling myself unravel inside, I still had to command my platoon.

When my two men went to Baghdad and the Green Zone, then, I went back out in my tank and led missions. Our area of Baqubah had been completely locked down, so we were now running missions within cleared-out areas, double-checking streets for IEDs and following up on any suspicious activity that was reported over the net. We bounced from street to street, checking on leads and providing support to Explosive Ordnance Disposal teams. The town was even more ghostly now, with large craters dotting the landscape and more houses collapsed under explosions. We rarely saw a single Iraqi, most inhabitants having either fled when al-Qaida had taken the town or when we had come to retake it. The days were quiet, hot, and heavy, and one day, as we returned from holding a position on the western side of town, my tank weaved back across the city and turned down the street of the house that I had destroyed.

I had not yet seen it. On the day of the missile strike, I was in the command position out on Route Highlands. In the days that followed, I had worked to clear other streets and had conducted brief patrols into other neighborhoods, but I had not been down that street until now. I had my driver stop in front of where the house had stood, and I opened the hatch above me and stuck my head out and stared at what used to be the front entrance of the home. All that was left was a single portion of wall, leaning slightly with a window frame still visible in it. All around it lay a jumble of crumbled brick and stone, and near the rear of the remains of the building, the metal of what may have been a bed-frame stuck up out of the debris, pointing skyward.

I looked at the ruins, noticing that some bricks had exploded out into the road. In the distance, I could hear another tank rolling down a barren street, and ahead of me, I could see a helicopter moving across the sky above and past where the house had stood. I realized that if the house had still stood, I would not have been able to see it. The house would have blocked my view, but now, above the rumble, I could see everything for a mile ahead of me. My view now was unobstructed, and all I could see was the haze of the blazing sun and the collapsed home that had once housed a family, that had once stood far from the sounds of war.

I didn't know how I was going to make sense of it. The remains of the house confronted me with the reality of the strike, and for ten minutes at that site, I began not just to think about it, but to feel about it. Pain tried to rise up through the numbness that I had erected within me, and I felt loss, and I felt emptiness, and I felt shame for feeling both of them. I did not deserve to feel anything. I had taken the lives of a family. Their deaths were not mine to mourn.

Their deaths were not mine to grieve. I had ended their lives, and looking across the yard to where their front door once stood, I shut myself off from it all. I could not think about it. I could not let myself feel anything about it. I had done this, and I did not belong here. They deserved a life, and I no longer deserved mine.

I lowered back into my tank, and one of my men said something. I did not listen to him.

"Ready?" someone else said.

"Let's roll," I said.

"We did what we were supposed to do," someone else said.

"Let's roll," I said again, "We've got work to do."

Our tank lurched forward, the road grinding beneath our treads, and I put on my earphones and listened to the sounds of the net broadcasting reports of other action across Baqubah. The clearing had been going well, and our company and our whole battalion had started to feel stronger and more relieved, even as I felt something empty and dark growing inside me. I should have been feeling the success of the mission. I should have been celebrating the overwhelming victory of Arrowhead Ripper in Baqubah, but I wasn't. I felt the house and its only wall, leaning into the sun and on the verge of final collapse, and I could not find a way to prop it back up.

On June 24, one of the Colonels of the Stryker Brigade addressed the media. He expressed his feeling that many al-Qaida members had fled Baqubah as the battle for the city began, and that many had slipped past us. Most of us suspected that, but we also knew that removing al-Qaida was the primary goal, so we had little concern about how that happened, even if we knew that we might be chasing them down later in other parts of Diyala. When a writer from Reuters newswire addressed the Colonel and wondered if the fight in

Baqubah had been as vicious as he had expected, the Colonel looked down briefly, then, lifting his head, said, "The fight so far has gone a little easier than expected."

He stared at the reporter. He did not blink. He turned back to the rest of the media, and nodded his head slightly.

"That doesn't mean," he continued, "that there isn't any fight left in them."

22

On August 4, in the heat of the Iraqi summer, I was awarded
an Army Commendation Medal with Valor. The award recognized my actions back in December, when the air was cool
and when my platoon had killed the large group of insurgents who had barricaded themselves in the house in Dojima.
I remembered the sense of success I felt then, but now, only
weeks after the end of our time in Baqubah, the event felt
like another life, like the life of an entirely different person.

My Brigade Commander presented me with the award.
Fifteen other soldiers were being honored for various accomplishments, including Roberts and Duvall, and the brigade
leadership felt it would be more meaningful if we had the
presentation at an outpost instead of at FOB Warhorse.
My Company Commander resisted, wanting to have it at
Warhorse so that more people from Delta could attend
the ceremony, but I had mixed feelings. I did not feel like
making the effort to travel to an outpost simply to have a
medal pinned on me, but I also did not want a big audience

for the occasion. Even when I was promoted from Second to First Lieutenant, I had been uncomfortable with the public recognition, but now, after the events in Baqubah, I found it almost unbearable.

All of us receiving awards lined up in front of the soldiers who were stationed at the outpost or who had come specifically for the ceremony. The Brigade Commander stood in front of us, made a few remarks, then began the presentation of the awards. An assistant read a narrative accompanying each soldier's medal, and when mine was read, I had to force myself to keep my eyes up and my body locked at attention. The reader described me as "heroically distinguished," then read a summary of the action:

On 14 December 2006, 2LT Meehan led his platoon to the town of Dojima in support of Iraqi Army forces in heavy contact within the town. Over the last several weeks preceding the engagement, sectarian violence between Dojima and the neighboring town of Zambor had led to the death and serious injury of dozens of residents of the two towns. Upon arriving in Dojima, 2LT Meehan saw that the IA forces were pinned down and were under heavy fire from the target house and had suffered several casualties. 2LT Meehan then moved a tank section forward under fire towards the house and after clearance of fires he engaged the house with 8 rounds of tank main gun which ceased all enemy fire. After ceasing fire on the house, numerous explosions were heard from inside the house as well as small arms fire "cooking off," which indicated that a large cache of weapons and explosives were inside the house. When the IA cleared the house after the engagement, they discovered the remnants of several heavy machine-guns, thousands of spent rounds, the remains of several explosive devices, and the remains of 30 enemy combatants. 2LT Meehan's actions during combat operations in Iraq contributed to the overwhelming success of the command's mission. His bravery is in keeping with the finest traditions of military heroism and reflects great credit upon himself, Task Force Lightning, and the United States Army.

I could picture it all perfectly. The fallen Iraqi Army soldiers pressing themselves against the house's courtyard walls. The desperation on the face of the American soldier who gave me a briefing. The collapse of the house and the report of the enemy killed inside. I remembered the pride of that moment, when I realized how successful we had been and how we had completely neutralized a battle that had gone out of control. But I could not feel it. Not anymore. I couldn't feel anything. I heard just the words, rising past the line of awardees and lifting above the outpost. They all floated away, and all I wanted to do was lower my head and walk away from it all. If I couldn't feel proud, I didn't want to be there.

My attitude must have shown. I hadn't been entirely precise in putting on my uniform that morning, and my hair was longer than it should have been. I was yelled at for the oversight, as though chastising me on the day when my accomplishments were publicly recognized would drive deep into me and make me feel shame. It didn't. A much deeper shame had already taken hold, and my only response to the man challenging my dedication and my honor was anger. More anger. More on top of the anger that had begun to rise and fill the hollow space left in me by my actions in Baqubah. December did not matter to me anymore. All I had was June. June 19. It's all that seemed real to me anymore.

On August 15, Operation Phantom Thunder ended, barely two weeks after my Brigade Commander thanked me for my heroism. Four days later Arrowhead Ripper officially ended. By all reports, the operations had been a resounding success.

Al-Qaida had been driven from Baqubah, and new attempts to fund development for the city were already beginning. New sources for water and new supplies for roads and city buildings were finding their way to the town, and some of the townspeople who had fled the city began to return to try to reclaim their lives. In all, our command indicated that we had killed more than two hundred insurgents. I never heard any final count on civilian casualties.

Immediately after the operation, word began to spread that a new set of orders was coming whose purpose was essentially to continue the success of the Baqubah offensive by expanding our area of control. The goal would be to regain control of the rest of Diyala Province. The Army would spread its fight northward, pushing out and killing al-Qaida in order to finally, we hoped, stabilize the entire province. We knew other insurgent groups might pose resistance as well, but our primary concern remained al-Qaida, knowing especially that JAM tended to work within organizational power structures instead of by overt, violent attacks like al-Qaida's.

My men were tired. We had been in our tanks for forty straight days during the course of Arrowhead Ripper, and during that entire time, my men had remained focused and dedicated, even as I began to doubt myself in light of the missile attack I had called on the house. To my men, I continued to show a face of strength, and I continued to run my platoon the way I liked it to be run – organized, communicative, and structured. We continued to have meetings, and we continued to focus on our daily jobs. The result was that during the forty consecutive days of the operation, White Platoon did not lose a single tank to enemy attacks or have one become disabled due to carelessness or IEDs. It was a remarkable feat. Maintaining a group of tanks in working order for forty days of an intensive operation is rare, if not entirely unheard of, and when the operation finally ended, my Company Commander rewarded my men. He sent them to FOB Anaconda for a day of R&R.

Anaconda had grown into a mini-America since our deployment began. Part of this growth was reality, based in the military's constant attempt to improve it and make it seem more and more like home. Another part of it, though, was perception. Our time in the field had simply made us forget what daily conveniences were like. So, my men went, and they spent the day at a large pool, swimming and basking in the sun. For lunch, they ate Burger King, and when they could, they ordered drinks by the poolside, taking it all in, trying to forget the war.

I stayed behind. I could not bring myself to go. I told myself that work still needed to be done and because our company was scheduled for Quick Reaction Force, I used that as an excuse to stay back. I said I needed to help set an example and work outside the wire to ensure that we maintained security while everyone else was gone. Beneath that, though, I had another reason, one that had begun to shape how I saw the war and how I saw myself in the war. It had begun to shape my decisions, and it led me to press myself harder, much harder, to avoid anything that might seem like rest or relief. I did not deserve either. I did not deserve to go to Anaconda. I did not deserve to swim and eat burgers. I deserved to fight a war, and I deserved to be in the line of fire.

While my men were at Anaconda, Sgt. Duvall returned from Baghdad and the trial there surrounding the insurgents we had detained in May. He and I met, and we discussed his testifying on my behalf, and he conveyed to me that the JAGs were impressed with how our platoon had run our detainee operations. The information we had provided the JAGs was water-tight. We provided solid sworn testimony, and we provided detailed and accurate pictures of the people we detained and the weapons we had found on them. We followed protocol, and the result was that the JAGs were able to secure convictions of the detainees.

Other platoons did not always follow the protocol correctly. One platoon which had been partly responsible for the cordon around Baqubah during Arrowhead Ripper, for instance, had nabbed nearly 400 alleged insurgents and al-Qaida militants as they fled the city. The platoon, however, had failed to follow some basic protocol, so, despite the sheer number of the detainees and despite the fact that they had been caught engaging our forces in a battle, all had to be released. Such problems infuriated our leadership, and it frustrated the JAGs daily as they tried to help the Justice Department and the new justice system in Iraq establish the rule of law.

I worked hard to follow the protocol, and I knew my men did, so when the platoon returned from Anaconda, I asked Duvall to brief them on his time in Baghdad. I wanted the platoon to hear directly from him the praise they had received, unsolicited, from the legal branch of the Army. Duvall explained how the military lawyers guided him through the legal process and how they relied on his testimony as expert witness. He told them how the pictures we had taken and the detailed and carefully written sworn statements had been at the center of much of the trial, and he explained to them how he had witnessed first-hand the significance of the reports. He reported on the trial, recounting details of the mission that some of us had forgotten but that had been well recorded, and how those notes and our ability to follow the appropriate guidelines ultimately led to the imprisonment of men who were responsible for the deaths of many American soldiers and Iraqi civilians.

I could see the pride in my men. The day at Anaconda had relaxed them, and instead of returning to Warhorse simply to mount up and head out on patrol again, they were this time greeted with a story of their success. Duvall related the story, and they asked him questions. They recalled their own roles in the capture of the enemy, and they reminded themselves of the good we had done. They smiled. They laughed. They lost, for a few minutes, the weariness of the days in Baqubah.

I felt some of the same satisfaction. I needed to feel like something had gone right, and Duvall's story provided me with the hope that maybe something could be different. Maybe, I thought, I had made some sort of difference. But, as I began to feel that, my chest tightened. I felt myself draw my lips tight against my teeth, knowing that I was clenching them, and I realized that no matter what I heard, and no matter who told me, I would not be able to forget what I had done. The capture and sentencing of those men could not lift the weight of those children's bodies from my chest. I could not find any place where that memory did not live inside me.

I felt numbness again, even as Duvall finished speaking and even as words of congratulation and praise poured out of my mouth in order to encourage my platoon. I was angry that I couldn't celebrate with them. I was angry that I couldn't find a way to get a break, to breathe, to feel okay. I was angry that I was alone and that I was the one who had put myself there. I couldn't connect, not through stories of success anyway. I had to find another way. I had to find a way to feel like I was joined to the group again, and at the same time send the anger out and away from me. And I could only figure out one way to do that. I would turn that anger into aggression and let it drive me. In order to get it out, I would let it drive deep into me to push me forward.

I would fight harder.

I would fight stronger.

I would feel something again, something that would place me back with my men and away from doubt and pain. I would be certain. I would be decisive.

I would ensure that I would be at the front of any future mission so that if God felt I deserved to die for killing that family and those children, the opportunity would find me. I knew a new mission would be starting. I would make sure I would lead us into it. I would not cower from what seemed to me now to be my fate. I would not hide from my sins.

I began to lose sleep. My mind drifted at night between the final moments of the family in the house and the penance that I would put myself through. I still did not talk to anyone about it all, and no one spoke to me about it. I showed a strong face, the face of a leader certain of his future and of his plans, but at night, alone in my CHU, I faced images of my past and of my future. I saw the children, each one, in detail, imagining their lives and creating whole stories for them. I created their futures for them, then punished myself for having taken it from them. I came to believe that my future could not stand in the face of theirs being lost. I did not deserve something they would never have.

Returning from a mission one day, exhausted from the heat and my lack of sleep, I surveyed at the wall of my CHU. I stood in the doorway and looked to the left and took account of the area around my bed. The poster of AJ still hung on one end. My Eagles poster hung close by, and over the head of my bed, a plaque that my Aunt Bernadette had sent with me to Iraq now hung. It had a cherub standing and looking out and away. A banner stretched across the body of the childlike angel, and the words "Angels Gather Here" were scrolled on the banner. My aunt told me she had had it blessed.

I stared at it. The face of the child cherubs filled the sign, round and plump. The blank space of the CHU wall next to it seemed to recede into darkness. I began to remember a story I had read in college in an English class. It was the story of a mutiny. Slaves aboard a slave ship turned on their captain, Aranda, and after killing him, strung him up as the figurehead at the bow of the ship. They covered his body with a tarp, and beneath him, they painted a new motto for the ship. I remembered the motto.

I walked over to my desk and pulled open a drawer. I dug through a tangle of pens and pencils, finally pulling out a red ink marker. It had a broad tip, so when I climbed on top of my bed and reached the pen high above my head and began to write, broad, sanguine letters stretched across the pale green surface of the CHU. I traced out each line carefully, each letter drifting downward, each word dropping lower than the next. Some letters fell to the right, and others turned back, spiraling down directly below the letters above them, until the final ones, tipping almost horizontal to the floor, seemed to fall away, finally separating from the words.

When I pressed the final letter into the wall, I was low on my bed, leaning on my side. I tilted my head up and back, looking at what I had written as though I were staring up at the figurehead of a ship riding high on the waves above me, its bow about to come crashing down. I saw each red line, and I mouthed the words to myself, remembering Aranda and the slaves who took his life.

"Follow Your Leader," the mutineers had written below Aranda's skeletal corpse.

23

The road, pockmarked with deep holes from IED explosions, stretched away in front of our humvees. Some holes were shallow, but many dropped six or seven feet deep. So many stood in our way that the road was simply impassable. In humvees anyway. I had a decision to make. Continue the mission on foot, seeking intelligence and attempting to track down members of an al-Qaida cell, or turn around and head back to the outpost. I looked down the road. The humvee idled beneath me, its engine vibrating. I scratched my chin.

"Let's go," I said, "We're going on foot. We need to get this done."

We were now a few days into our new mission, and in fact, no one would have blamed us if we had turned around. We had been moved as a unit to an outpost at the edge of Baqubah. We knew we wouldn't find some High-Value Individual hiding out in the houses lining the road that stretched out in front of us. No one would have expected us to take the risk of going on foot. We had a mission, though.

We needed to contact the people living in those houses, and we needed to try to collect information from them. We were expected to do our jobs, and our jobs meant moving down that street and pushing through obstacles. So we were going. I wasn't going to shy away from a challenge so simple as holes in the road. I was not in the business of turning away from any challenge. I did not deserve to be.

We dismounted, and I led my men down the street. Now the middle of September, the heat of the Iraqi summer had not abated. We sweated beneath our body armor, soaking our clothes simply by walking. We wore Camelbacks to carry our water, and we sipped from them often. If we happened to pass by a grove of trees or some sort of shelter, we lingered in its shadow, as though an extra few seconds out of the sun was our greatest gift. We did not say much to each other, and when we did, we kept it brief and clear. We did not waste our energy on words. We thought about the weight of our armor, our water-filled Camelbacks, our weapons, our ammunition, and, for some, our packs, even though we knew well that we should keep our minds off of our bodies, that we should turn our thoughts outward to prevent fixating on the weight and heat.

My men had endured a lot in the past few months, and I admired how they continued to do what I asked them. They did so professionally and efficiently, even though I could tell that our morale was beginning to slip. I'm sure some of them sensed my own despondence, and they certainly felt the increasing lack of initiative in the company. Much of the rest of the company had already fallen into a sullen daily routine, with several platoon leaders effectively avoiding their work and asking little of their men. Entire platoons sometimes lingered in the courtyard of our outpost, biding their time. For them, the war had ended in Baqubah. They had no intention of doing more.

I understood why. Shortly after Arrowhead Ripper had finished, our company received word that our deployment was being extended. Instead of the prescribed twelve months, we would be staying longer. No one would say for how long – extension orders never included deadlines – but most of us assumed that it would likely be for another three months.

We had already expected to stay past our assigned time. Most other companies over the past few years had been extended, and word had leaked from stateside that we would be as well. Yahoo News had stories about it that our wives and families read before we received official orders. It really only sunk in, though, after we heard it from our Commanding Officer. Despite how practical most of us, as soldiers, were, we also held a small hope that something would be different for us. Of course it wasn't, so we shouldered as best we could news of the extension. We went about our business, and we hoped to be home for Christmas. I hoped to be home for my anniversary on December 17, knowing well that the odds of that were slim. No one knew what would happen, but most of us spent little time worrying about it.

The extension, however, came within days of the company learning that we would be moved from operating out of FOB Warhorse to operating out of a small outpost in Buhriz. Buhriz was a section of Baqubah that had been a stronghold of al-Qaida, and most of its citizens remained loyal to the terrorist organization throughout our deployment. It had been a rallying point for the organization and had only been abandoned when the surge and Arrowhead Ripper finally allowed our forces to penetrate deeply into it. I had guarded the outpost in my tank the night, early in our deployment, when Bravo had been under heavy mortar fire, but I had never actually been inside the outpost itself until our assignment there.

It was a wasteland. A former Iraqi Police Station, it had been taken and burned by al-Qaida. When U.S. forces seized it back from al-Qaida and made it into an outpost, they had little time to clean it or repair its broken buildings. The structures were still charred. Black soot clung to us when we brushed up against the walls. The latrine was simply a hole in a dark box that straddled a bucket. The bucket was emptied daily and its contents burned in the only courtyard on the outpost. Burning shit filled the air each evening just outside the door of where we slept, a single room in a ruined police station. We were crammed into tight quarters, and we smelled shit each night as we drifted to sleep.

The combination of the extension and our move to the Buhriz Iraqi Police Station sent the company morale spiraling downward. Most had imagined the mission in Baqubah as a kind of last stand, a final big operation that would effectively end our deployment. They imagined that after Arrowhead Ripper, we would run small missions around the FOB to maintain the fragile security we had established. Most believed that the majority of fighting was behind them. The move to the Buhriz Iraqi Police Station, however, suggested the possibility of new battles. We would be conducting missions into areas that had not yet been secured, and we would be moving at times to the south, far beyond the places that we had come to know intimately. We seemed to be starting over just a couple of months before we were to leave, and no one really wanted to do it. No one wanted to leave the relative comfort and certainty of the region of Diyala that we had helped to secure.

I certainly didn't. The prospect of trying to generate new local contacts frustrated me, but more importantly, being away from Warhorse meant minimal contact with home, and losing the thin thread of connection to home terrified me. I had been relying on AJ for support in the weeks after the missile strike, and working at the outpost ensured that I would have very little, if any, contact with her. When I heard about our move to Buhriz, then, I imagined myself finally drifting away, finally losing the only tether I had to something outside of me. At the outpost, all I would have was the ruins of war.

The only way I could imagine making it was to continue to focus on my work, to continue to run missions and try to drive out the enemy, even if it meant taking some risks to do so. Al-Qaida still had a real presence in this area, especially to our south, and though it did not have the strength or will it had in the weeks before Arrowhead Ripper, it still tried to disrupt the establishment of the rule of law. The Army wanted to finally root out the last of the al-Qaida forces in the area, but with our deployment clearly on the downward slide to going home, many of us just didn't feel like doing extra work or showing much initiative. If I did, it was only because I couldn't stand being alone. I couldn't stand listening to my own mind tell me about the mistakes I had made. I just could not sit all day at the Iraqi Police outpost. I did not want to spend days in the black, burned-out reminder of our failures.

I drew Roberts into my plan to keep us all busy, and he and I worked hard to keep the morale from slipping too far in our particular platoon. We continued to hold meetings simply to keep lines of communication open, and we passed on any information that was conveyed to us in briefings with company and battalion leadership. We also insisted on the men maintaining their gear in good working order, and we focused ourselves on conducting our missions. I knew that as long as the men had work to focus on, they would be less likely to dwell on the extension or on the fact that we had been moved to a place outside of our comfort zone. It kept me busy and, except at night, it kept my mind off of the children I had killed. I told myself that I was simply being a good leader. After all, I was doing what the Army wanted and needed and what the local Iraqis deserved – I was securing our area. I was providing opportunities for the men to succeed and accomplish something and ensuring a dependable routine. But, the truth was that I was doing it to keep myself out of the shadows.

On that September day as the sun burned into us and we came to the deep holes in the road, I wanted to make sure we kept going. Certainly, returning to the base after having just left a few minutes before would have accomplished nothing, and it would have communicated to the men that we were now on a downward slope to our departure from Iraq. I did not want to send that message to my men, and I did not want to give myself time to be alone. So, we walked past and through the large holes in the road and started going door to door, seeking out intelligence.

I was nervous about my decision. Being out in the open not only meant exposing ourselves to snipers or other insurgent fire, but it also meant we would be less protected from IEDs. Walking on foot through an area that had been an al-Qaida stronghold was not something any soldier looked forward to, but doing it without the immediate support of the armored vehicles was especially anxiety-provoking. So, I called my men together and told them that we needed to be especially alert to anything out of the ordinary and that we needed to do whatever we could to stay off the roads, where IEDs were most likely to be buried. We would move from one house's yard to the next, staying away from the road and, as much as possible, within the property boundaries of specific homes. If all went well, we would gather more information and return to the outpost with strong intelligence and a better sense of what this area of Iraq, still largely new to us, was like.

We had been on the trail of the leader of this region's al-Qaida cell, and we knew we were getting closer to him. He had begun to leave Buhriz for several days at a time, avoiding a town that had once been his stronghold. His prolonged absence meant he might be harder for us to find, but it also meant that many of the locals began to feel less loyal to him. While we were on the street providing food and water and sometimes simply cash to the people, he had abandoned them, leaving their town a wreck and providing little in the way of resources to help rebuild it. He knew we were gathering intel on him. He must have known we were getting closer. The enormous holes in the road were a sign of that. He was erecting greater and more numerous obstacles for us to surmount. He was making our daily routines more difficult without confronting us directly.

The more obstacles he put in our way, the more fixated I became on him. He became my reason to conduct missions and keep myself out of the quiet loneliness of the Iraqi Police outpost. I focused only on him, and when we had an opportunity to find information on him, I took it. I was aggressive, I was persistent, and I was desperate. I didn't care about the risk to myself. I didn't deserve to worry about my own well-being when others had died at my command. Finding that man, I convinced myself, would help me undo what I had done in June. Killing or capturing him would mean that I had finally done something right again, that I had finally justified my reason for fighting this war. Killing him would finally give me a reason to push back the memory of those children who, like ghosts, haunted my dreams.

We moved from house to house, then, doing soft searches. My men would enter the house before me, led by Deboe. His team would begin to clear the building, and as they did, I entered with my translator and a security detail. The locals knew the routine, and few felt threatened by the searches. The families gathered in the living room, and as my men quickly glanced through rooms, basically just to give the appearance of searching, I would talk with the families. I would ask them how they were doing and what their main concerns were. I would ask them if any particular projects to the city would be most useful to them and if they had good supplies of food and water. We would chat, and as the conversation continued, I would ask them if they had any information that would be useful in tracking down the insurgents.

Some households were, obviously, more forthcoming than others, but most were exasperated with the war and simply wanted to find the best solution to ending it. Oftentimes, it was clear to them that we were that best solution. I always provided families with food and water, and if they provided strong intelligence, I would often leave them other gifts, frequently money. It was an exercise in judgment. I wanted to show appreciation for the people who helped us and who were trying to find ways to end the fighting, but I knew as well that I could be being manipulated. We had to weigh any information that they gave us with what we already knew, and ultimately, I had to make judgment calls, decisions based not just on experience and evidence, but on a kind of trust that we were trying to build.

I tried to follow up with families if I knew I could provide some service for them to help secure that trust, to show them that I wasn't simply wanting to buy them off. I wanted intelligence from them, but I also wanted them to have better lives. I tried to show them that I was concerned for their welfare, and I tried to make the case that the sooner that we were able to root out al-Qaida, the sooner we would be able to provide them with even more services so that we could eventually leave. So now, five years into the war, many of them were more than willing to provide information. They eagerly anticipated our arrival so that they could give us the latest news.

If I knew someone or a particular family had taken a significant risk in providing me with especially dangerous information, I would help them create a cover so that they would not be the target of al-Qaida retribution. My platoon developed some strategies to try to ensure the safety of the families that helped us. We might leave the house yelling at them, or even slapping the patriarch of the household over the top of the head. We might publicly threaten them so that others would perceive us as angry at them. Sometimes, we would simply leave them with a written survey that asked them questions like which public works project they wanted accomplished or where they wanted a school opened. They could then show the survey as evidence that we had simply come to ask for ways to spend money, not solicit intelligence.

In all, it had proved extraordinarily effective, and on this day, as we made our way down the row of houses, we received credible information that al-Qaida was operating a hospital for its fighters in the neighborhood. When I sought out more information about the hospital from other families, I continued to get corroborating stories about it, effectively confirming not only its existence but its location.

We found it with very little effort. Housed in a crumbling brick-and-plaster building, once white but now brown after years of being exposed to the dusty Iraqi air, it was similar to a storage container found on oceanic transport barges. It stood off an alley and near a grove of trees, and it was marked with a symbol al-Qaida used for its hospitals, a snake wrapped around a martini glass. The doors leading into it were padlocked, and when we shattered the lock, the doors swung open to expose a spartan interior. Along one dark wall stood a line of cheap lawn chairs. Along the opposite wall near the rear was a bed, and across from it, next to the chairs, shelves and cabinets holding medical supplies and drugs rose up from the floor.

No one was inside, and it was unclear when it was last used, but it was certainly still in operation. The medical supplies were current, and recent used bandages lay on the floor. The blood on them was still bright red.

We removed the medical supplies and searched the building for any intelligence that might be useful. We found no useful information, so we left with the supplies, locking the doors again with our own lock, and returned to some of the families we had met with earlier. We distributed the supplies to them and thanked them for cooperating with us. We recorded the grid coordinates of the hospital and radioed back to the outpost to report our find. We had been working especially closely with Special Forces in recent weeks, and we sent them the information.

Uncovering the al-Qaida hospital was a boon. Shutting it down meant that an insurgents' operation had been discovered and eliminated, and it would force them further from the area. It meant that we were getting closer to our man because it demonstrated that the local population was providing us with precise and more important information. It also reinforced to my men that the walk on foot into the area meant that we were doing the right thing and that we should be doing more than simply waiting in our vehicles for our time to end. We could still try to make some difference in this new area. We could still catch an important bad guy.

Equally important, it taught me that I needed to start to continue to adapt to the circumstance. The obstacles to traveling were becoming bigger and more challenging, and traveling in humvees in this area would simply be ineffective. We would be on foot, and that meant we had to take new measures in executing missions. While on foot, we had to, whenever possible, avoid traveling along the road. The road meant IEDs, so we had to keep off of it whenever we could. Instead, we would travel from house to house by jumping fences and walls in the backyards of the homes we searched, moving from yard to yard, entering houses by the back doors. Jumping the walls was exhausting, all of us being weighed down by our armor and the weapons and packs we carried, but it was far safer and equally efficient. So, I knew that when I came back to the area, I would need to be more prepared. Next time, we'd bring more water to help keep us hydrated during all of the walking and wall-hopping, and next time I wouldn't come just in humvees and be forced to travel without armored support. Next time, I'd come with tanks so that we wouldn't be alone out in the city.

24

I was intent on finding the al-Qaida leader. He was my only focus. The idea of killing him was the only thing that gave me some meaning for working in the war. Knowing he was out there kept me from thinking of the other things I had done, and I needed to find something to keep myself from turning too far inward. I hoped one more mission would give me the final, detailed intelligence I would need in order to finally get my man. I hoped one more mission might help me forget the family I had killed.

A week later, we were heading into a small enclave called Dwebb, south of the Buhriz Iraqi Police Station outpost. Only one road led into the area, and that road, I knew, was riddled with deep holes and other obstacles. Roberts and I met to discuss our plan for entering the neighborhood and how best to tackle the problems we had faced just the week before. We understood the risk we had assumed by going on foot. Walking in the sun, proceeding on the ground, was far from ideal, especially when the only armored support we had, the humvees, were parked, useless, half a mile away. So, we developed a plan to drive down the road as far as we could in both humvees and tanks, and when the humvees could proceed no further, we would dismount and, alongside the tanks, go house to house on foot. One tank would move slightly ahead of our position, and the other would move directly across from us, paralleling our progress. The tanks, of course, would travel the road, but those of us on foot would go yard by yard. The week before had taught us that, despite the hassle, hopping fences was far safer than walking the IED-laden roads.

The night before the mission, Deboe, Roberts, and I briefed the men. Deboe would continue to lead forces into the houses, and Roberts would man the tank running next to us. I would interact with the locals and elicit information that would be recorded by an intel soldier. I talked to the men about the overall mission, and Roberts then discussed the tanks' role in the mission and the medivac plan in the event that someone was injured. Deboe clarified the roles of each of the men on the ground and how we would enter the houses. After fielding questions, Deboe then took the men who would be on the ground and divided them into their teams and checked to ensure that each man was properly equipped. Each needed a camelback, his eye protection, gloves, and armor. Each needed his weapon and eight extra clips of ammunition, and the platoon needed a portable radio backpack and a shotgun, which could be used to blast our way into buildings. As Deboe checked his men, Sgt. Duvall took the men who were assigned to the tanks and ensured that the vehicles were prepped. Each had to be fueled and supplied with ammunition and two days' worth of food and water. Roberts and I continued to talk about the mission, finetuning it and double-checking all of our maps and routes.

I awoke the day of the mission feeling as ready and as prepared as I had ever felt. I knew my men were ready, and I knew we had done everything we could to execute our plan. I opened a bottle of water and rinsed off my face, then pulled on my ACU pants and an Under-Armor shirt and went outside, climbed to the roof of our outpost building, and jumped rope. I had started exercising on the roof in the morning, long before the heat of the day and just as the sun rose on the horizon. As I jumped rope, I watched the sun emerge, casting light across the rooftops of Buhriz, and I thought about the day ahead. I wanted the man we were after. He was all that mattered to me, and he was the only thing keeping me from falling into the lethargy of the company and the darkness that crept up on me at night as I thought about the operation in Baqubah. I tried to focus only on the goal of getting the guy who had been evading us, and I tried to make sure we were all ready and that we would be successful. I knew there were risks in trying to chase him down. I knew there were risks in going by foot, but I thought that just by planning, just by following an exact mission, we would all be safe.

After a trip to the Command Center, I returned to the Buhriz Iraqi Police Station. I pulled on my body armor, and over it, my ACU jacket. I grabbed my gloves and my goggles, then found Roberts and went to join the men. All were business-like. All were focused. I climbed into a humvee, then called in a check to all the other vehicles. When all responded, I called out over the radio.

"Let's roll."

The engines revved, and our two tanks and two humvees left the small outpost compound and turned south toward the village of Dwebb. We bounced along the dirt-and-gravel road, passing the ruins of Baqubah to our east and some smaller towns, essentially suburbs, to our west. The area had not even begun to recover from five years of war, including, most recently, the surge, and Operation Arrowhead Ripper had left many of the buildings looking like abandoned warehouses.

Every structure had holes in it, whether large ones from RPGs or cannon fire, or small ones from small-arms fire. Some had collapsed totally, their roofs drooping into the rubble of crumbled walls. Others had sections of walls knocked out, rammed in by vehicles or explosions. None had glass windows.

We left the outpost shortly after one o'clock, and we only made it a few miles south before we had to abandon the humvees. Deep craters from IED explosions blocked our way, and only the tanks and men on foot would be able to go any further. We weren't exactly sure why the local al-Qaida fighters had started to use IEDs to blow holes in the road instead of attacking us with them. Some of the craters were months, maybe years old, but most were brand new, detonated deep in the night when no one was around. IEDs that had been manufactured, and in some cases planted, in order to attack us were now being used simply to create obstructions to our progress, and we only had one real answer to why. They had chosen simply to block us instead of to attack us. They had decided, perhaps because so many of them had fled or been captured or killed, that risking an assault on us was too risky. More likely, the al-Qaida cell leader we were pursuing did not want to draw too much attention to himself. Killing a U.S. soldier would do precisely that, so instead of inflicting casualties, he opted for creating frustration in order to bide his time.

So, with new large holes in the road before us, we dismounted. Those of us on foot moved to the side of the road and watched as the first tank crossed a set of craters and led the way. We followed, skirting the road, staying well away from the edge of it. Our other tank rumbled abreast of us, moving slowly in order to ensure that it could provide immediate support if we needed it.

Only one major road runs through the village of Dwebb. Houses line the west side of the road, and a canal runs along the east side of it. When we began to travel south on foot, we walked along the west side until we came to the first house. Low, made of brick and plaster, the structure had a flat roof and open windows. Deboe and his team went in first. They entered through an open doorway and announced their reason for being there, then fanned out throughout the house and yard. I followed shortly afterward, scanning the living room we entered into first, checking with Deboe to make sure the house seemed secure. Outside, Roberts's tank rumbled, and I could hear Deboe checking in with him over the radio to keep him apprised of what was happening inside the house. Roberts, in the tank staying parallel to us, radioed back, reporting that all was quiet outside.

The first house, and the next, and then each one after that, went smoothly. Many of the families inside seemed happy to see us, and we were receiving good intelligence. I shook the hands of the men I spoke with, talking to them about their daily lives and the lives of their families, and I congratulated my men after each house so that they would know that I felt good about how the mission was proceeding. When I finished interviewing families, and when my men were prepared to move on, we headed to the next house. We left nearly each home through the back door, scanning the backyard of the next building and then climbing over walls or fences into it. We moved from backyard to backyard, following the routine we had established the week before, avoiding the road and potential IEDs.

The day dragged on, the temperature rising every hour and reaching well over 110 degrees. I poured whole bottles of water over myself and down my back, running through eleven of them within just a few hours. I saw the sweat on my men's faces, and some of their cheeks turned red in the heat of the day, their faces glowing beneath their dark glasses. By the time we had come to the final house, we could all feel the muscles in our legs cramping, and a couple of the men had begun to sit down while I talked to members of households. They simply wanted to rest their bodies for a moment before we moved on.

We had been out for more than four hours by the time we reached the end of the neighborhood we were canvassing. The final house of the street was separated from the rest of the homes by a short stretch of open field and a gravelly lot. We had been to the house before, and I knew that the man who owned it would have good intelligence. I wanted to make sure we made it there, even though it meant crossing into the open and extending our mission a bit longer. I looked across the lot, knowing that we would probably have to use the road to get to the house. Shimmers of heat rose up off of it. A dry wind blew against my face. We were all tired. We were all burning up. We had come a long way. None of us wanted to go the last fifty yards on the road.

Deboe spoke up. "How about the canal?" he asked.

I looked at him and then turned my eyes to the canal across the road. I hadn't considered it, and looking across the street toward it, I wondered why it hadn't crossed my mind. It was a good idea. The canal was barren and dry, and we knew al-Qaida often traveled down it in order to avoid the IEDs they themselves had placed on the roads. Running parallel to the road, it made a safe freeway for them. Now it struck me as a safe freeway for us. It made sense to use it. We would simply follow the canal to the final house, climb the banks out of the dried waterway, cross the road to the house, and do our final interviews. Then, we would head back.

The canal was probably seven feet deep. Made of earthen walls and strewn with rocks and knee-high, dried weeds, it served as a storm-water management system, an irrigation canal, and a trash heap. Old bed-frames and piles of refuse lined it, waiting for the next storm to wash them away. We descended into the canal in our teams and turned south in the direction of the final house. Our lead tank had already moved forward, and the tank flanking us moved slowly along the road, tracking our position in the canal.

We walked a short distance until we could see the edge of the house rising up on our right. The route had proven far easier than all of the wall-hopping of the previous few hours, and I told Deboe he had come up with a great idea. I felt like we had avoided the last real threat to us by circumventing that last stretch of road of the neighborhood, and though the sun beat down on us, I knew our day was coming to a close. When we came even with the final house, we climbed up the earthen walls of the canal and crossed the street to the building. The family there, knowing us, greeted us with tea. My men conducted their obligatory search, and I, feeling relaxed, removed my helmet and sat down to talk with the family. Some of my men joined me, and we all talked about what the man had recently learned. He told us about the al-Qaida leader's increasingly infrequent visits and about rumors he heard about where the cell leader traveled when he came.

While the father of the house talked, his young son and daughter stared at me from across the living room. I looked at them, and I smiled. I reached in my pocket and pulled out a couple of bottles of Gatorade. I knelt down and leaned toward them, waving for them to come over. Each took a step, then hesitated. Their mother, lingering behind them, laughed, and told them to go ahead, and they tentatively came and took their drinks. The boy, wide eyes staying on me as he took his gift, smiled. I took off my glove and rubbed the back of my hand across his cheek. He leaned into me, reaching his arms around me, and hugged me. I looked up to his mother and smiled. I looked around at the family. The mother and father grinned. The daughter drank from her Gatorade bottle, humming a tune between sips while she skipped around. The boy moved back toward his parents, and I let the entire scene fill my mind with images of a home that seemed to have found some peace. I wanted to push out other images. I wanted the boy's joy and his smiles to crowd out all the shadows. And, for a moment, it worked. All I felt was the reality of his touch and his family, and the family of June 19 left me.

I lingered. When the head of the household invited me and the rest of my men outside, we moved to a shaded porch. Most of us finished our tea there, savoring a light breeze that blew across the porch and cooled us. We stopped sweating. Our muscles stopped throbbing. We reflected on our day, talking to the family about what we hoped to accomplish for them. We had received good information. We had followed our plan precisely, and we had ended it in the midst of a family who welcomed us and wanted to help us. Some of my men were laughing, joking around and teasing each other. Earlier, one had stumbled when climbing the wall of the canal, and another had fallen while climbing over a wall. All of it was funny now, and we felt the day ending in success.

By the time we left, the sun was tracking down toward the horizon. We needed to get back to the outpost, and from there, we knew we would be heading back to FOB Warhorse for a night. We typically spent four nights at the outpost, followed by a two at Warhorse before returning back to the outpost for another four-day stint. Tonight was our turn to return to Warhorse, so we all wanted to get back to our humvees and get back to the outpost to make our report and then head immediately to our own CHUs and our own beds at the FOB. I talked to a couple of my men and decided that we would follow the canal back to the humvees. Instead of walking the road or leaping wall after wall, we would follow al-Qaida's own tracks in the bottom of the canal and find our way home.

We scaled down the steep walls opposite the final house. Rocks popped out from beneath our boots and tumbled into the bottom of the canal. We all began to sweat again, only seconds into the heavy sun of the late afternoon. In the canal, the sunlight reflected off of the walls and tore into us from every direction. The dirt of the walls and floor baked and cracked. Half of my men proceeded down the west side of the canal, and the other half proceeded down the east side. I walked down the center with Deboe and my translator. I found myself laughing at the quips of some of my men, and I felt the weight of the day start to fall off of me. All of our planning had worked. We had gotten the information we had come for, and we had done it efficiently and safely. I began thinking about finally nabbing the bad guy. It seemed like we were getting closer. We were certainly gathering more information, but we were still, apparently, far from him. We would have more missions to run. We would still have work to do, and I would not be alone.

Ahead of us and to my left, just above the edge of the canal wall, I could see our lead tank. Behind it and over my left shoulder, I could see the turret of Roberts's tank, and I could hear its engine growling. The sky was starting to turn from the glaring yellow of the day to the burnt orange of the coming evening, and everything, except the tank and the occasional comment from my men, was quiet.

Everything was still.

Everything was hot.

I took a step, and there was a flash. The ground erupted beneath me, and a fire filled the air.

I felt my body flying forward and my leg ripping skyward. I felt a rush of heat against my face, and I saw dust and the orange sky lift and tumble above me. For a moment, I felt myself suspended, hanging above the canal, the empty sound of dead air filling my ears, and then I felt my body hit the ground.

My head snapped downward, and my chest bounced once against the earth. The left side of my face smacked the ground, coming to rest on gravel. Without lifting my head, I looked back and to the right to where I had just been standing. I had been pitched forward by a blast, and five yards back I saw Deboe lifting himself off the ground, his head down but turning, surveying the scene around him. I heard my translator screeching in pain, his voice clear above a dull ringing now filling my ears. I saw other men's boots running around in a haze of dust and heat. Everything was shifting around. Everything was crawling with motion.

My arm seared with pain, and my back throbbed. I heard men start to yell to each other, and as they did, the ringing in my ears got louder. The sun seemed brighter, and the ringing rose to something I could feel, like heat against my body. I could see it, blinding and unbearably loud. It drowned out the yells of my men. It overwhelmed the pain in my body. It filled everything around me, pitching and stabbing into me.

I looked for somebody. I wanted someone to say something to me. I wanted somebody to silence the ringing and call my name. I wanted someone to come close to me and touch me, but the canal and all my men blurred and drifted, and in a final flash, the sun went black and the sound in my ears went away.

25

By the fall of 2007, more than 3,200 American soldiers had died in Iraq. They had died from direct engagement with the enemy. Firefights. RPG attacks. Tank engagements. They had died from indirect attacks. Bombs. IEDs. Storming booby-trapped houses. They had died from friendly fire, accidents, and desperation. They had died from suicides, murders, and the cold inability to keep going, to keep fighting. They had left their stories behind, some of them never told, some of them never even imagined by those who loved them, and now, as the war seems to wind down, they will be the stories that some try to tell, some try to resurrect. Others, like the stories of the more than 50,000 Iraqi civilians, may never have voice, at least in our country. They will never find some expression for what they have lost and what they never had a chance to see.

I can't tell the story of the children I killed. I don't know who they were or who they were hoping to become. I don't know what they dreamed about or where they one day wanted to go. I don't know where their family came from, and I don't even know their names. I never will. None of us ever will. I only know that I'm the one who ended their lives, and when I was blown up to the sky, part of me didn't want to come back down and open my eyes on the Iraqi land. Part of me didn't want to ever see my own life again.

When I opened my eyes once more, I was slung over Deboe's back, and he was carrying me up the wall of the canal. I could feel his shoulder pressing into my ribs, and I could feel my arm burning. The loud ringing in my ears continued and made it hard to hear. As we crested the edge of the canal, Deboe slipped, and I reached out with my free hand and helped him pull us both up and over the embankment. Pain lurched through my body, and I felt myself drift away again.

I regained consciousness moments later and opened my eyes. I saw Roberts on his tank ahead of me. Deboe rushed me up to it, and Roberts, his huge frame towering over me, grabbed me by a set of straps running across my back and lifted me up and over the edge of the vehicle, dangling me like a puppet and gently lowering me into the hatch of his tank. I slumped down against the wall, smelled the familiar stuffy air of the interior of a tank, and felt the vibration of the engine against my back. I closed my eyes. Everything went quiet.

I dreamed of being on the field of the Drexel Hill Raiders, my football team. I was lowering my body and digging deep under the shoulders of the other team's offensive lineman, getting leverage beneath him and pressing him up on his toes until he lost his balance and I broke free and bore down on the quarterback. I leaned forward, squaring my shoulders and preparing for impact, and when I hit, I heard the roar of the fans in the stadium erupt around me. I felt the quarterback's body crumple under mine, and I drove him into the ground.

I felt satisfaction. I felt certainty. I felt my own power, and as I passed to and from consciousness, I lost sight of the war. All there was was my body, searing with pain, but launching like a missile across enemy lines.

I opened my eyes and looked up. I heard the sound of helicopters. I was now outside the tank, and I was lying on the ground of a soccer field adjacent to the outpost. I could see members of Blue Platoon circling around me and my men, trying to help. A shadow passed over my face, and I looked up and saw the silhouette of a Blackhawk. I watched its dark form descend until the sun came free from it and forced me to turn my head to shield my eyes from the light. Small pebbles pelted my face, whipped up from the soccer grounds by the helicopters' rotors. I felt hands beneath my legs, back, and head, and I felt my body being lifted and loaded into the bird. Inside it, more hands grabbed me, pulling at my uniform, ripping it open. I saw a man, his face directly in front of me, his nose virtually touching mine. He was saying something. My head hummed and fell, and I closed my eyes again.

I woke when I felt my body being pitched forward and rushed through a hall and into a wide, open room. A man, a doctor, was asking me questions, and I felt my uniform being cut off of me. More hands pressed hard against my skin, along every inch of me, like I was being searched. Someone kept saying, "Stay with me here. Look at me, Lt. Meehan. Stay right here," and I kept watching the person who was saying it. The voice sounded far away, and next to it, I could hear the screaming of my interpreter. I turned in the direction of his voice, and I could see him and hear him telling them he wanted to stand up, that he didn't want to talk to them. He wanted them to leave him alone. He wanted to go to the restroom. They were trying to restrain him, telling him they needed to help him. He was a native Iraqi who had lived for twenty years in the United States before joining the war to help free his own country from Saddam. He was speaking to them in English, but between his words came screams that were deep and primal.

I knew I was in the emergency room at FOB Anaconda in Balad. The hands on me, the voice of my interpreter, and the smell of alcohol and sterility pulled me up and out of the canal. I tried to focus, but the room blurred and my ears still rung. One ear seemed to be filled with something, as though it were blocked with cotton. I felt a nurse wipe at it with a white towel, and when she pulled the towel away, I could see streaks of blood on it.

I became aware that I was naked, and when the nurses turned me on my side to look at my back, I felt my body tense. One nurse pressed his fingers along my spine and my lower back before gently setting me back down and lowering a light sheet over me. I felt another person working on my arm, and I watched as he twisted the arm up slightly and lowered a pair of forceps toward it. I felt the cool metal press against my skin and then pull away, and a rush of pain spread from my wrist to my shoulder. I saw him extract a chunk of bloodied metal the size of my thumb with the teeth of the forceps, shrapnel from the blast that had lodged in my muscle and flesh. I turned to my right.

Another man, an Iraqi police officer, was being treated. I didn't know who he was. He wasn't from our mission, and I didn't know him from any of our operations. I didn't know where he came from, but urgency hovered over the men working on him. Their hands moved rapidly, their voices sounded strong and certain but desperate. I could see the heart rate monitor next to him, and it blipped slowly and irregularly. I saw them lean down over him, reaching in to him, pulling and pushing, ravaging his body. I saw them press down on his chest. I heard the monitor flat-line and looked to it and saw the thin blue line draw straight across screen.

No jumps. No motion. The doctors and nurses moved in on him one more time, a flurry of hands and arms pressing down, hard, panicked, then one nurse stood upright and her head fell. The others stood. Straight. Still. The entire room came to full attention for moment, honoring the man who had died as their hands pressed down on him and tried to find his life, and then they walked away, one nurse lingering, pulling a blanket across his body and over his head.

I turned away. I saw a man in uniform moving across the room toward me. He strode with purpose. When he came close to me, I saw his face, drawn and powerful. The Brigade Commander, Col. Sutherland, stood over me, his uniform perfect and clean. Next to him stood the Brigade Sergeant Major, Sergeant Major Felt.

I was confused. The Brigade Commander should have been elsewhere, not at Anaconda. He had work to do. I wondered why he was there. I tried to say something, and I wondered out loud at the strange coincidence that the day I was injured he happened to be there. I apologized he had to see me hurt and on my back. He interrupted me. He said he had come specifically to see me and my men. The minute he had heard about the blast, he had left his base and flown to Anaconda to meet us. He may have landed before I had even arrived.

He expressed his pride in us and our mission, and he told me how he was honored to lead men like me, who risked their lives to conduct their missions. He held up an award, and I stared at it. He had in his hands a Purple Heart, and he told me he was privileged to be able to give it to me. He held it in front of me, and then he pinned it to the pillow next to my right ear, my uniform having been cut from my body. He waited to talk to me, even as doctors and nurses continued to swoop down on me and take my blood pressure and pulse, even as they checked to see if I was going to be okay.

I was proud of my award and honored that the head of the entire brigade had come to see me, but I was also embarrassed. I couldn't imagine how I would be worth making that trip for him. Traveling from base to base in a helicopter in Iraq was a combat mission, real risks attendant to flying during the day, so I felt embarrassed that I had done something that would cause him to take the risk of flying out to give me an award and thank me for service. I wanted to enjoy the moment, but I couldn't fully. I didn't feel like I deserved the attention, and the pain in my body still made it hard to focus on him or anyone else. I still heard the ringing, and my back ached. My arm stung, and I was having trouble making sense of what had happened. But, the Colonel's presence in the bustling of the ER around me assured me of one thing: I had survived. Looking at that man die next to me, hearing my translator's pleas for help from across the room, listening to the words of encouragement from the brigade leader, I knew I had been spared. I did not know why or how. I did not know what was going to happen next. But I did know I was not going to die. I knew I had been lucky. And it did not make me feel better.

In the days following the blast, I learned more about what had happened. Deboe had returned to the site and had found a wire buried in the dirt. The wire sat millimeters above a detonation device, and when my foot, or perhaps the foot of the translator, stepped on it, it made contact with the device, completed a circuit, and the IED was detonated. The blast ripped through our platoon, knocking most of us to the ground, but injuring mainly just me and the translator. The day of the explosion was September 22 – exactly two years to the day after I had become active duty in the Army.

An examination of the site revealed that the IED was an anti-tank mine, a powerful IED whose purpose is to disable or destroy tanks. No one knows how we survived the hit.

Apparently, I absorbed most of the force of the blast, the force of the explosion catapulting me in the air and leaving me with a severe concussion, a ruptured ear drum, a wounded arm, a knee injury, and severe compression on the discs in my back. Shrapnel blasted into my arm and the body armor on my lower back. The armor had done its job, so my back was only bruised. My interpreter, though, had had older body armor. Most of the platoon's armor had been upgraded just before our deployment, but he had not been with our company during that time, so he had missed out. The shrapnel sliced through his armor, penetrating his back and stomach and puncturing his colon. Deep wounds had opened inside him. Within two hours of his arrival at the hospital at FOB Anaconda, he was airlifted to Germany for further surgery, then on to the United States.

My men had responded quickly and professionally in the aftermath. They did everything exactly right, to the degree that by the time Deboe got me to the tank for evacuation, Roberts had already reported the hit to battalion and choppers were in the air speeding our way. They had stabilized our translator, and they had moved quickly to get us to the medivac site so that we could be evacuated immediately to Anaconda. I, evidently, talked about playing football throughout the evacuation.

Before that moment, everything had gone well. We had had a good day. Perfect even. We had gotten good information on the al-Qaida cell leader. My men had worked the streets well and had not complained about the heat or the walking. All had been perfect until I had tripped the wire, until I had found the retribution I had come to feel I deserved.

Now one of my men was being taken to Germany for surgery, and I didn't know if he would make it. When they finished with me in the ER and rolled me into the Intermediate Care Unit, I reflected on what had happened. Somehow I had survived and, given the type of IED, I had escaped with relatively minor injuries. I knew I was hurt. I knew I wasn't going to be all right anytime soon, but I knew I could have been killed, and, sitting in the hospital watching the doctors and nurses save lives, I didn't understand why I hadn't been.

I felt something growing inside of me. It felt like a disease, palpable and invasive, and I felt it reaching throughout me and pulling me inward, away from the world and the war and toward something dark, and deep, and lonely. I grasped at it sometimes, as though I were hoarding it and keeping it from others' eyes, and late at night, when other soldiers around me were sleeping, their breathing laboring through their wounds, I sometimes imagined myself sneaking out and away into the Iraqi night, clutching my secret to my chest.

I tried to find some way to talk about it with AJ. I had called both her and my father after I had left the emergency room, but I pulled my secret close to me, refusing to talk about why we were on that mission, why I was pushing so hard to find the cell leader. I would not risk saying, releasing into the world, that I was working to fight off the deaths of those children, and I would not risk telling them that I had been punished for June 19 and lose the slim connection I had with home.

In the days that followed, that connection seemed increasingly difficult to hold onto. AJ was exhausted and concerned, and she often felt she needed to provide support to my family. She listened to everyone – my brother, my mother, others – and she tried to reassure them, even as she felt increasingly alone and deeply separated from me. She tried to reach out. She tried to ask questions and tried to find some way to touch me from across the globe. She wanted to know that I was okay, and she wanted to know that when I returned, everything would finally be back the way it should be. We would be happy. We would be newlyweds. We would be in love.

I did not reach back for her, though. I sat for long hours under the white sheets of my bed, sometimes sleeping, but often simply awake and staring across the room. I was in a room with other soldiers recovering from injuries, but I did not speak to them. Often, I did not even notice them. Instead, I wondered why I had survived, and I wondered if I had finally been punished for what I had done on June 19, the day that I had taken the lives of innocent children. I also wondered if my life had been spared because I had not yet suffered enough.

The doctors and nurses continued to ask me questions for the next few days, trying to discern the severity of my injuries. They were earnest, and they looked at me with compassionate eyes. My head still ached, sometimes with blinding pain, and my ear still had almost no hearing. I felt sick sometimes, especially if I moved quickly, and I hated standing up because I knew that sometimes I would faint. But when they asked me about symptoms, I lied. I told them what they wanted to hear, and I asked them time and again when I could return to my men. I wanted out of the hospital. I wanted to leave before my feelings overwhelmed me. I wanted to leave before someone discovered that I was keeping a secret, before someone discovered that I was no hero and that when that IED blew into me, all I could think about, all I could remember, was that I had bombed a house full of children.

A day before they discharged me and sent me back to Warhorse, one doctor asked me a series of questions about my work as a soldier and about my ability to lead. He asked about my family and about my relationships with my wife and with my soldiers. He asked me about my drive to keep going and my desire to fight the war, and when it was all done, and I sat across from him hoping to find a way back to my base, he looked at me.

"You just used the word 'worthless' to describe yourself more times than I can count," he said.

I watched a nurse walk past us and disappear behind a curtain.

"I think you're depressed, and I don't want you outside the wire. In fact, I don't think you should leave the hospital."

I heard some sort of monitor beeping somewhere. The doctor kept his eyes on me.

"I need to leave," I said.

"I'm not sure you know what you need."

"I know I need to be back with my men."

He stared at me and then looked down at some chart in his hands. I insisted that I be allowed to leave, arguing that I was physically suited to be released. That was a lie, but it held some power. We went back and forth before he finally consented to my leaving on the condition that I stay inside the wire. Again, I protested, but he wouldn't budge. He said that as long as I followed his orders on my medical profile, I'd be able to return to Warhorse and my men soon, so I agreed, and within a day I was back on a helicopter heading to my CHU.

26

I'm not sure what I expected when I returned. I suppose I thought that just being among my men would cheer me up. But it didn't. Instead, I felt more isolated. I felt like they knew my secret and were talking about it when I wasn't around. I felt like they were judging me as a leader for having continued missions in our area of operation while other platoon leaders simply sat on their asses and waited for the time to pass. I felt like they could see through me and saw my motivations for keeping our platoon outside the wire. Not the good motivations. Not the ones about trying to help, trying to maintain my sense of duty to the mission in Iraq, but the darker ones, the shadows that fell over me in the slow days at the outpost and forced me back out into the searing light of the Iraqi sun.

Sgt. Roberts was now leading the platoon, continuing our missions in order to try to gather intelligence on the al-Qaida leader we had been tracking. When we heard that Special Forces had used our intelligence, including intelligence we had gathered on September 22, to track down and kill him, the men felt a real satisfaction. We had gotten our man. He had made a final stand against Special Forces, drawing weapons and firing at them, but they had responded with decisive force and killed him. Our intelligence had finally pinned the man who had been controlling our area and who was, ultimately, responsible for the IED that had hit my platoon.

I should have been happy, but I wasn't. I felt some slim satisfaction that our information had finally amounted to something, but the weight of the days pressed down on me, and I realized that I had been robbed of my purpose and my excuse for staying busy. I watched my men coming and going from their missions, and in between, I slept or sat at my desk, looking at the posters around my bed, looking at the message I had written for myself bleed down along the wall. "Follow Your Leader." I had nowhere to go.

My body ached, and my headaches intensified. Sometimes they were so severe that I puked. When I stood up, I would have to steady myself. Any physical exertion, anything that caused my heart rate to rise, would sometimes cause me to faint. Ringing still filled my ear, but when it abated I felt no relief. In the silence, I heard a dark voice telling me that I had failed. It reminded me that my life had been spared. It reminded me that I had not spared others.

I spent all of October alone, replaying June 19 and September 22 like films in my mind. I watched them over and over again. The desert light of Warhorse waned to darkness each night, and I sat in the silent room of my CHU dwelling on my failures. I stopped eating. I stopped lifting weights. I stopped joining the men for dinner, and when one would come to ask me to find my way out into the evening, I found a reason to be alone. I could feel myself spiraling downward. I found myself turning away from people who reached out to me.

In October, I received word from home that I had been honored in a ceremony at the Philadelphia Eagles Stadium. I had been named one of the Seventy-Five Greatest Living Philadelphians. Word of the award from home came around the same time that I was honored with a military citation. I was awarded the Bronze Star to recognize my "exceptionally meritorious actions during combat operations." The top brass would be giving it to me at the outpost, the place I associated with my own failure as a combat leader.

Instead of lifting me, both recognitions fell hard on me. I did not attend the ceremony for the Bronze Star. I traveled with others who were also being recognized to an initial ceremony to receive it, but when that ceremony was aborted, I did not return to receive my star at the rescheduled event. The first time I went, my men were at the outpost, conducting their missions and continuing the work we had been doing before I was injured. They greeted me enthusiastically, glad to see me outside the wire. They wanted to see me immersing myself again in the military rituals that, in part, define us as soldiers, and some of them I think were just glad to see me outside of my CHU.

Many of them had come to see me in the long days I spent in my CHU. Deboe regularly showed up, checking in often and practically organizing the rest of the platoon to swing by frequently. Roberts kept me informed about how the platoon was going and what kind of missions the men were running, but he always tried to make sure I knew he would listen to me if I wanted to talk. Dave Nguyen, who had left our unit, actually checked in with AJ to make sure she was coping with my change. Poppen coaxed me out of my self-pity, at times forcing me to get out of the CHU and eat and watch TV with him and others in the platoon.

I knew that I was deeply depressed. I was aware that I didn't feel like I deserved to be seen with anyone else or, at times, even to be alive anymore. I was aware that my own shame was a dim shadow of the real tragedy of the death of the children, that my sadness was a ridiculous, insignificant fact in the face of the real fact, the real horror of the war, and thinking of that made me more depressed, more ashamed, and more disconnected from everyone around me. I lived in the face of a deeper silence than the one I imposed on myself. I lived in the silence I had called down on the children, and I could find no way to reconcile it, no way to make myself believe that I deserved to be alive when they no longer lived.

I began to think about my Purple Heart and all that it stood for – the injuries in the line of duty and the sacrifice it represented. That sacrifice seemed insignificant. That award, and even the Bronze Star, reminded me of the people I had killed. I had chosen to live my life in a war zone and hoped to make a difference. I had in some broad way sacrificed a life back home with AJ, and I had put myself at risk. But that seemed insignificant in light of what I had done. I had survived an IED blast, miraculously, but no miracles had come to save those children from me. No divine hand had reached down from the skies and plucked that missile from the sky. That family in June had died under my command and under my orders. I did not want a heart or a star to show to the world. I did not want some metal pinned to my chest so people would assume that I was a hero, that I was a great American. I wanted to find some way to change what I had done. I wanted to fix my mistake. I wanted those children to be alive. So, when the others went to have their awards pinned on, I stayed in my CHU and sat on my bed. I sealed my Purple Heart in my desk on the other side of the room, and I remembered all that I had done. My Bronze Star, miles from me, dangled from the hands of my Company Commander waiting for someone to pin it to.

I understand that our military ceremonies recognize everyone who fights in the war and that it serves to motivate other soldiers to achieve, to lead, to fight. I understand that some of my men may have been disappointed in me and that they may have felt like I was minimizing our importance as a platoon. I understand that now, and I understood it then, but that day, I could not move from my CHU. I could not have men look at me who knew what I had done. They knew I had called in the missiles that day, and they knew I continued to lead men into missions into areas of Iraq still partially under al-Qaida control. They knew that I had pushed forward, seeking out the enemy at all costs, and if they knew all of that, they would see that award as an emblem of military leadership. They would see it as a sign of the right actions, of the behavior that should be most desired and that would be most rewarded.

I could not make myself the example of great military action. I would not have myself held up as a leader to follow.

October passed so slowly that I knew I could not bear another month like it. We had heard we would now, with any luck, be home by the end of November, so I decided, against doctor's orders, that I was going outside the wire each day. If all went well, I would be too busy to listen to the ringing in my ears and the voices that I secreted away. If something went wrong, if retribution finally fell down on me like thunder, then at least I would know that the ringing and the chatter in my head would finally end and all of Iraq would turn to silence.

27

I do not know how most of my men spent their first days home. I have never asked, and I most likely never will. I know that they, like me, probably tried to reconnect with their wives and families and tried to find some way to feel joy. Maybe they did. Maybe they laughed and cried and held their loved ones and made love to their wives and girlfriends. Maybe they drank champagne and celebrated with ice cream and apple pie. Maybe they just rolled in their beds with their lovers, intertwined, interwoven, interconnected. Maybe they felt the war wash off them and the light of a new beginning fill their lives and launch them forward into some ineffable blue.

I did not. I tried to. I wanted to. Desperately. But I did not. During the last few weeks in Iraq, I had gone on patrols with my men. Simply walking was sometimes exhausting for me, and at time, migraines would overwhelm me and I would slump onto the shoulders of one of my men. I could not have looked good, and I'm sure my men grew tired of my physical exhaustion, but I made the choice to suffer through the physical stress of being on patrol instead of suffering with the silence of being alone. So, my platoon spent our final weeks of late October and most of November covering some of the same towns we had worked before we had been sent to the outpost, and when our replacements arrived, we tried to orient them to the area. We told them which local Iraqi men we had formed relationships with and which towns we thought still might give them trouble. Our replacements, though, did not much care. They were an engineering outfit. They had been sent as a kind of stop-gap measure until a more significant combat crew could arrive, so when we talked to them, they politely listened, then turned their minds to other things and settled in as we, just as Thanksgiving arrived, waited in the flight line and listened for the Chinooks that would finally carry us out of Iraq.

I arrived home to a new house. We had bought it while I was deployed, and I had as yet spent no time in it. AJ's parents had helped her settle in, giving her house-warming gifts that transformed our house into a home. The house was custom-built for us, and almost everything in it was new. New furniture. New dinnerware. New paintings and photographs for the wall. New linens.

The whole house sparkled. It shined. It was everything Iraq was not, and when I walked into it, I wanted to leave. I could not find my bearings. Nothing seemed like it was mine. Nothing seemed like it related to my life, my experiences, my war, and it all seemed so staged. It was, in truth, the house I had dreamed of. It was beautiful and new. It was full of warmth and care. But, I found myself wishing for the dry air of Iraq and the rusted bunk of my CHU. I found myself searching for the remnants of a life of war and of barely getting by. It was all I deserved. Our new custom house was a perfect contrast to my metal space in Warhorse, and it simply reminded me daily of how undeserving I was of it. It broke me apart, and no one, especially AJ, could find a way to put me back together.

We did our best. She tried to find out where I had gone and who I had become. She tried to understand why June weighed so heavily on me and why, sometimes at night, I was afraid to turn off the television. AJ did not know that, rising up from the darkness, children waited for me, hoping I would be awake when the last program on the television turned to black. She did not know that each night I took sleeping pills and I would wait and wonder if a child would appear. He came for me, desperate and real, and he watched me, knowing I did not sleep.

I was aware that I was becoming a stereotype. I could not believe that I was turning into the wounded vet or the broken soldier whom so many movies and books portray with ridiculous clichés. He sits alone in the house staring out the window, or perhaps he holds a gun in his hand, contemplating his reasons for living. He cries, sometimes for no reason, and his lover, reaching out and caressing him, can do nothing. He responds only by knocking her hand away.

I knew all of this, and when I felt night pressing in on me, I would turn the volume on the television higher, fighting off both the image of that child and the image of me suffering like some pitiful caricature. I did not want to be that guy. I did not want anyone to know that I was that guy, and I could only imagine one way not to be him. I had to shut off completely. I had to turn away utterly from everything that connected me to that place and that time in my life. I would not drift toward melodrama. I would not become Hollywood's fallen hero. I would instead write myself a new script and act out a role I was supposed to play as husband and son and brother. I would numb myself to the reality of Iraq and stay within myself. From there, I would suspend my life and watch it like some drama acted out with no director and no direction.

My family knew that the war had taken something from me, and they could sense my distance, even while I tried to act the right part. My sister held me once and told me that she missed me. My brother frantically tried to find ways to make me laugh, to engage me in the world of our friends. I told them I was the same, I told them that I would be just fine, and I told them that we needed to find a way to celebrate the lives we had ahead of us. We had to change things. Improve them. Take control. And we all decided New Year's would be that time. We all decided we would start a new year together and begin our new lives then.

AJ and my family planned a welcome home celebration for New Year's Eve. We had had a few gatherings already. AJ and I returned to Philly before the holidays to be near our families, and we spent Christmas at my grandmother's. We spent most of it sequestered from the rest of the family, though, talking on the stairs leading to another level of her house. We found little to say to other family members, and, above the sounds of presents being opened and the fire crackling, we tried to find something more to unite us. Family wasn't enough. Our past wasn't enough. Love, something I had always been told would save me even in the face of my greatest fears, could not withstand the way the war ripped at us. I didn't know how to reach back out to AJ. She didn't know how to find light among the shadows that had fallen across my life. We fought anger and desperation, trying to avoid directing it at each other.

The anger, though, sparked several days later when AJ and I went out with Matt and Dave, my friends from high school. Dave was now a newlywed, having been married when I was back home during my furlough in the spring, and before we all headed out, I decided I would wear my uniform. It was not a good idea, and there was no real reason to do it, but I felt like I needed to do something to reconnect to my time in

Iraq. Within just a few minutes of entering the bar, I knew I had made a mistake. A man sitting next to us looked me up and down, pursing his lips and spinning the ice in his glass with an obsessive twitch of his wrist.

"Your awards are bullshit," he said.

I heard venom in his voice. I knew, somehow, he felt some pain like mine, but I could not respond. All I could do was stare at him and feel a burning in my chest. I wanted to level him, to utterly and completely destroy him, but I could not move. I felt darkness welling up inside of me. I felt terror and grief freeze me, unfamiliar, too long shut out and now too difficult to pull up and feel, too buried to know how to free. I felt myself lean back, away from him. He knew about me. He knew my secret.

Bouncers were on top of him before he could say another word. One grabbed him by the collar of his shirt and pulled him straight up and out of the chair. Another grabbed him by the front of his jacket and pushed him down, taking his legs out from under him. They dragged him to the door, shaking him as they went, and threw him into the parking lot. One of them came back to the table. He had been in the Army. He didn't stand for talk like that.

I talked with the bouncer for a moment, then looked around for AJ to introduce her to him, but she was gone. I heard someone shouting from near the door, and my brother Patrick grabbed me by the arm and told me I had to get outside. AJ was in the parking lot. She was hitting the guy. She was yelling at him, slinging her arms at him, battering him. He retreated, and we went out and pulled her away.

I knew where her anger came from. She was protecting me, I know, but the anger was deeper than that. It was rage over what she couldn't control. It was pain over what she had lost. It was hatred of war and what it had done to me, and most of all that energy and hurt and anger was meant for me.

By the time New Year's Eve arrived, the incident was a joke among friends and family. I laughed at it, applauding my tough wife in front of my friends, but that brief exchange with that man and seeing how AJ had collapsed under the weight of the war ripped the final ounce of pride from me. The one time I had tried to show pride in my job again, the one time I put on that uniform and wore those medals, I had been insulted and attacked and told that everything I had done was worthless. I had been ridiculous to wear it out. I don't even like when other soldiers parade their awards around, but I needed to find some way to bring the war home and find my way back to some sense of pride, some sense that what I did mattered. I needed validation, and I shouldn't have sought it that way. I felt myself grasping for some external sign of my worth, and as I stammered and tried to find some way to confront him, my wife had stepped in to protect me. She had turned all the rage she had harbored and lashed out. It was rage for me. It was emptiness and hurt that I had caused that had transformed into anger, and as I waited, feeling the pain of my own hypocrisy and the shame of my career wash over me, she had acted. On New Year's Eve, I remembered that I had been still and that I had lost the power to respond. I realized that my service, which I once had shown with pride, had become a mark of failure. I turned further inward and further away from any hope that I could ever feel okay again.

I could sense desperation in all of my family and in AJ. They wanted me back, and I think they believed that if I could just see how many people loved me and how many people were proud of me, I would change back to who I once was. So, for the New Year's Eve celebration they rented a big room in a Dave and Busters that overlooked downtown Philly and the Ben Franklin Bridge. The lights on the bridge glowed in the night, blue and white, and beneath it, boats had anchored awaiting a fireworks display that fired over the Delaware River. From our room in the restaurant, we could see it all. We had our own private bar and buffet with crabcakes and satay and mounds of cheese and fruit. We had our own private waiters, who scurried around filling glasses with champagne and clearing dishes from tables. We had the expansive view of the bridge and the river, and we had family and friends who had traveled from all over the United States to come welcome me home. My Rat from VMI, Jeremy, was there with his friends, and my extended family was there, some who had come all the way from Montreal to show me their support. Some of the soldiers who served with me had traveled to join us, and a reporter, Brian Freeman, who had followed my career since high school, had come, now a friend and no longer just a newsman.

I wore my Class A uniform again, and I tried to play the part I knew I was supposed to play, but AJ and I were hurting, and I had not been able to get past the encounter in the bar a few days earlier. My sister-in-law and AJ prepared a display of my awards and my accomplishments near the entrance to our private room. On a table covered with a maroon table-cloth, a glass display case held my medals, polished and pure. Next to it, a series of photos, images of me in Iraq, and an Irish flag. I set up my own table nearby, a memorial to the soldiers who had died. Pictures of the men I knew who had died sat next to a rifle, a helmet, and boots, all stacked together with a set of dog tags hanging from them.

My friends crowded around the tables, talking about everything they saw. They asked me questions, and I tried to answer them clearly and professionally, wanting them to know that I had done my job and that I had done it as well as I could. They asked about the Purple Heart, and I told them about the blast and my injuries. They thanked me for my service. They told me how thankful they were I had survived. They told me that I was a hero and that I should be proud. I thought about June 19, and their words mingled with the sounds of the waiters, clanging dishes, and the indistinct buzzing of the crowd.

We all drank, and I felt some of the war lift off of me. As midnight drew close, I went to find my wife. She was talking to a friend at the bar, and when I came to her, I knew that she had been talking about me. I knew that she had been talking about the person I used to be and the person I had become, but I did not care. I just wanted to be with her when the New Year finally arrived. I wanted to believe that somehow that moment would make a difference, even though I knew that it wouldn't. I wasn't in a movie. New Years don't begin with the chime of a clock. For some, they never do begin.

I pulled AJ away from the bar just as the first fireworks began. I led her through the crowd so that we would be near the center of the window and our view would stretch wide in front of us. I wanted us to see it all and take it all in. I wanted us to blend in, melt away, and forget what had happened. I wanted us to feel something besides sadness and grief and rage. I wanted us to see a stream of light shoot skyward and forget about the war as the New Year began.

As the crowd celebrated the final seconds of 2007, the fireworks intensified, filling the air with explosions of light and color. Champagne glasses rose and clinked. The countdown, chanted, intensified, and the voices became more determined and reckless. People began to count in unison as the seconds ticked away.

The numbers fell, lower, lower. Fireworks filled the sky above the bridge.

Our friends and family pushed in closer around us. Their bodies pressed into ours, collapsing in toward the window, in toward the show. A solid buzz of their voices, hopes and dreams, promises for the future, filled the room.

I pulled AJ closer and pointed at an explosion of light. Fire, colored and gemlike, danced across the sky and crowded out the darkness. The display reached its climax, and the crowd erupted into cheers. I felt the voices rush through me and the light press against my face, and I leaned in to kiss AJ.

I felt her breath. I felt her lips. I felt her body fall into me, and I tried to feel her warmth, her touch. I tried to make the New Year begin.

The fireworks began to fade. Blue smoke drifted and turned in the night sky, illuminated by the glow of city lights and the sparkling bridge. I heard the buzz of family around me, kissing, touching, celebrating, dreaming of a new beginnings, hoping for new lives. Someone touched me, a hand reaching across bodies and resting on my shoulder. AJ's arm wrapped around my waist, and I wondered if all the buzzing would come true. I wondered if it would ever overwhelm the ringing in my ears and if the smoke would clear and the night sky would open up and invite me in. I wondered if it would swallow me whole, and if it did, whether I'd find one last flash of light to show me the way home.

EPILOGUE

I was a legacy. My father had been in the Army. My mother's father had been a Marine in the Korean War. My father's father had been in the Navy in World War II. Another relative, my Uncle Eddy, had also become a Marine. All had enlisted. All had chosen to serve, but I was the first and only officer. That one difference, though, did not matter. We shared a common history. We all had stories to tell.

Today, I'm sitting in my home in Ft. Hood. It is September 22. It is still hot, and the Texas live oaks are still green. It has been one year since I was hit by the IED. It has been three years since I became active duty. It has been ten months since I returned to the States, and in that time, I have not yet found a way to leave the war.

I have been home since December. I watched the winter rains of Texas fall in February, and in May, I watched thunderstorms roll across the hill country, bearing down and lashing out at the landscape. I waited for June 19 to come, pretending that I would not notice it, but knowing that I would and knowing that on that day, just as today, I would fall backward into the thin space between me and Iraq and I would wonder if my life was still worth living, if my life was worth the lives of all those other people.

On July 3, a day before Independence Day, a doctor finally diagnosed me with Traumatic Brain Injury. TBI. When the doctor made the diagnosis, he apologized. They should have recognized the injury earlier, he said. They should have known that my head had been scrambled. The acknowledgment of that injury validated that I was not imagining the ongoing headaches, the confusion I often feel, the strange inability to recall and find the right word, and the constant ringing in my ear. I've been told that I'm essentially deaf in that ear now, and I have begun to receive regular treatment for my back injuries, usually a series of shots injected directly into the discs in my back. It is supposed to relieve the pressure. It is supposed to relieve the pain. It's hard to tell if it does.

I have been placed on a series of eight different medications, and I take seventeen pills every day. Some are pain-killers whose job is to numb the injuries to my leg and my back. Some are for my headaches and supposedly relieve the migraines. Others are for the other pain I have. The nightmares. The depression. The constant fear and uncertainty about who I am, who I will become, and how I will ever learn to cope. I've been moved to a medical unit where I will be given a medical discharge. I go to work each day and often am just told to go home. They don't know what to do with me, or with any number of other injured soldiers.

Suicides on the base have escalated, and now the Army is quick to put any of us in the unit on a kind of heightened state of observation if they sense any change in mood. More meetings. More consultation. More simple check-ins. More hoops, all to ensure that one more of us doesn't die, that one more of us doesn't try to find his own way out of the war.

The men I served with have continued with their lives. My Company Commander has been promoted to Major and is pursuing a Masters degree at a university in Hawaii. Sgt. Roberts has remained in the military and works as an instructor at Fort Knox. He is soon to be a father. Deboe has received his orders to be redeployed, returning to combat in theater for his third tour. As I write these words, he is preparing to leave in less than a month. Garnica has been spared redeployment. He suffered injuries from the IED blast that were not immediately obvious to any of us, and he can no longer serve in combat. At the time of the IED blast, I had not been aware that he had been injured, but the explosion that sent me tumbling and that had nearly killed our translator slammed into his back and caused four slipped discs. His pain increases daily, and doctors have told him that he will someday likely be confined to a wheelchair. Dave Nguyen has come to visit me several times. He continues to live his military life, trying to find a way to negotiate the war. Our translator, who was most seriously injured at the time of the blast, returned to the States shortly after being flown to Germany, and in the States he had surgery to repair internal injuries. He has found his way home to Michigan.

I have tried to talk to some of these men about my experiences, and I have begun to rely on others as well to help me. I've reached out to friends and family, and some of them have shown me something like peace. Others, though, I should not have reached out to. Some had suffered in the war too. They had felt the loss, the terror, the pain, and when I reached out to them, they couldn't provide the support I needed. They couldn't fill the void that had developed inside of me. I needed to find my own way home. I needed to find some way to reaffirm who I was and who I could be and remind myself that I was more than just a soldier wounded in a war.

AJ has borne the brunt of that search to redefine myself. I have tried to remember that the war lingers in our relationship, but I have not been the strong husband I always thought I would be. In trying to find comfort, I have hurt her, and despite this, she has continued to reach out to me. She has continued to help me find a home. I don't know why she has endured it all, but I know at night, the two of us lying together, I only want to feel somehow like we did before I went away, and I want us to find a way forward.

I need to find some peace for myself. The gentle touch, the soft words, the moments of hope that AJ and others give me comfort me, but they do not change me, and they do not last. I know that I have to find some way to make sense of the war and what I did, and I've come to believe that I'll only be able to do so with time.

I don't know how I'll wait for it. It's only been a year, and still, when I try to talk about what I did that day in June, while the sun beat down on us and scalded the Iraqi sky and missiles that I called crashed into that house and tore life from the earth, I stop, and I pull back, and I try to find a reason why we were there. Why I was there. Why I was in that war.

Part of me wants to say something definitive. To pronounce. To proclaim. To declare with final certainty whether I support the war. But I realize what happens the minute I do. If I say I'm in favor of this war, I'm a monster. I'm a zealot who blindly follows the orders of an oil-thirsty government that has no regard for others. A duty-bound beast. If I don't approve of this war, I'm either an unpatriotic soldier who has forsaken his country and his fellow soldiers or a traitor who has been too easily swayed by questions that my military training and love of country should have taught me to ignore. Either way, I haven't provided the right answer. Either way, I've gone far beyond duty.

So, I can't tell you if I approve of this war. I'm too close to it. We're all too close to it. It's raw. We still feel it. All of us. How can any of us possibly say anything clearly, unambiguously, and unequivocally? How can I possibly tell you if I should have fought this war? I have too many questions. I have too many memories to sort through and make sense of.

Maybe at some point I will know what to say, and maybe then I'll have finally found some way to understand it all. Until then, all I have and all I can tell you is my story, and my story is this:

I went to Iraq to serve my country, and I think I made a difference. But while I was there, I killed people who did not deserve to die.

That is all I can tell you. My approval or disapproval of this war is not what matters.

It's not at all what matters.

And it's not at all why I've told you my story.

Fallen Soldiers in Baqubah area during my deployment. Gone but not forgotten . . .

Juan M. Alcantara

Matthew L. Alexander

Alexandre A. Alexeev

Zachary D. Baker

John Barta

Donnie R. Belser, Jr.

Ryan R. Berg

Anthony M. Bradshaw

Leeroy A. Camacho

Branden C. Cummings

Ebe F. Emolo

Anthony B. Ewing

Nathan P. Fairlie

Kevin Gaspers

Jay R. Gauthreaux

Orlando E. Gonzalez

Jonathan D. Grassbaugh

Nicholas A. Gummersall

Jason R. Harkins

Blake Harris

Schuyler B. Haynes

Andrew J. Higgins

Levi K. Hoover

Drew N. Jensen

Kareem R. Khan

Jerry R. King

Garret C. Knoll

Damon G. Legrand

Joel W. Lewis

Darryl W. Linder

Kenneth E. Locker, Jr.

Rodney L. McCandless

Ronnie G. Madore, Jr.

Jonathan A. Markham

Randell T. Marshall

Anselmo Martinez III

Joshua P. Mattero

Barry W. Mayo

Scott A. Miller

William C. Moore

Michael T. Mutz

Casey W. Nash

Dan H. Nguyen

Jason Nunez

Brice A. Pearson

Robert R. Pirelli

Michael A. Pursel

John D. Rode

Michael J. Rodriguez

Vincenzo Romeo

Joshua G. Romero

Adam J. Rosema

Eric Ross

Ryan D. Russell

Jonathan E. Schiller

Carl L. Seigart

Ian W. Shaw

Eric R. Sieger

Richard A. Smith

Clarence T. Spencer

James E. Summers III

Jason Swiger

Jacob M. Thompson

Francis R. Trussell, Jr.

Iosiwo Uruo

Michael L. Vaughan

Jason W. Vaughn

Kile G. West

Anthony White

Jesse L. Williams